ANCHORED

God Uses Sailing Couple to Pioneer In-depth Bible Study in the Caribbean

Chuck & Micki Harding

PRESS

ANCHORED
by Chuck & Micki Harding

Printed in the United States of America

ISBN 9781600344619

Unless otherwise noted, Bible quotations are taken from the *Holy Bible*, New International Version, NIV, Copyright © 1973, 1978, 1984 by International Bible Society.

Scripture quotations marked NKJV are taken from the *Holy Bible*, New King James Version, Copyright © 1982 by Thomas Nelson, Inc., The New King James Bible, New Testament, Copyright © 1979.

Scripture quotations marked NLT are taken from the *Holy Bible*, New Living Translation, Copyright © 1996, 2004, 2007 by Tyndale House Foundation.

Map credits:

2010-2011 Cruising Guide to the Leeward Islands. Copyright © 2009 by Cruising Guide Publications, Inc. and Chris Doyle.

Cruising Guide to Trinidad and Tobago Plus Barbados and Guyana. Published by Chris Doyle Publishing & Boaters Enterprises Ltd. in association with Cruising Guide Publications. This edition published in 2006.

To all CBSI Caribbean leaders who follow God's calling to be disciple makers for Jesus Christ—you were the inspiration for writing this history of His faithfulness. May God continue to be glorified through your sacrificial servant leadership.

He is Faithful!
1 Thes. 5:24
Chuck & Micki

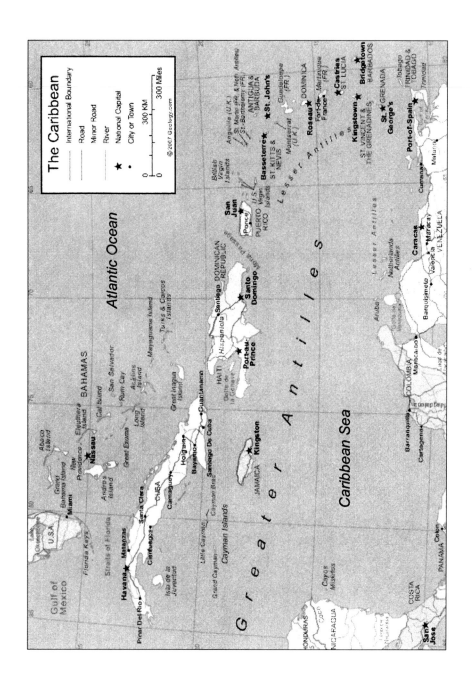

Contents

Foreword

Chuck and Micki are God's called servant leaders who have faith-fully served Him as CBSI "Calebs" to the Eastern Caribbean for more than 10 years. There is no greater joy than to be used by the Lord to train and equip national leaders to reach their people with God's Word and the opportunity, through regular study of it, to grow in faith in Christ or embrace it for the first time. The Hardings have watched God develop CBS International in the Eastern Caribbean into a region-wide ministry incorporating several island nations. I hope this adventure story of two surrendered Christ-followers step-ping out in faith will inspire others to invest their lives in making disciples of the Lord Jesus Christ. The Eastern Caribbean is being transformed through the Word of God! Well done, good and faithful servants!

Camilla

Camilla L. Seabolt
Executive Director
Community Bible Study
Colorado Springs, Colorado

Chuck and Micki

Introduction

We had college educations, a growing manufacturing business, a beautiful home, business and personal travel to many places—dreams come true for many! But we felt empty. Christmas was approaching, and we thought church might help, so from the local newspaper we chose a church near our home, one different from both our denominational backgrounds.

Micki had gone to church her whole childhood but never experienced the love of Christ as in this church! Skeptical at first, wondering what the people wanted from us, we still continued to attend. The Bible was preached every week, and the message was brought to life with creative dramas and pointed music. At age 37 Chuck, an atheist, was attracted to the joy of the people and their confidence in the Bible. Pastor Clancy Thompson cared enough to challenge Chuck to read the Bible rather than scoff at Christianity as mythology. Meeting with Clancy weekly, Chuck questioned his way through the Gospel of John. When he came to the irrefutable truth of the resurrection in John and read *Man Alive* by Dr. Michael Green, however, his atheistic philosophy began to crumble. On April 19, 1980, Chuck accepted the truth of the Bible and became a follower of Jesus Christ.

Two weeks before that, during an Easter Sunday drama, Micki came to understand that Christ died on the cross in her place. She recognized the filth of her prideful thinking that she was a good person deserving God's blessings. At that moment in her mind, she pictured herself kneeling at the foot of Jesus' cross, confessing her sins, asking Christ to forgive her and take control of her life.

God poured His love into our lives through this caring church family. For five years Chuck was mentored weekly by Pastor Clancy. During that time we struggled to follow Jesus while dealing with severe trials and troubles in our everyday lives. But God had provided a way through it...His Word. As a couple we began studying many "how to" books, learning what others had gleaned from the Bible. What is a Christian marriage? What does a Christian home look like? Then, on a cross-country airline flight, Micki providentially sat next to a lady doing a Bible study lesson. This woman was studying what God said rather than what another person was saying about God and His ways. Once back home, Micki searched out and joined a local class. Studying the Word of God directly made a profound difference in her life—so much so that when a men's class was organized, Chuck joined, and his life was likewise changed. Soon Chuck was invited into class leadership. Micki was a small group leader in a women's class at that time. God then moved us into various leadership roles until 1992, when He called us as founders and Co-Teaching Leaders of the first co-ed single young adult's class in the Detroit, Michigan, area. God blessed the class, growing it to a vibrant 300 members with many leaders—and marriages! We were humbled by the privilege given us to help young men and women grow in Christ through in-depth Bible study, and we thought this cross-cultural Gen X ministry was "ours" until retirement. But God had other plans.

Our eight years of teaching that class was preparation for a greater step of faith. We had "escaped ministry" with summer sailing vacations aboard our sailboat *coram Deo* in the Eastern Caribbean. It was during these trips that God revealed the next step in His calling on our lives. If we would step out in faith to pioneer Community Bible Study International (CBSI) to make disciples of the Lord Jesus Christ through caring, in-depth Bible study, He would bless the people of the Eastern Caribbean through us. God's faithfulness in that journey is the subject of this book.

From the inception of CBSI in the Eastern Caribbean in 2001, our goal was for it to become a Caribbean ministry, not an American ministry. Our calling from God was to pioneer CBSI in-depth Bible study and help the West Indians establish it as an autonomous or indigenous ministry. Our objective was that classes would continue to honor the Name of Jesus Christ by making disciples of Him long after we would leave the islands.

In May of 2008, with the formation of CBSI Caribbean Incorporated, we passed the baton of leadership to the treasured men and women of eight CBSI island nations. It was then we realized that we were the only ones who knew the "whole story" of God's faithfulness in bringing CBSI to this beautiful part of His creation. Our first idea of a ministry history was that of a timeline recording when CBSI classes began on the various islands. In conversations in October of 2010 with both veteran and new CBSI Caribbean National Coordinators, however, God sprouted the seed in our hearts for a full-blown story of His faithfulness to us and to the people of the Eastern Caribbean in pioneering and anchoring in-depth, systematic study of His Word through the life transforming process of CBSI.

We have written this book in the hope that you, Eastern Caribbean CBSI leaders, will realize the disciple-making tool in your hands today, is not from us, but was brought to you by the love and faithfulness of God alone. May you and all disciple makers who read this account of His faithfulness be encouraged in knowing that when God calls you to a particular work, He faithfully meets all your needs according to His glorious riches. May these accounts of God's faithfulness help you realize that before God can do anything through you, you must step out in obedience to His calling, trusting in Him alone to fulfill His purposes in and through you. Then, as you walk in God's irresistible calling, you will know experientially that *"The One who calls you is faithful and He will do it."* *(1 Thessalonians 5:24)*

Chuck and Micki unloading groceries from dinghy to *coram Deo*.

1

The Calling

***"Delight yourself in the Lord and He will give you
the desires of your heart."***
(Psalm 37:4)

"Good book you're reading!" Chuck said to the ticket seller at Nelson's Dockyard in English Harbour, Antigua. We were there on a sailing vacation and wanted information on a bus to St. John's, Antigua's capital city. The young man was so engrossed in reading his Bible that he wasn't aware we were at the window. We cleared our throats to get his attention. Then Chuck spoke up. That was June 23, 1993, and the man was Ted Martin. He was reading in the book of Deuteronomy, and this was no chance meeting. It was a God-ordained appointment that several years later would put us on the adventure of a lifetime!

We are Chuck and Micki Harding, two ordinary people who are passionate about two things: in-depth Bible study and sailing. We both became born-again believers in Jesus Christ in April 1980 and were immediately discipled by our pastor and spiritual father, Clancy Thompson. Clancy pointed us to the Bible as the manual for living. He said he would never tell us how to live or what we can or cannot do. Instead, he would point us to God's Word to discover for ourselves how He wanted us to live.

Clancy invited us to be part of a Navigator's 2:7 series. In it we memorized key Bible verses and learned to dig into the Word mentally each day, choose a verse or two on which to meditate and pray for God to show us how to apply it. This was good but not enough for Micki, who hungered to study the Bible, to understand the words on the pages. So she prayed for God's help.

God answered that prayer on a flight from Detroit, Michigan, to Palm Springs, California, en route to a business convention. Not long after takeoff, the woman sitting next to Micki pulled out a Bible Study Fellowship (BSF) lesson along with her Bible and proceeded to read and answer study questions. Though Micki tried hard to stay focused on work she wanted to finish before the flight landed, she interrupted the woman and asked about her study. The two talked about Bible study for the rest of the four-hour flight.

Upon returning home, it took Micki about two months before finding the only BSF class in our area, about a 45-minute drive away. It was this weekly, in-depth Bible study that God used to transform Micki's life—so much so that one time, when she felt it was too time-consuming and told Chuck she was thinking of quitting, he said, "No! I like the person you are when you're in BSF!"

A few years later, when a men's BSF class opened in our area, Chuck became a member. Soon he was asked to pray about becoming a Discussion Group Leader. After a year as a Discussion Leader, he became an assistant administrator and then a Substitute Teaching Leader. In 1990 Micki joined a prayer group to start a women's BSF class in our town. When the class was piloted, she became the Class Administrator and then Substitute Teaching Leader. Two years later we were approached to start and team-teach a BSF Young Adult class for singles ages 18 to 35. Initially we were hesitant, since we had never ministered to that age group. Also, we do not have children of our own and were not Christians as young adults. What did we have to offer? However, after meeting the five young people who had been praying for a year and a half for a teaching team to step forward, God laid a "love debt" on our hearts for the young adults of the area. ***"Let no debt remain outstanding, except the continuing debt to love one*** *another,"* says Romans 13:8. And in John 3:16, Jesus says, *"For God so loved the world that He gave His one and only Son."* According to the Bible, love is action. If we believed God laid a love debt on our hearts, were we willing to give our time and our God-given talents to teach those who desired to know God's Word?

God confirmed the calling through our BSF study in Esther. *"For if you remain silent at this time, relief and deliverance for the Jews will arise from another place, but you and your father's family will perish. And who knows but that you have come to royal position for such a time as this?" (Esther 4:14)* If we chose not to step out in faith, God would raise up another teaching team, and we would lose the blessing!

We obeyed, loved the young adults and poured ourselves into teaching God's Word. Our aim was to help them apply what they learned. Then we watched amazed as God transformed their lives week by week. As we steeped ourselves in God's Word daily, preparing to teach and to lead, we were filled to overflowing. Our lives too were being transformed. We were given a purpose and meaning as never before.

Micki felt this would be our ministry until we were old and babbling, no longer able to teach! Chuck maintained an intense schedule with his two brothers in a vibrant manufacturing business. Though he worked from home a full day each week to prepare for teaching and leading, God grew and blessed the business.

Ministry is much like viewing a mountain range. You think what you see is all there is—until you crest one of its mountains and see a completely new range! Teaching a Bible Study Fellowship class, having access to the training and materials of this excellent organization was that first mountain range. BSF, we learned, is "A Season of Preparation for a Lifetime of Ministry," and we would see this fulfilled in our lives. We poured our lives into the BSF Young Adult ministry, even in the months when class was on break. To prevent burn-out, we were strongly encouraged by our BSF Area Advisors to take time away from the ministry during the summer recesses. "Get out of town and do something you enjoy," they said. "Be refreshed and restored."

We both loved sailing. One year, with family and a friend, we had chartered a sailboat in the British Virgin Islands (BVI), where we sailed and swam in the beautiful waters of the Caribbean, having the best time. This we decided would be our "get away from ministry." Or so we thought!

It was in 1993 on one of those vacations "getting away from ministry" that we met Ted Martin, nice looking, outgoing and fun-loving. After Chuck's comment about the "good book" he was reading, we told him we were Bible teachers. In his early 30s and a Christian for just two years, Ted was eager to talk about the Lord and learn more from the Bible. He asked how long would we be in Antigua and whether he could follow us around. For the next two days, as Ted showed us the sites of English Harbour and Shirley Heights, we continually discussed the Word. When he would meet up with us, he'd say, "Got my sword!" Then he would pull out his pocket Bible. Active in reaching the youth, he asked for tracts to hand out, and we promised to send him some. On the night before we sailed from Antigua, Ted met us on the dinghy dock with a bag of fresh mangos and bananas. Thus began our God-given love relationship with Ted Martin. Over the years we sent tracts, books to encourage and help him work with youth and Bibles for his family. But we didn't see what God had in store. We had not yet reached the top of that first mountain range.

At the Annapolis Boat Show in October of 1994, we bought a charter sailboat, a sloop-rigged Hunter 430. We had had no plans to purchase a boat—we had no time to maintain one! However, the deal presented to us was never offered before or after. The boat was to be built and delivered in January of 1995 and put in the Sunsail Charter fleet based in Tortola, BVI, with a five-year lease contract. A charter fleet is like a timeshare with boats. We would get six weeks of owner's time in the summer to sail in the Eastern Caribbean or at other Sunsail bases around the world. We compared the costs of chartering for that period of time versus the monthly lease payments we would be paid, and it made sense. The lease income, plus the residual value of the boat after completion of the contract, would more than pay back the purchase cost. Annual summer chartering would be essentially free!

We were concerned, however, that this purchase would distract us from our ministry, so Chuck sought counsel from Brent Barnes, a friend and our Sunday school teacher at the time. Brent pointed him to Psalm 37:4. *"Delight yourself in the LORD and He will give you the desires of your heart."* He then said, "If God places a desire in your heart, He will use it for your good and His glory." How prophetic these words were!

On July 1, 1995, we sailed into Antigua on our maiden voyage aboard sailing vessel *coram Deo*, a Latin phrase that means "before the face of God." We had been in touch with Ted Martin, so he was expecting us. We spent a short time with him, his wife Ann Marie (who is Parks Commissioner for Antigua and Barbuda) and their 3-year-old son TJ before sailing off to return *coram Deo* to Tortola, BVI.

The following summer we took our owner's time sailing in Turkey, so it was June of 1997 before we returned to Antigua. It was then God began working in our hearts about the need for Bible study on this island. On this trip we were able to stay on island for 10 days. A few days before our departure we were joined by Steve Orsini and his friend Colin Maiorono. Steve was a leader in our BSF Young Adult class. The four of us had great times together with the Martin family, but the last night was the eye opener. After a seminar at the Martins' church, Ted, Ann Marie and their friend Yolanda joined the four of us onboard *coram Deo* for refreshments, Bible study and prayer. We led by taking just a few verses of Scripture, teaching our Antiguan friends how to pull out the facts, reflect on the meaning to the people in biblical times, and then consider ways to apply the truths or principles to their lives. It was an incredible time of sharing, studying and praying that went on until well after midnight.

The next morning, as Steve and Colin went off to finish their SCUBA Diving Certification, we went to Nelson's Dockyard to say good-bye to Ann Marie in her office. She was ecstatic! She said she could not sleep after Bible study and was up until 5 a.m. praising God for what she had learned through just a few verses of Scripture.

When was the last time you stayed up all night praising God for what you learned in Bible study? In the States we have all kinds of in-depth Bible studies from which to choose: Community Bible Study, Bible Study Fellowship, Precepts, Navigator studies, Beth Moore and others, but none of these was available in the Eastern Caribbean. We promised to have Bible study next time we visited.

In the summer of 1998, we took our Sunsail owner's time in Tonga and New Zealand. While we were there, Ted Martin tried to contact us. Thinking it was an emergency, we anxiously returned his call. He announced that Ann Marie was pregnant and saying the baby was due in January and that they wanted us to be godparents. They would even hold off the christening until June so we could be there. That was the year we reached the top of a mountain in that first range, where we would begin to see more of what God had for us.

In June of 1999 Chuck sailed *coram Deo* from Tortola to Antigua on a men's outing with his brother-in-law Chris Doherty, a nephew Mike Harding and friend and fellow-BSF leader Les Posey. Because of family commitments Micki flew to Antigua to join Chuck for baby Alexia Martin's christening. Upon our arrival we learned we were not the only godparents but two of eight! How fun! After the christening festivities and some sailing, we held a night of Bible study for Ted, Ann Marie and six of their friends in the historic Officers' Quarters of Nelson's Dockyard, using the same three-question method as before. As we ended the study, Sharon pleaded for us to hold one more study before leaving the island. We changed our plans and held another study. Twelve persons attended, including a young man, Boris Teague, whom God would use in our future.

We had a spirited discussion on Genesis 21:18-21 and a powerful prayer time. When it ended, not one person stood to leave. They all sat looking at us. Malvaire finally spoke, "Now how can we have this kind of Bible study here?" In response Micki said, "Pray. You pray, and we'll pray. God will send someone." It was by these events that evening that we began cresting a mountain in that first range.

This would be just the first of three islands, where we would see the need for in-depth Bible study. Another of the godparents was Andy Brown, a good-natured friend of Ted's in his early 20s from Anguilla, an island about 100 miles northwest—not far off our course to BVI. At Andy's insistence, we laid over in Anguilla on our way north. Upon our arrival he picked us up when we dinghied to shore. On the way to his home, he stopped to help with audio equipment for a revival tent meeting that night. He introduced us to Pastor MacDonna, who would be leading the meeting. When pastor learned we were Bible teachers, he wanted to talk to us about the need for a Bible school on Anguilla. Wow! Here was another island asking for in-depth Bible study!

From Anguilla we sailed to *coram Deo's* home base, Soper's Hole, Tortola. Another of Alexia Martin's godparents was Nath Browne, a long time friend of the Martins and wife of Antiguan Rev. Charlesworth Browne, who pastored in BVI. Nath, fair-skinned and attractive, had worn a stunning beaded hat for the christening, looking absolutely regal. Some of us dubbed her "Princess Di." When she left Antigua, she forgot her hat, so the Martins asked if we would deliver it to her.

Upon arriving in Tortola, we phoned Nath, inviting her and Charlesworth to meet us for dinner so we could return her hat. As we enjoyed dinner at Pusser's Landing overlooking the boats in Soper's Hole, we had an animated conversation about the Lord, their ministry and in-depth Bible study. We shared many of the stories of transformed lives in the BSF Young Adult class. As we walked with them to their car, Charlesworth commented on how encouraging and meaningful our time had been. He expressed his desire to make a true difference for Christ, and he said he knew God brought us together for a purpose. But for what, he didn't know. Remember how Mary, the mother of Jesus, had treasured things said and pondered them in her heart (Luke 2:51)? We walked back to *coram Deo,* wondering what God was doing. We were now almost cresting the mountain where we would see farther!

That summer we were doing the *Experiencing God* study by Blackaby and King in our quiet time. The study emphasizes "Knowing and Doing the Will of God." Repeatedly it speaks of looking to see where God is at work and joining Him there. We are not to ask Him to bless what we want to do but see where He is working. Doing this means being willing to adjust our lives to His direction. "Not my will, Lord, but Yours."

Returning to Michigan, our hearts and spirits were stirred. God had given us a deep love for the Caribbean people we had befriended. We thought of the excitement of Ann Marie Martin after that first Bible study in 1997, staying up all night praising the Lord! There was that question posed to us as we prepared to leave Antigua: "How can we have this kind of Bible study here?" Then we heard the interest for deeper study of the Bible in Anguilla and the comments of Rev. Charlesworth Browne in Tortola.

"God, what would You have us do? People on three islands are hungry for the in-depth study of Your Word, and none is available. Lord, is this where You are working and want us to join You?"

Coram Deo's charter lease would conclude in January of 2000, and we would be free to sail as much as we wished. We had dreamed about living aboard, but was that what God would have us do? The next generation in Chuck's family business was chomping at the bit to take the reigns and willing to buy out our partnership. But what about our BSF Young Adult class, with a leadership of 30 and a class size hovering at 300. Would someone be willing to take on this commitment?

We sought godly counsel from Pastor Dave Andersen, a former pastor of our church, the president of Envoy International (which promotes world missions) and our Adult Fellowship Group teacher. Dave said what we desired to do by taking in-depth Bible study to the Eastern Caribbean is something needed all over the world. A mountain of that first range had been crested! We could now see that God would have us act on the love that He had placed in our hearts for the people of the Eastern Caribbean.

Continuing to pray and willing to adjust our lives to God's direction, in August of 1999 we gave notice to our BSF Area Advisor of our resignation at the completion of the next study in May of 2000.

That is, we would move on if they could find a replacement couple. We were both struggling with the thought of leaving a ministry that was so fulfilling and life changing! We enjoyed the challenge and vibrancy of teaching the young adults and loved the men and women that God brought into our lives through it. By Christmas our replacements were found: Tom and Jeanne Snyder would be trained in January of 2000 to take over when we stepped out.

Our Caribbean friends Charlesworth and Nath Browne in Tortola, Andy Brown in Anguilla and Ted and Ann Marie Martin in Antigua were informed that God had answered prayer. He was making a way for us to relocate to the Eastern Caribbean to begin in-depth Bible studies. They were elated! When doubts would creep into our thoughts, we would receive a call from one of them telling us how they were counting the days until our arrival!

We approached the Executive Director of Bible Study Fellowship, in person and by telephone, about introducing and establishing BSF in the islands. BSF, we were graciously told, is focused on working with large population areas for their international classes, mainly in large cities. So this study program would not be available for the small populations of the Eastern Caribbean islands. Believing that when one door closes another will open, we continued to pray and plan, trusting God to provide materials for us to use. God had called us, and when He calls, He equips. Therefore, we waited while looking for His provision.

One Sunday in March of 2000, God arranged a serendipitous meeting in the church vestibule between Micki and a friend, Judy Scott, who wanted to know how the plans were coming for our new ministry. Micki explained that God was bringing together all the details, but as yet we had no materials to use! Judy, a Community Bible Study Children's Supervisor in a local class, said that at the prior week's Leaders Council, the CBSI Caleb program was introduced and seemed to be geared to just what we desired to do. She agreed to call CBSI the next morning and have Caleb information sent to us.

Community Bible Study (CBS), very similar to BSF, is active in our area and does not have the population restrictions of BSF. The CBS International motto is "Everyone in the world...in the Word." After receiving and reading the information about CBSI's Caleb Connection Ministry, we called and talked to CBSI Director Paul Young, who was enthusiastic about us working in the Eastern Caribbean since no one else was working there.

We then spoke with Caleb Ministry Director Gordon Spaugh and learned that Calebs, named after Caleb of the Bible, were generally people near retirement or already retired and looking for a new challenge from the Lord. As recorded in Numbers 13, Caleb was one of 12 men sent by Moses to explore the land of Canaan, which God had promised to give the people of Israel. Only Caleb and Joshua returned with positive reports. Caleb said, *"We should go up and take possession of the land, for we can certainly do it." (Numbers 13:30)* Because ten of the dozen spies feared the Canaanites and did not trust God's protection, the Israelites spent the next 40 years wandering in the desert. Of that entire generation of Israel, only Joshua and Caleb actually crossed into the Promised Land.

After taking control of the land, Caleb said to Joshua, *"'So here I am today, eighty-five years old! I am still as strong today as the day Moses sent me out; I'm just as vigorous to go out to battle now as I was then. Now give me this hill country that the LORD promised me that day. You yourself heard then that the Anakites were there and their cities were large and fortified, but, the LORD helping me, I will drive them out just as He said.' Then Joshua blessed Caleb son of Jephunneh and gave him Hebron as his inheritance." (Joshua 14:10-13)*

That was us, sort of old and still strong! We filled out the Caleb application and other paperwork. Within a short time Gordon notified us of our approval as Calebs to the Eastern Caribbean. Can you believe it? God married the two passions of our lives—in-depth Bible study and sailing! Psalm 37:4 promises, *"Delight yourself in the LORD, and He will give you the desires of your heart."* This was above and beyond what we could have ever asked for or imagined!

Besides becoming CBSI Calebs, we approached our pastor, Doug Schmidt, at Troy Baptist Church (now called Woodside Bible), asking for missionary status to be granted us by the church. We wanted our home church to support us in prayer and hold us accountable, but we did not ask for financial support. Who would be willing to support two people living on a sailboat in the Caribbean? Besides, God had already provided for us financially through the sale of the business. The Missions Committee approved us.

We set our faces to finishing the teaching of the BSF Young Adult class not just somehow but victoriously. God provided for the many hard and painful details of leaving home, family, business and a ministry with young adult men and women whom we had grown to love as "our God-given family," our spiritual children. As we daily continued to saturate ourselves in His Word, His promises and challenges came alive. *"And everyone who has left houses or brothers or sisters or father or mother or children or fields for My sake will receive a hundred times as much and will inherit eternal life." (Matthew 19:29)*

"Jesus replied, 'No one who puts his hand to the plow and looks back is fit for service in the kingdom of God." (Luke 9:62)

"Anyone who loves his father or mother more than Me is not worthy of Me; anyone who loves his son or daughter more than Me is not worthy of Me; and anyone who does not take his cross and follow Me is not worthy of Me. Whoever finds his life will lose it, and whoever loses his life for My sake will find it." (Matthew 10:37-39)

Prior to the final decision we met with Micki's sister Louise Doherty and her husband Chris. Since the bulk of the care of their elderly parents would fall on them, Micki wanted their support in this step of faith. Chris said we would be living his dream on the boat. Once Louise realized all that God had put in place, she said we "couldn't not go."

When God's call is confirmed, obedience is the only right answer. Departure day, Sunday, May 28, 2000, arrived. Our dear long time friends Bill and Bonnie Reeves drove us to the airport. As we winged our way to Tortola, Micki looked at Chuck and said, "What have we done? We've told all these people. What if God doesn't do anything?"

Brother-in-law Chris Doherty caught yellowtail snapper while sailing from Tortola to Antigua.

Sailing crew to Antigua (l to r): nephew Mike, brother-in-law Chris, Chuck, friend Les.

Proud parents and godparents. Back row: Ted (father);
Middle row: Chuck, Nath wearing hat (Tortola), Malvaire,
Yolanda; Front row: Ann Marie (mother), Micki holding
Alexia reaching for her mom, Sharon wearing hat,
Andy (Anguilla); cousin and TJ in very front.

Antiguans who asked for in-depth Bible study. Future TL and
ATL Ted and Boris are tall men in back row.

**Come aboard *coram Deo* to relive our
adventure of a lifetime!**

2

The Beginning

"In his heart a man plans his course,
but the Lord determines his steps."
(Proverbs 16:9)

With faith the size of a mustard seed but armed with the love and faithful call of God, we landed on Tortola, British Virgin Islands (BVI), on the evening of May 28, 2000. We were welcomed with open arms at the home of Rev. Charlesworth and wife Nath Browne, who presented us with keys to their house and Nath's car to use while there.

Our thinking was that we would take the first six months to settle into our new lifestyle as live-aboard sailors, often called cruisers or "yachties," and begin the CBSI ministry in January of 2001. We had not yet been trained by CBSI. Training was set to take place at the CBSI Ministry Service Center in August. The hurricane season was on us, and our boat insurance coverage required *coram Deo* to be located in Grenada or farther south from June to November. It was not time to start the ministry...or so we thought.

The first week was spent examining the boat, ordering further work done, getting our BVI drivers licenses, negotiating with BVI customs agents over unjust charges on shipments of our boat stuff (which are supposed to be duty free) and meeting with immigration officials to be approved for doing missionary work in BVI.

It *just so happened* that Rev (nickname for Charlesworth) had recently assumed leadership of the BVI Christian Council. In the midst of our busy first week, he announced that Chuck was scheduled to make a CBSI presentation to the council on June 10. God was launching the ministry. So much for our plan! *"In his heart a man plans his course, but the Lord determines his steps." (Proverbs 16:9)*

Now added to our To Do List was preparation for that introduction and a plan for an inaugural prayer group—which, the Lord willing, would result from it. We called Caleb Director Gordon Spaugh to get authorization to make a CBSI introduction and discuss what such an introduction entailed since we had no CBSI training! On top of this, we were preparing for "Caribbean Adventure 2000." Fourteen of our BSF young adult leaders were joining us on June 3 for a farewell week's sailing vacation. It was planned to be an enjoyable conclusion to the dynamic ministry that had been the center of our lives for the last eight years—a time of letting go of the former and fully embracing our new CBSI Eastern Caribbean ministry.

Looking back on that first week in the Caribbean, we can see that God was giving us a preview of the schedule to expect in our future. When the Lord is at the helm, hang on!

With only enough time to move our clothes on board *coram Deo*, we welcomed our 14 guests. We chartered a second yacht, ironically named Bonic Witch. Chuck captained this 50-foot yacht with a crew of nine while Micki captained *coram Deo* with a crew of five. God blessed us with incredibly good weather, great group devotions and lots of laughter and love! A highlight of the week was attending Rev's Zion Hill Methodist Church. As we gathered in front of the platform and were introduced, together we sang "Great Is Thy Faithfulness," a classic hymn fitting for what lay ahead. After service Rev and Nath came aboard *coram Deo* for lunch and a fun afternoon sail—a melding of former co-laborers with the new.

On Saturday, June 10, as many of our God-given "spiritual family" prepared to leave for the airport, Chuck was off to make the first CBSI presentation in the Eastern Caribbean to pastors in the BVI. The Christian Council endorsed CBSI, and a meeting was scheduled for the following Tuesday to form a prayer group with the goal of starting a class on Tortola.

With time before the next meeting, we began setting up house-keeping on *coram Deo*. On Sunday afternoon we excitedly made our first official sail as "live-aboard missionaries," sailing three hours west to St. Thomas to pick up our new dinghy and outboard motor. The dinghy is like a family car, and with only one in our family, single-mindedness was required. It was a 10-foot RIB (rigid inflatable boat) with an aluminum bottom and weighed about 80 pounds, making it easy to haul onboard with our spinnaker halyard, a line running over the top of the mast designed to raise the spin-naker sail. The outboard was a 15 horsepower Yamaha. Chuck had installed a motor lift on the stern rail, a wonderful back saver! With our new ship-to-shore transport on board, we sailed back to Soper's Hole for Sunsail to complete their boat work and for us to prepare for the prayer group meeting Tuesday night.

Eighteen persons attended the inaugural prayer group for Tortola, including Rev. Comet Chalwell and three other pastors. After we again introduced the mission and process of CBSI, Madlene Blyden, a lay leader, volunteered to lead the group, which would meet every other week. The prayer focus would be for God to raise up leader-ship to begin a class in September, when we could return for training.

The Tortola Sunsail base was unable to replace all the mal-functioning parts and equipment on *coram Deo* and instructed the base in St. Martin to accommodate our needs upon our arrival. After good-byes to Rev and Nath and clearing BVI Customs and Immigration in mid-afternoon on Friday, June 17, 2000, we eagerly sailed out of Soper's Hole bound for St. Martin. The adventure of a lifetime had begun!

It took about three and a half hours to move out of the protected waters of the Sir Francis Drake Channel into the open waters of the Caribbean. With an 80 mile sail beating into strong winds, we estimated the passage taking up to 22 hours. The swells were six to eight feet pretty much on our nose as we entered the open waters. As we slammed into the waves, the plunging and falling motion was extremely uncomfortable. Chuck went on deck to secure the dinghy better. Back in the cockpit, he began to feel queasy—the beginning of the captain's bout with seasickness!

Initially we encountered a couple of mild squalls (sudden, short-lived but violent localized wind and rain), but by the end of the crossing, we had endured five. The third, hitting after dark, was the doozy! With Chuck mildly seasick, Micki was at the helm. It took all she had to ride it out. Not wanting to disturb him, she waited too long to call him to shorten sail. The winds were whipping, the driving rain was blinding and *coram Deo's* deck was pitching in the big seas! On deck but still suffering from seasickness, Chuck began furling or rolling in the jib (forward most sail). Due to the rotten condition of the sail combined with the extreme conditions, the clew (back corner) of the jib ripped out. It could not be reset. Not to worry, or so we thought—we have the mainsail and an engine! With Chuck's seasickness now worse, Micki stayed on watch. After a time, the engine started slowing down and cutting out. Chuck knew it had to be a fuel problem and that the filter needed to be replaced. However, when he had tried ahead of time to get spare filters from Sunsail, they said they had just done the maintenance and told him to pick up spare filters in St. Martin. For most of the night, Chuck could not restart the engine.

The autopilot (which automatically steers a set course) was a major help to Micki. Not having to be constantly at the wheel, she got about an hour and a half sleep. In the middle of the night, however, the autopilot quit, forcing her to hand steer.

By early morning, with the jib useless and the engine out, we were left with only the mainsail to move us the last 40 miles. To sail to our destination, we had to tack in one direction for miles and then back. Against the seas and current we were making about four and a half knots but not getting much closer to St. Martin. So we prayed, and Chuck went below to see what he could do with the engine. Micki continued to steer and prayed for wisdom for Chuck, as commanded in James 1:5-6, *"If any of you lacks wisdom, he should ask God, who gives generously to all without finding fault, and it will be given to him. But when he asks, he must believe and not doubt, because he who doubts is like a wave of the sea, blown and tossed by the wind."* This is not a hard prayer to pray and believe in when you are literally being blown by the winds and tossed by the seas! Micki prayed for God to give Chuck insight and wisdom in solving the problem. She reminded God that Chuck had a desk job before this ministry and had mechanics to fix diesel engines. "You have all wisdom, Lord, and You are the only one available out here!" Like Elijah, she prayed a while, then called down and asked Chuck, "Anything yet?" He said, "Not yet," so she prayed again. After a while she'd call down and ask, "Anything yet?" "Not yet," he'd say, so she continued to pray. This went on for hours.

About 11 a.m. after repeatedly trying to clean the clogged filter cartridge, Chuck bypassed the primary filter and ran with only the engine filter, hoping this would not clog the injectors. After what seemed like an eternity, the engine started! We kept it at the most efficient fuel usage because it appeared we were running low on fuel!

The engine continued to run, our fuel lasted and we motored into Marigot Bay, St. Martin, at dusk after a 29-hour crossing. Another concern as we approached the island was that it would be with some daylight. The cruising guide said there were two unlit buoys in the bay on which you can sit after they sink your boat! We saw the buoys just before darkness fell. *"And my God will meet all your needs according to His glorious riches in Christ Jesus."* *(Philippians 4:19)*

Chuck was feeling better, we were safely at anchor and took looooong showers. Nothing like a fresh water shower when sea spray has formed you into a human salt lick!

Initially Micki entitled this sail, "The Crossing from Hell." But then, recalling a conversation we had with Rev before leaving Tortola, we looked at it with new eyes. The discussion centered on the question, "Do we really believe the God we say we believe in?"

Yes, we do. It was plain to see His hand and provisions in every mile of our crossing.

One more thing about that crossing. We received a farewell gift on the Tortola Sunsail work dock—a stowaway rat. Yes! We discovered the droppings of the unwelcome guest just before our departure. We sought help from the Sunsail manager to get rid of the rodent. He said they knew of the rat on the premises and that it was a smart one. No one had been able to trap it. Basically he said, "Good luck!" We needed to get moving south, so we sailed with a rat on board. In all the pounding seas, Micki figured that rat would be sorry he picked *coram Deo*!

The next morning we radioed the St. Martin Sunsail base, and it sent out a guide boat to lead us through the shallow, narrow channel to their dock. As we motored, weaving around masts and boat rails sticking up out of the water, we had a sobering reminder of the devastation of Hurricane Lenny seven months earlier.

Tied to a mooring near the dock, we began a thorough cleanup, as everything on deck was covered with salt and felt greasy. As we worked together, Micki mentioned that she forgot to put on suntan lotion. Being thoughtful, Chuck got the lotion and, without warning, squirted it onto Micki's back just as she dipped his water activated PFD (life vest) into a bucket of water. It worked! The CO_2 cartridge went off, blowing up the vest in the bucket! Micki screamed and jumped, thinking the bucket was exploding. Comic relief was just what we needed! Micki was laughing more than Chuck since it was his PFD.

The St. Martin Sunsail manager, Nick, was unavailable to meet us on the Sunday morning of our arrival. He was busy teaching his adult Sunday school class in the Simpson Bay Marina. Yes! God providentially placed one of His own to oversee the work needed on *coram Deo*. Upon meeting Nick on Monday, we talked about his class, church and pastor and told him about our CBSI ministry. When we changed the subject to our horrendous crossing and equipment failures, Nick took a personal interest. We gave him a list of repairs, including rat removal. He inspected *coram Deo* and added to our list. Assigning four of his workers and two sail makers, they set to work.

Our planned one-week stay in St. Martin stretched into two weeks due to the amount of work. Not only was the jib repaired, but due to the worn out condition of the mainsail, a new main was ordered, to be built in Barbados and delivered to the Sunsail base in St. Vincent for pick-up in October. For our use in the meantime, Nick hired a sail maker to redo a serviceable mainsail from another boat to fit *coram Deo*. The shipwrights worked daily, replacing our water heater, compass, jib roller reefing system, main and jib sheets, fuel filtering system, anchor windlass and more.

Also, the rat was exterminated! However, in its two weeks on board it had chewed books, toilet paper, shoes, swim fins and, later we learned wiring, when our depth sounder began reading erratically! Nick hired two exterminators. The first attempt was a trap baited with peanut butter and banana—Caribbean rats preferring this to cheese. The second spread poison paste. The night when the trap was set, Micki was reading in bed with Chuck sound asleep beside her. A few minutes after turning off the lights, she heard the trap door slam and scurrying feet on metal. "We got him, Chuck, we got him!" Micki cried out, waking a groggy husband. Checking the trap, he saw, sure enough, that we had it! Chuck picked up the cage and started up the companionway stairs to dump the rat overboard. The rat was frantically racing around the cage, the cage tipped slightly, the rat flew against the trap door, and it opened! The rat was under the floorboards in a flash. We were dumbstruck! Inconceivably, it got away! There was not much sleep for Micki that night.

The next morning we accepted the fact that God was in charge of all things, even rats, and determined not to let the stowaway distract us from what God had called us to do. We did not like it, especially Micki, but we would trust God even in this.

Two days later, at about 10 a.m. during our Bible study devotions on deck, Micki spotted the demon rat walking across the cockpit floor. Not speaking, she nudged Chuck and pointed to the rat. Chuck grabbed the nearest implement, a metal winch handle, and stealthily circled around on the cockpit seats. He then swung, knocking the rat out of the cockpit onto the swim platform, finishing him with a lightning quick smash to the head, propelling him into the water! We did a celebration dance in the cockpit, yelling to all that the rat was dead!

Think of it: this was mid-morning under full sunshine, and rats are nocturnal. We discovered later that the rat ate some poison in the starboard lazarette. It was God's further protection that it did not die in some impossible-to-get-to place, giving us a decaying stench for weeks.

Even before the rat became fish food, we were able to stay on mission. We had contacted Andy Brown's family, who were eager for us to return to Anguilla. With the Sunsail crew in the midst of our boat work and the rat on board, Micki was particularly happy to take the ferry six miles north to Anguilla. Andy met us at the dock, driving us to his family's home, where we were welcomed to stay with him, his mom Rose, Granny and sister Andrea. The first night was a long one, as Andy, Andrea and Micki worked until midnight photocopying materials for the following morning's presentation.

At 4:40 a.m. on Monday, June 26, 2000, we met with a group of 19 believers at a regularly scheduled prayer meeting at Christian Fellowship Church. This group, primarily women, had been meeting Mondays through Fridays from 4 to 6 a.m. year round for two years. We explained the CBSI mission and process and then prayed with them for God to raise up the needed leadership, meeting place and additional people to participate in the class. The reception was wonderful, as was the time of prayer. They expressed the need for in-depth Bible study, to become well rooted in God's Word, as the solution to their social problems, especially those of young people. Since Clara was already leading the group, she agreed to dedicate Thursday mornings to CBSI.

Then the excitement within them came out. One woman suggested that Andy Brown be the Class Coordinator. Andy and two other young men began brainstorming on how to promote CBSI. In a future email from Kirk Hughes, we learned that Andy and a friend, Claudius, and himself had dedicated Tuesdays as "fasting days" for a CBSI class.

Buoyed by God's faithfulness, we set sail for Antigua the evening of June 30, 2000. With no rat aboard and with new equipment, new headsail rigging and a very serviceable mainsail, we made the nearly 100 mile crossing from St. Martin to Antigua without incident. We arrived in English Harbour the next afternoon.

After a restful night we met with Ann Marie Martin in Nelson's Dockyard, asking her for contacts for a CBSI introduction. Out of that came a meeting with Bishop Dorsett of the Church of God of Prophecy, also head of a group of evangelical ministers. We met him in the tiny office in his store in St. John's. As Chuck presented the CBSI literature and began explaining the process, the bishop interrupted, asking, "You're the man on a boat?" Chuck agreed. Bishop Dorsett said Rev. Comet Chalwell told him about a man on a boat starting Bible studies. The bishop had visited Tortola shortly after the formation of the CBSI prayer group there.

Bishop Dorsett went on to say that Antigua did not need more churches. "There are two, three or four churches on every corner," he declared. "We don't need more evangelists either. Many Antiguans have been saved 20 times over! What CBSI has to offer is what my people need because their lifestyle does not match their words." His denominational responsibilities included 19 islands and nations in the Caribbean. "I'd like you to take this to all my people," he said. "What about Guyana, Surinam and Curacao?" We sat dumbfounded, thinking we would have to convince this man to listen to what we had to offer, and here he was flinging open the doors of the Eastern Caribbean and beyond! All Micki could think was, "Wow! We're only two people on a boat."

A few days later, at a meeting of the Interdenominational Intercessory Prayer Group in St. John's, our reception was not this welcoming! At the end of a two and a half hour time of praise, worship and deliverance, we were given five minutes to make a presentation. Chuck did a quick overview of CBSI while Micki distributed brochures and a sample lesson and announced that we would be making a full presentation the following Monday, 7:30 p.m., at Ebenezer Methodist Church. The Pastor leading the meeting said he realized CBSI was an interdenominational work. Then he said to Chuck, "And what church do you belong to?" Chuck replied that we are born-again believers and that regarding the CBSI program our church affiliation did not matter. He persisted with his question until Chuck said, "Troy Baptist." He then told us to go to our own people on the island. The wife of this pastor had invited us to speak, but apparently they were not on the same page.

On July 10, 2000, we rented a car and drove to Ebenezer Methodist Church, arriving half hour early for the 7:30 p.m. meeting—our normal practice when leading a meeting. The room was locked, and no one was around. We eventually found the caretaker, who unlocked the room, and we set up a circle of chairs, organized our materials on a table and waited. Seven thirty came, and no one was there. Where was Ted? We had followed him until he veered off to pick up a friend. We prayed. At 7:45 we still had not seen a single person. Fifteen minutes later, when not even Ted had arrived, we became concerned, wondering if he had been in an accident. Finally, at 8:15, two women arrived, Joy and Vivian, whom we had met the day before at Ted's church. Then, slowly, people began trickling in—Michàl and Ted with Naldin, Sharon and Yolanda. At about 8:45 we decided to start the presentation, and then, a short time later, Boris and Franklyn came in. When we had gone through our explanation, we spent time clarifying and answering questions, especially for those who missed part of the presentation. After some discussion, they agreed to form a prayer group to seek God's guidance for leadership and a venue for an interdenominational CBSI class in Antigua. Franklyn Braithwaite, a close friend of the Martins and a sail maker in Nelson's Dockyard, volunteered to lead the prayer group, which would meet on Monday nights. Though a small group, it represented three denominations, and its members were mighty in prayer! From their prayers that night, it was clear that they would be committed and believed God would answer.

Within one month after the first presentation in Tortola, from June 10 to July 10, we experienced God's faithfulness by prayer groups established on three islands! All three groups expressed interest in starting classes in September. We were elated! But we were also wondering how this was going to happen!

Therefore, we emailed our prayer warriors back in the States to pray for wisdom and discernment in calling God's chosen leaders for each group and arranging our schedule to train and shepherd three classes on different islands. As 1 Thessalonians 5:24 says, *"The One who calls you is faithful and He will do it."* But we must pray! Steve and Jane Colyer from our home church volunteered to distribute our eNewsletter, *coram Deo* online, to those interested in receiving it via email. Steve, a website builder and fellow leader with Chuck in BSF, hosted our web page on the church website. People were added regularly until well over 200 supported our mission in prayer. In 2005 Bob and Terrie Mathison, two of our spiritual children, took over the responsibility from Steve, and to this day they distribute *coram Deo* online. We are indebted to the Colyers and the Mathisons for their faithfulness in helping us keep our prayer team updated on the ministry and, more importantly, on our vital prayer needs.

With the prayer groups formed and hurricane season upon us, it was time to get out of harm's way. Boat insurance has an exclusion area, known as the "hurricane box," during the months of July to December. The box encompasses all the Caribbean islands above 12° North latitude, which is southern Grenada. We prayed for a safe weather window to sail from Antigua, and God quickly provided.

On July 12, 2000, with people in three island nations praying about starting CBSI classes, we set sail for Deshaies, Guadeloupe, about 30 miles south. From there, while fast tracking, we still enjoyed beautiful sails, island hopping to Dominica, Martinique, St. Lucia, St. Vincent and the Grenadines (SVG) before sailing into Tyrrel

Bay, Carriacou, on July 26. Carriacou, the largest of the Grenadines, is part of Grenada and about 14 miles north of it. As we sailed out of Tyrrel Bay, headed for our final destination in Grenada, a rain shower passed quickly. When it passed, there was the most beautiful rainbow, which seemed to start at the bow of *coram Deo* and wrap around to the stern. The reflection of the colors on the water was breathtaking! We thanked God for His promises that the rainbow represents and for His daily faithfulness as we stepped out in faith.

On July 27 we arrived in Mount Hartman Bay in southern Grenada, after cautiously reading and following the markers through the reefs. With a week until our flight home to Michigan, on August 3, we had much to organize and prepare. This was unfamiliar territory to us, and we knew no one! Day by day God faithfully provided for our needs...and more.

Recommendations from other cruisers guided us to a boat service to watch *coram Deo* as well as oversee various projects in our absence. We rented a secure mooring to keep the boat safe even in a serious blow. Then we received an unexpected ministry confirmation.

Micki needed to take care of some business in St. George's, the capital. We radioed for the taxi driver we had hired the prior day, but by the time Micki was dinghied to shore, the driver was busy and turned her over to Percy Glaud. In the car on the way to town, Micki asked about churches in the area. The conversation led to talking about CBSI, and Percy, a humble and reserved man, perked up! He said he had an evangelist friend, Norma Jeremiah, we must meet, and he invited us to go with them to Happy Hills Berean Church on Sunday. Micki readily accepted the invitation.

Knowing we were new to Grenada, Percy arrived early on Sunday morning and took us on a short tour of the area around Mt. Hartman before picking up Norma for church. Norma, outgoing and one who loved to talk about her Lord, helped in founding the little church in Happy Hills. The people stole our hearts that morning!

About 100 mostly young adult men and women attended that morning. We arrived on time, and as we entered the church, Norma marched us up to the second pew as people reached out to greet us all along the way. Once the service started, Pastor Paul Miller had Norma introduce us. Then, while the congregation sang praise songs, we were called to the front, where every person came forward, welcoming us—some shaking our hands but most hugging us. What bright countenances they had as we looked into their eyes, saw the joy of the Lord and experienced His love through them! Later in the service pastor asked Chuck to come forward to bring a word to the congregation. Chuck explained God's new calling on our lives and a little about CBSI. God had faithfully arranged for CBSI to be introduced in Grenada before we even got the salt washed off from our trip down the island chain! Pastor Paul was visibly disappointed when we told him we were returning to the States for a few weeks. While we assured him we would contact him upon our return, God had radically different plans in store.

Only 68 days had elapsed between our flight to Tortola to move aboard *coram Deo* and this return flight home. On that flight to Tortola, we were questioning. "What have we done!" we exclaimed to ourselves. "What if God doesn't do anything?" Sixty-eight days later, as we boarded a flight home, we could hardly take in all that God had done! We were living a completely different lifestyle aboard *coram Deo,* living before the face of God—the faith adventure of a lifetime. Groups on three islands were praying and waiting for our return. With all we saw God doing, we hardly had time for this trip back for business and training! God's faithfulness was overwhelming.

In hindsight we realize that God used these beginning times and circumstances to train us and prepare others for the amazing things He was about to do! No one had tried what we, with God's grace, were hoping to accomplish. When we became Calebs in 2000, the CBSI ministry was just developing. There was no road map for them to give us! Two years later, St. Vincent Associate Teaching Leader Chiefton Charles would introduce us as "pioneers" for CBSI in the Eastern Caribbean. He was on target because we were breaking new ground, providing in-depth Bible study in these islands by following the faithful leading of God's Spirit one step at a time.

God knew we needed time to catch our breath. Back home in Michigan we had a wonderful time with family and friends and finally received our CBSI training.

Since our training at CBSI headquarters in Reston, Virginia immediately followed the CBS 25th Anniversary Teaching Directors Conference in nearby Washington, D.C., we were invited to be part of this great milestone celebration. With famous journalist Cal Thomas and Prison Fellowship Director Chuck Colson as key-note speakers, we were motivated and challenged. Gifted vocalist Steve Green inspired us with soul-stirring times of worship, and we learned Steve Green's wife was in CBS leadership. Cool!

The amazing backup singers for Steve Green were from the Reston Bible Church choir, near CBSI Ministry Service Center. Wanting to hear more of these singers, our hosts agreed to attend the Reston church on Sunday. Early Sunday morning, however, they called saying plans changed, and we would attend Cornerstone Chapel in Leesburg. Initially we were disappointed, but once we were into the Cornerstone service we were impressed by Pastor Gary Hamrick's teaching. He gave an excellent overview of the Book of Daniel in about 45 minutes!

Then, departing from his normal practice, Pastor Gary stepped into the congregation at the end of the service, and there we were introduced to him by our CBSI host. When he heard we were ministering in the West Indies, he exclaimed, "You must meet Verrol Blake in St. Vincent! He knows everybody in the Caribbean." From behind us, a man asked, "Did you say St. Vincent? I'm from St. Vincent. I'm here with my pastor, who is visiting his daughter at Howard University." This man's pastor, Desmond Fessal, head of the Baptist seminary in St. Vincent, approached, and we were introduced. His church, we learned, is minutes away from the Sunsail base where we would pick up our new sail in October. He urged us to call him when we arrived in SVG.

It *just so happened* that our church choice was changed, so we would attend one with ties to the Caribbean. It *just so happened* that Pastor Gary decided to step into the congregation after that service, and it *just so happened* that he knew Verrol Blake in St. Vincent. It *just so happened* that a young man from St. Vincent was in that church then, standing where he overheard the conversation, and introduced us to Pastor Fessal, who *just so happened* to be visiting his daughter at a nearby college and who *just so happened* to live minutes away from where we would pick up our new sail. It could have been delivered to a number of different islands, but it *just so happened* that Nick in St. Martin ordered it to be delivered to St. Vincent.

While we were awed by Cal Thomas, Chuck Colson and Steve Green the day before, this sovereign and faithful confirmation topped all of that! What, then, did God have awaiting us in St. Vincent?

All of this encouragement and inspiration came before our training! We were eager and ready! New Acting CBSI Executive Director Damon Martinez joined Caleb Director Gordon Spaugh in our training. Both were enthusiastic and encouraging. They introduced and reviewed the CBSI materials—brochures, lessons and manuals—for our use. Through this training we could see that our years in leadership, experience in training and shepherding leaders and teaching in-depth Bible study were a foundation for this next step in ministry. It would definitely be more challenging in a foreign culture, but we were encouraged and confirmed that God had put us exactly where He wanted us and would use what He had invested in us over the years.

There was one last concern before we left CBSI Headquarters. How long were we willing to commit to this work? Damon and Gordon asked if we would be willing to follow through with a work of God once it began. We thought about it and committed to a year, to see how it went—on the boat and in the ministry. Within three months we knew the boating lifestyle was for us, and we grew more and more in love with Caribbean people. We extended our commitment to five years and later to 10 years, or as long as God directed.

As we left training with the realization that this would be no walk in the park, Micki was reminded of a remark made by one of our young adult leaders, Mike Seventko, when we disclosed our call to the Caribbean. "You always told us that when God calls us out of our current leadership position, it will be to something more challenging," he said. "You taught us this principle, and now you are doing what you taught." How important it is that we walk our talk! Everything we do as leaders teaches something!

Motivated and inspired, we looked for a way to respond more quickly to open doors. In our contacts with the prayer group leaders, we were led to believe that God had raised up teaching leader candidates for Tortola and Anguilla and that there was growing enthusiasm in Antigua. So Chuck, ignoring what little he had learned about cross-cultural ministry, implemented a plan to cover all of the open doors in one quick trip around the Leeward Islands. And at a bargain! American Eagle Airlines had a "circle the Caribbean" fare allowing a traveler to stop for a few days at a number of intermediate destinations. So on September 6, 2000, rather than fly directly to Grenada as scheduled, we interrupted our flight at San Juan, Puerto Rico. From there we flew to Tortola for a three-day training seminar, then on to Anguilla and Antigua to repeat seminars before returning to San Juan on September 17 and then return to Grenada to rejoin *coram Deo*. Whew!

The three-day training seminar we implemented included the components we considered essential to start a class. In the first session we modeled a CBSI class. After explaining the format, we passed out lessons for everyone, assigned questions and gave time to do the assignment. Micki then led them through a short time of discussion to get a "feel" of the discussion group. Chuck followed with a short teaching on the passage. In the second session we trained on the Discussion Leader role and in the third on the Teaching Leader and Associate Teaching Leader roles, including the eight-step preparation of a teaching. Pretty intense!

Upon arriving in Tortola we learned that the "teaching leader" was not committed. Seventeen people attended the first seminar, but only two single young adults returned for the next two, and they had not been in the prayer group. They had heard the announcements about CBSI leadership training in their church. At the end of the third seminar, they committed to join and bring others into the prayer group and would pray about taking a leadership role.

In Anguilla, the situation was more encouraging. Seventeen also attended that first seminar. Six stepped forward as leadership candidates and were present at the next two seminars. As a result, the six agreed to do a six-week study of 1 John among themselves, reviewing the various leadership roles and taking turns leading and teaching while praying for God to identify persons for the specific roles. Regrettably, this group abandoned the study when no one was willing to commit to teaching, not even one lesson!

We flew on to Antigua, where 23 people attended the first seminar. Ten turned up at the second seminar and returned for the third. At the end of the training, Gerald Henry stepped forward as Teaching Leader and Michàl Charles as Class Coordinator. Similar to Anguilla, Gerald would lead the leadership team through the six-week 1 John study, praying for God to identify the Associate Teaching Leader and Discussion Leaders.

It certainly was an ambitious schedule! We felt if God was in it, He would provide the strength for us to do it. And He did. But we believe He allowed this to teach us that this strategy would not be effective in the Eastern Caribbean! It would have been a great plan in Midwest U.S.A., but Caribbean people move at a slightly slower pace. Oh, the flights were safe and reasonably on time. But the people were not ready. Since they had never seen an in-depth Bible study like CBSI, they had a difficult time understanding the format and how all its pieces work together. Their experience of a Bible study was at church, where the pastor studied the Bible and spoon-fed what he learned in his study without expecting any effort in participants. The concept of personally studying the Bible and answering questions in preparation for the weekly meeting was very unusual. Some had done studies from books that expounded on scriptural topics or examined a book of the Bible with lessons learned from the author's viewpoint, but no lay people we met had experienced direct, personal study of God's Word.

What we learned in the weeks ahead was that this work was not like instant coffee! We would need to return to these islands to motivate, encourage and coach until the leadership teams were strong enough to stand on their own. It was going to take time and organization, and we needed to be faithful shepherds to those who stepped forward in faith to lead in CBSI!

Arriving back in Grenada September 17, 2000, after our "circle the Caribbean" whirlwind, we were picked up at the airport by Percy and Norma, and they took us to Mt. Hartman Bay dinghy dock. New friend Gary Simmers, from sailing vessel Elusive, was waiting with his dinghy to haul us out to *coram Deo*. It was great to be home! The new upholstery completed while we were gone looked fabulous! The three boxes shipped from Michigan were on board—we did not have to wrestle with customs officials, then try to get the 70-pound boxes on the boat. The Lord took care of it all!

Up early the next morning after a great night's sleep, we met with our boat watcher to review the completed work assignments. Sean Thomas, a young boat worker, had cleaned and polished the fiberglass and stainless steel. We worked all day unpacking and organizing. Flat bed sheets that friend Mary Andersen made into fitted sheets fit! The carpet pieces that former young adult leader Brandon made for the sole (boat floor), looked great. However, the freezer was still warmer than the refrigerator, and our battery power was low, and it was not charging properly. The saying that "cruising is a time spent in exotic places working on your boat" was proving to be true!

One of our questions when moving on board was whether our Hunter 430 was the appropriate boat to carry out our mission. It was a great vacation boat but left much to be desired in storage, systems and sea kindliness. Micki was losing patience with the daily scene of boat parts exposed for repair and Chuck's tools spread around the living area.

While grumbling to himself about the batteries and other boat issues, Chuck met Mickey Smith from sailing vessel Discovery, a 1984 Hallberg Rassy 49-foot ketch-rigged sailboat made in Sweden. Mickey said he would be selling her the following spring. He then looked at Chuck and said, "You want to buy a boat?" In jest Chuck said, "Sure! What do you have to sell?" So Mickey invited us aboard to look. We took him up on his invitation. The boat was obviously well maintained and had everything we were working to achieve on *coram Deo*. But this larger boat seemed overwhelming with its space, equipment and superior construction. Though 11 years older than *coram Deo*, it was more solid, comfortable and functional. We had a lot on our plate, but Mickey's offer was food for thought.

We continued our boat work on Monday and began hearing about a possible hurricane developing. Thinking more about Mickey's Hallberg Rassy, we radioed to see if we could take another look. When we went aboard, we met Mickey's wife Ann, as well as their daughter Cassidy and son Christian, who had just returned from visiting family in Florida. Amazingly, we learned that Mickey and Ann had lived in Ortonville, Michigan, 10 miles north of our current home! Furthermore, before getting married, Ann lived down the street from our previous home! We all had to move to Grenada, 3,000 miles south, to meet! After spending a couple of hours on the boat, both of us liked it more than the first time. It was more like a home than a "camper" like the Hunter, so we determined it was something to pray about, but at the moment it sounded as if we needed to prepare for a potential hurricane!

By Wednesday the storm developed into Hurricane Joyce and was on a track for Grenada. On Thursday she was still tracking for Grenada, and Mickey and family said they were heading south 70-plus miles to Trinidad. Maybe we would catch up with them there. Our other options were a protected "hurricane hole" anchorage in Grenada and sailing off to Venezuela.

While waiting to make a decision, our boat worker, Sean Thomas, was boat watching another 49-foot Hallberg Rassy moored behind us. We told him about our interest in the Smiths' vessel, so Sean invited us to come aboard sailing vessel Hestia. While we were there with Sean, a rain squall with 37-knot winds blew through the anchorage. We watched *coram Deo* bucking and sailing at anchor while we were riding out the weather comfortably—another positive for the Hallberg Rassy.

Once back on *coram Deo,* two of our sailing friends radioed us, encouraging us not to leave for Trinidad. In an updated weather report they heard that Hurricane Joyce was dropping in latitude and moving more toward Trinidad. Rather than follow the Smiths, we decided to wait another day and continue to pray for wisdom. On Friday morning there was lots of VHF radio chatter. Joyce was not turning. Mt. Hartman Bay was in her path! Some people were talking about getting axes and machetes to nestle boats into the mangroves. Our friend Gary on "Elusive," an experienced Caribbean cruiser, was talking about leaving for the island of Margarita, off the Venezuelan coast, 139 miles to our southwest. He understood there was a mild weather window for the next 30 hours. We radioed him, asking if we could tag along. Having prayed and wanting to take the safest measures, we had a peace about following the wisdom of experienced sailors.

So at 11:55 a.m. on Friday, September 29, 2000, we followed Elusive through the marked channel out of Mt. Hartman Bay and headed toward Margarita. Five to ten miles out we looked back and saw clouds and a rainbow just south of Grenada. The overnight sail was smooth and exciting even with the problems of weak batteries and non-working running lights. We had never seen the sky so filled with stars. It was awesome! It was hard to believe we were running from a hurricane!

When it became dark, we began two-hour watches, with the one off duty sleeping in the cockpit, close at hand if needed. On Micki's 5 to 7 a.m. watch, she saw the sun rise over the still waters and the faint coastline of Venezuela. A new adventure in a new land! At 7:45 a.m. Chuck was below trying to nurse some life out of the batteries when Micki yelled, "Whale off the starboard bow!"

Approaching Isla Margarita, Gary radioed that we were bypassing the planned Porlamar anchorage. A heavy swell was expected, one that would make the anchorage uncomfortable, even dangerous, so we continued 24 miles to Cubagua Island. We anchored there at 1:05 p.m. — 25 hours and 10 minutes after leaving Mt. Hartman. It was a beautiful anchorage with a gorgeous beach, but we were too tired to appreciate it. We took a nap, got up around 6 p.m. for a spaghetti dinner and went back to bed. We would explore this beautiful place tomorrow.

At 5:40 a.m. we were abruptly awakened by shouts outside the boat. Gary, on Elusive, was alongside saying the weather report was not good and that we needed to move 42 miles south to Laguna Grande. Hurricane Joyce was tracking between Grenada and Trinidad, expected to continue west, aiming directly at us! We said, "We'll be right behind you." Within 10 minutes we had the engine running, raised the anchor and joined a parade of 12 yachts heading south to the Golfo de Cariaco, where we would tuck into Laguna Grande. The lagoon, full of small bays just large enough for one or two boats to anchor in each, was cut into a desert peninsula off the northern Venezuelan mainland. So there we were, anchored in our own private bay, safe and working on our running lights and batteries while watching the weather.

We praised God when Hurricane Joyce dissipated before even reaching Grenada. Mt. Hartman Bay reported the highest winds at five knots! Actually, the greatest scare was in Laguna Grande, where a bat flew into a boat and bit a lady four times while she slept! She awoke covered with blood.

After three wonderful days, we followed Elusive out of the beautiful anchorage of Laguna Grande and headed for Margarita. We motor-sailed through the Golfo de Cariaco until we had enough wind to sail and cut the engine. Four dolphins appeared and played in our bow wake! When the winds changed direction, we restarted the engine. After about an hour the engine conked out. Recognizing the signs of a clogged filter, Chuck went below to change it while Micki sailed where the wind took us. Even after changing the filter we couldn't keep the engine running, so we tacked our way to the Porlamar anchorage, making about three knots.

Radioing Gary about our engine problem, he said they would go into Porlamar, anchor and await our call for help with anchoring. When we were about a mile out, Gary came out in his dinghy, and tied it to *coram Deo's* port side to act as a tug. As we headed for a spot to anchor, Micki turned into the wind, Chuck furled the jib and dropped the mainsail and then the anchor. Gary then put his outboard in reverse to help set the anchor.

But that wasn't all. Our engine problem was a dirty fuel tank. Gary spent two days helping Chuck clean it. After removing the diesel, the sludge needed to be removed from the tank. Chuck's arms were to short, so there was Gary, up to his armpit, cleaning our fuel tank! If that wasn't enough, his wife Sharon prepared dinner for us onboard Elusive at the end of a very dirty day. Gary and Sharon are God-given friends who helped us learn the ropes of the sailing lifestyle! *"...for your Father knows what you need before you ask Him."* *(Matthew 6:8.)*

Before returning to Grenada we all did some serious shopping on Margarita, a vacation Mecca for Venezuelans. There are large hyper-markets with prices half those in the Eastern Caribbean islands, so we stocked up. We also fueled up with seven cent-per-gallon diesel, carefully filtering every drop!

On Friday, October 13, 2000, almost two weeks after running from Hurricane Joyce, we sailed back to Mt. Hartman Bay, Grenada. We immediately replaced our problematic house batteries and completed a number of other projects. While we did make contact with Pastor Paul Miller, we could not stay because the groups in Antigua, Anguilla and Tortola were waiting for our return.

On a sunny October 30, we once again sailed out of Mt. Hartman Bay, heading north and having a great time of worship, playing praise music and praying just about the entire 21-mile length of the island! Arriving 38 miles north in Hillsborough, Carriacou, we anchored briefly to clear Grenada Customs and Immigration before making the short sail northwest to Union Island, where we cleared St. Vincent and the Grenadines Customs and Immigration. International law requires any visitor to clear in upon entrance and clear out when leaving each nation, even small island nations.

We took a couple days to enjoy the idyllic Tobago Cays, with its clear turquoise waters and magnificent snorkeling! From there we made the half day sail north to Bequia, purchasing battens for the new mainsail we were about to pick up. Sailing across the Bequia Channel, we entered Blue Lagoon at the southeast end of St. Vincent. We docked at the Sunsail base where the staff installed the new mainsail.

Meanwhile we telephoned and met up with Verrol Blake, the contact given us by Pastor Gary from Cornerstone Chapel in Leesburg, Virginia. We explained the CBSI mission and process to Verrol and his gracious and pleasant wife Norma. They expressed a desire to help us get CBSI established in St. Vincent. As a director of the Evangelical Association of the Caribbean, a missionary with Ambassadors for Christ and well known radio preacher and local pastor, he really did know a lot of people in many denominations throughout the Caribbean Christian community, just as Pastor Gary had said! Verrol provided the names of persons in many of the islands. It was an encouraging time of Christian fellowship with people so willing and eager to help.

The Blakes then took us on a tour of the Atlantic side of the island, Fort Charlotte overlooking the Caribbean Sea, the church where their son Allister was assistant pastor, their new church plant in Buccament Bay and a bakery where we bought wonderful bread loaves. Returning to *coram Deo* for a late lunch, we continued discussing CBSI and how God could use it to make disciples for Jesus Christ around the Caribbean. Verrol told us about the annual Christian Leadership Retreat he hosted in St. Vincent, with leaders attending from across the Caribbean. He invited us to attend in July of 2001 to make a CBSI presentation. Though July is in hurricane season and St. Vincent is in the hurricane box, we saw God opening another door and began making plans to attend.

We also contacted Pastor Desmond Fessal, whom we had met in Virginia, and at his invitation we attended a convention of his Mid Missions Baptist denomination. In talking to some of the pastors there, we detected little interest in an interdenominational effort.

Finally, with our new mainsail in place, we day-sailed up the island chain, making stops in St. Lucia, Martinique and Dominica. From there we sailed the windward shore of Guadeloupe, dealing with pretty high winds and seas but making it safely to Antigua.

Dropping anchor in English Harbour just before dark on Thursday, November 16, 2000, we had arrived in time to attend the CBSI leadership session Saturday night.

We were encouraged by the eight leaders with consistent attendance and intense and spirited discussions. However, after observing this team for two more weeks, it was clear to us they did not grasp the principles underlying the format and the roles of the specific leaders. We needed to invest time in training to help establish CBSI on a solid foundation in Antigua.

Speaking of solid foundations, we decided we needed a better foundation at sea. On our sail out of Prince Rupert Bay, Dominica, we knew we had to sail west for some time before heading north. Strong gusty winds shoot down the high mountains at the north end of the island. When we thought we were out far enough, we steered north. Suddenly a high wind caught our sails, knocking us on the port side, throwing both of us across the cockpit. *Coram Deo*, a lightweight vessel, popped back up, and we were able to get her under control but we were left bruised and shaken.

Once in Antigua, we emailed our friend Bill Reeves and our brother-in-law Chris Doherty to check out the reputation of the Hallberg Rassy, its seaworthiness and the price we were quoted. Chris replied, "It's in my coffee table book, *Great Sailing Yachts*." Both men agreed, saying, "Buy it!" After much prayer and upon their advice, we emailed Mickey and Ann Smith with an offer to purchase Discovery, as we had discussed in Grenada. They accepted the offer, and we agreed to meet them in Florida in March of 2001 to finalize the deal. We would sail our Hunter to Florida and sell her there. With our future path determined, we returned to Michigan for Christmas.

Our work was cut out for us when we returned to Antigua January 8, 2001. Upon our arrival Gerald Henry resigned as Teaching Leader. Also, the exterior painting of the hull of *coram Deo*, ordered prior to our departure, was barely started! Since we could not live on board during the painting process, we were graciously invited to stay with the Ted Martin family. It was a wonderful time of building our relationship with Ted, Ann Marie, eight-year-old TJ and our two-year-old god-daughter Alexia.

The previous September, when we had flown in for the training seminars, we had approached Ted to become the Teaching Leader. After all, hadn't God providentially brought him into our lives for such a time as this? He said no—that he was an evangelist, not a teacher. However, when Gerald Henry resigned, Ted was silently asking God if he had missed an opportunity originally meant for him. As Chuck and Ted were talking one evening after dinner, Chuck asked Ted if he would reconsider praying about the Teaching Leader position. Ted acknowledged his dilemma and agreed to pray.

While Ted was praying, we trained the leadership team by going through the 1 John study a second time. Through this God was teaching us that modeling appropriate leadership in the weekly training sessions was what these men and women needed. They had no experience or examples from which to draw. After all, the closest class was about 2000 miles away!

Ted had virtually disappeared for nearly a week. Here we were living with him under the same roof, yet we never saw him in the house! He had withdrawn into his "prayer closet" and was struggling. One evening as we sat reading in the living room, Ted came to us and said, "All the lights are green. There are no red lights." We were elated! For seven and a half years we had watched him grow as a man after God's heart simply through the faithful study of His Word.

Ezekiel 22:30 reads: *"I looked for a man among them who would build up the wall and stand before Me in the gap on behalf of the land so I would not have to destroy it, but I found none."* This was not true for Antigua. God found a stalwart, gap closing man in Ted Martin.

Young adult Bible study leaders who joined us for the "Caribbean Adventure 2000."

Micki cranking our washing machine. The dripping water later caused a rat's demise.

**The Antigua prayer group. Ted on left next to prayer group
leader Franklyn; future ATL Boris on far right.**

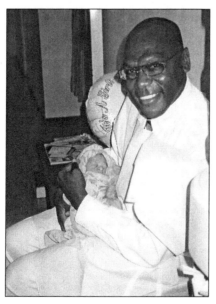

**Rev. Charlesworth Browne holding
newborn twin son Brenstan.**

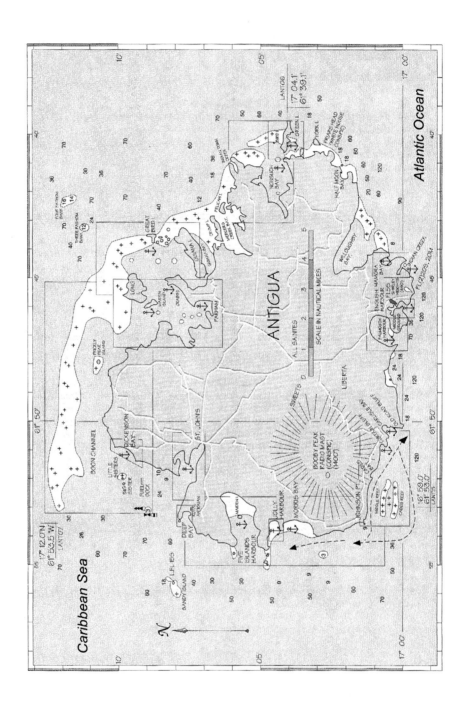

3

Antigua

"The One who calls you is faithful and He will do it."
(1 Thessalonians 5:24)

The first CBS International class in the Eastern Caribbean was born February 17, 2001, on Antigua under the leadership of Ted Martin.

A semi-arid island known for its 365 beaches and as a yachting center in the Leeward Islands, Antigua is only 14 miles long and 11 miles wide with a population of 68,000, but would have an impact throughout the Eastern Caribbean way beyond its size. For us this first class was like the birth of a first child! The One who called us was, is, and will always be faithful. He did it! And He gave us the privilege of being part of His work not because we were special, but available.

In John 15:5 Jesus said, *"apart from Me you can do nothing."* Thus, every detail had been bathed in prayer not only by us and the Antiguans involved, but by over 200 family, friends and prayer warriors who chose to receive our *coram Deo* online and support us in prayer. In the early years of our Caribbean ministry, we sent people specific prayer requests and gave updates weekly, at times more often. Looking at one sent on February 4, 2001, we listed eight encouraging answers to nine prayer requests. So it was an exciting time, not just for us, but for our prayer partners!

With Ted Martin's acceptance of the Teaching Leader position in mid January of 2001, Mitch Nicholas, a serious minded and well-spoken customs officer, began praying about the Associate Teaching Leader position. We were elated when this godly young man was called to the emerging team. With teachers in place, we approached others in the leadership training group to fill the needed roles. Franklyn Braithwaite, friendly, helpful and the prayer group leader, became Class Coordinator. Avondale Lake, soft-spoken and dependable, became Associate Class Coordinator. Linda Hogan, a sweet single woman in her twenties who worked at the Methodist Book Store in St. John's, and Edith Oladele, a strong woman of faith with a heart for Africa, agreed to be women's Discussion Leaders. Additionally, Edith opened her home for the Leaders Council meetings. The men's Discussion Leaders were Boris Teague, a mid-20s construction worker who would walk, run, or hitch-hike if he could not get a ride to meetings, and Mr. Cordelle Brown, a quiet, faithful middle-aged man. With the leadership roles filled, it was essential each leader understood his or her specific role before start-up.

And speaking about understanding, although the Antiguans speak English, each island has a unique dialect. When talking one-on-one, especially if we had been on island a few days allowing us time to adjust to their speech pattern, we could usually understand what people were saying. However, in a comfortable group setting like leadership training, they would rapidly speak in dialect and leave us clueless! They could easily tell by our expressions when that happened. In turn, there were times when they would ask us to explain American slang.

Since Ted had not been in the earlier training, we took advantage of any time we could get with him. If he were running errands, one of us would ride with him, answering his questions and teaching. We also had one-on-one training sessions in his home or on *coram Deo* anchored nearby in English Harbour. He was a quick learner with a mind like a steel trap, remembering the tiniest of details.

Having studied the life of the Apostle Paul recently through the teaching of Romans, we adopted Paul's missionary pattern. Whenever he arrived in a new area, he approached the Jewish synagogues first, the local centers of traditional Hebrew religion. Similarly, we sought endorsements from established church groups. This included the Evangelical Association, with the more charismatic churches, and the Christian Council, an assembly of the mainline churches. Before class was launched, we did receive their endorsements that CBSI was a benefit both to the church and to the country. It is important for the church leadership to understand that CBSI's sole mission is to "make disciples of our Lord Jesus Christ in our communities through caring, in-depth Bible study, available to all." CBSI does not compete with churches or church organizations, but comes alongside to help provide spiritual growth and further equip people to better serve in their churches. However, organizational endorsements did not necessarily speak for individual pastors or churches. Initially we offered only "CBSI interdenominational classes," not church-based classes, so the class would not come to be identified with a particular denomination. We learned of a fear on the part of many pastors that we needed to confront head-on. Missionaries had come to these Caribbean islands saying they would start Bible studies and instead established churches through Bible study by "sheep stealing." Needless to say, it took a few years before CBSI gained credibility with many in the church establishment.

The Antigua leaders did their part in talking to pastors and getting the word out about CBSI. They encouraged all who had attended the prior September's CBSI introduction meeting to attend the first class scheduled for February 17 and bring friends and family. Those with media contacts arranged free television, radio, and newspaper exposure. When we were interviewed on the secular Antigua Broadcasting Station during the evening drive time, we gave our ministry background and explained the role we would have in CBSI in Antigua. When Kenny, the interviewer, asked us to make suggestions for listeners who wanted to study the Bible, we shared the three-question approach to Scripture study: *What does the passage say? What did it mean to the people in biblical times? What does it say to you and me today?* Kenny also asked us to explain the CBSI study process—not just once, but several times. He was interested in what an actual class night would look like. We plugged the start-up date and emphasized that the class would be taught by Ted Martin, an Antiguan. Ted was popular in many parts of this 108 square mile island. Ride in a car with Ted and you would hear people calling, "Hey, Ted!" or honking automobile horns in greeting everywhere on island.

Other interviews followed with local television as well as Christian Radio ZDK. We created a bulletin insert for the churches and hand delivered 3,000 to five denominational leaders, driving the length and width of the island. This was not like driving in the States! We might turn a corner and find two Caribbean wranglers herding a dozen horses, or stop to let cows cross, or swerve to miss one napping in the road or follow a herd of slow moving goats. Chuck's favorite driving delay was coming to a halt and waiting for the driver of a car ahead, stopped and talking to someone in an oncoming car or to a person standing on the road nearby!

In the weeks before class, we also assisted Ted in making phone calls and filling out the paperwork to secure a public school as a place to meet. The red tape took longer than we anticipated, so Ted obtained permission to use the Methodist Hall in St. John's as an interim class location.

One week before class began, we scheduled a leaders workshop as a final review. We had prepared materials for Ted to lead the review of the training and coached him to encourage his leaders to be ready to see God do great things. Just as Joshua told the Israelites as they anticipated crossing the Jordan, *"Consecrate yourselves, for tomorrow the LORD will do amazing things among you." (Joshua 3:5)*

As we drove to the workshop we were exhausted! But as we watched the first CBSI Teaching Leader in the Eastern Caribbean lead his leaders, we were energized and praised God! Ted had learned well his role of leading, gaining their immediate respect.

There was a time of review where the leaders answered questions relating to the CBSI process and their specific roles as Discussion Leaders and Class Coordinators. They came through with flying colors! This was our high five from God. They got it, or at least most of what we taught them! Thank you, Lord!

We had created a role-play of a Discussion Leader making his first phone call to a class member. Chuck was the class member and Boris Teague the Discussion Leader. They had a script, but Chuck, seeing how well Boris was doing, started ad-libbing. Without hesitation, Boris handled all that Chuck threw at him. It reminded us of the comments at the end of the Discussion Leader pages of the CBSI Training Manual: "This is God's ministry, not ours. If we waited to serve until we felt ready, we would probably never do anything. God's method has always been to entrust His work to sinful, redeemed men and women. He does not call the equipped, He equips the called." This team was as ready as they needed to be! God would do the equipping as they stepped out in faith!

*C*oram Deo online went out the next day to encourage our prayer warriors about the exciting leaders workshop. We asked for prayer for the next step, the Leaders Council, signing off with Ephesians 3:20-21: ***"Now to Him who is able to do immeasurably more than all we ask or imagine, according to His power that is at work within us, to Him be glory in the church and in Christ Jesus throughout all generations, for ever and ever! Amen."*** The LORD heard and answered!

It was no surprise to us that Ted was suffering from a migraine headache as he prepared for Leaders Council and his first CBSI teaching, an overview of the Epistle of 1 John. We warned the team, as we had warned leaders in previous Bible studies: "Be prepared for enemy attacks. You are now armed and dangerous! You are taking on a responsibility that will transform your lives and those you lead. It will be as if you are walking around with a big red X on your backs. The enemy will throw everything at you to distract, to discourage, and to convince you that you have no time for this ministry. All of a sudden you'll get extremely busy at work. Things will happen in your families demanding more of your time. Be warned. Don't be surprised, and don't let him win! Know where the attacks are coming from and press on in the strength God will give you." We concluded *"because the One who is in you is greater than the one who is in the world." (1 John 4:4)*

Even with the migraine headache and cold symptoms, Ted persisted in his preparation, according to God's power that was at work within him. On Thursday, February 15, he led his first Leaders Council with passion and enthusiasm. The leaders were excited about Saturday night! But the eye-opener for us was an awe-inspiring realization that came over Boris Teague.

At the end of the meeting, Ted gave Micki an opportunity to talk to the Discussion Leaders about the privilege and responsibility God was giving them in leading the men or women in their small groups. She said God was entrusting them to invest in the spiritual lives of each person who would come and be placed in their groups. You could have heard a pin drop. Boris, sitting to Micki's left with his face in his hands and with such awe in his voice said, "Never thought of it like that. Wow! God trusting me—with these men."

He got it! Boris grasped the significance of what God was calling him to do! It took us years to realize that Discussion Leaders are front-line people in Bible study. They stand in the gap for the men and women in their groups. They encourage. They pray. They challenge. They help them grow in confidence in studying God's Word. They help them apply what they are learning to their personal lives.

Boris committed and has never turned back. He passionately embraced the awesome privilege and, yes, the daunting responsibility of his calling by God to be a Discussion Leader. When we initially invited Boris to be part of training, others took us aside to warn us. "He never sticks to anything," said one. "As soon as something else new comes along, he'll leave." That never happened. In the years to come, every time we visited the Antigua class, the men talked about Boris, his interest in them, his contacts with them.

"You did not choose Me, but I chose you and appointed you to go and bear fruit—fruit that will last." (John 15:16) We did not choose Boris, Jesus did. In April of 2003, Boris traveled to Barbados where we trained him as Associate Teaching Leader after Mitch Nicholas left class to attend Bible College in the States.

A blessing at that historic first Leaders Council was our "spiritual daughter," Heidi Lynn Holz from Michigan, a joy-filled, organized angel of God. She was assistant secretary and praise and worship leader in our young adult Bible study. Heidi stayed aboard *coram Deo* creating class recordkeeping forms—registration, attendance and finance forms for the Class Coordinator, discussion group attendance forms, a sample certificate of achievement, etc. This was needed because CBSI worldwide was in the exciting early stage of ministry development with some of the more mundane administrative essentials left up to those in the field. During the praise and worship time at the first Leaders Council, Heidi played keyboard. What a gift that Heidi was there to experience with us history in the making for CBSI in the Eastern Caribbean!

On Saturday, February 17, 2001, the leaders arrived early for set-up and pre-class prayer. At a lull in the activity, Micki found herself alone with Associate Teaching Leader Mitch on the outside deck overlooking the busy street. After some small talk, Mitch turned and spoke quietly, saying, "When I first met you two, I thought, who do these white people think they are, coming here and telling us how to study the Bible?" He paused and continued, "But then when I saw you working so hard, driving all over the island, willing to do whatever it took to help us, I knew you were real."

Wow! We had experienced love from all the Antiguans, except Mitch. Micki had felt he was distant throughout training and this explained it. Micki's eyes filled with tears as she touched his arm and thanked him for his honesty. People started walking up the stairs for class, so with healing in their hearts, Mitch and Micki began welcoming those who came.

The start time was 7 p.m. and some people, uncharacteristically, began arriving 20 minutes early! The leaders were greeting people at the door, making out nametags, answering questions, doing whatever needed to be done. The musician did not show up, so Heidi accompanied the uplifting time of praise and worship.

The two of us gave an introduction to CBSI with a brief history, explaining the unique five feature approach, providing lesson one of the 1 John study, encouraging those in attendance to do a little of the lesson every day to get the most benefit, advising them to answer from the passage studied and not with their "pet" Scriptures. As they did their lesson, we explained, they would hear God speak to them personally from the Bible. Then, when they would come to class, they would be encouraged by and learn from those in their group. In this way, they would learn to apply the Bible to their own lives week-by-week and would learn to share with their friends and family what God taught them.

To add credibility, we had Mitch and Discussion Leader Linda give personal testimonies of their short CBSI experience with the studies during training. Shy Linda Hogan came alive with her testimony and inspired everyone!

Then Ted Martin, with joy and enthusiasm, gave a Spirit-empowered first teaching! It was right on! The people were excited. Many came up thanking us for bringing CBSI to Antigua. Afterwards, Ted asked Heidi if his feet were still on the ground!

The class was born with 48 men and women from a number of denominations eager to study together in the first organized in-depth Bible study in Antigua. Ted encouraged everyone there to bring family and friends the following week. Since they had only two trained female Discussion Leaders and around 30 women who registered, those two groups were full. Another Discussion Leader was needed immediately. The leaders had a quick meeting. They noticed Holly Bennett, an on-fire young woman of God, standing around excitedly talking to people about this great new Bible study. Ted took her aside, telling her of their need. Holly was trained that week!

This was just the beginning of what God would do in Antigua and the rest of the Eastern Caribbean!

After the second class meeting we sent out the following *coram Deo* online:

Similar to what the Apostle John says in his first epistle, we have seen Him, we have heard His voice, and we have experienced His touch!

We wish every one of you could have stood with us in the back of the large church hall last Saturday night to observe the second meeting of the Antigua CBS International class. Your misty eyes would have seen Boris' group of 10 men as they dug into their first discussion, Boris exclaiming, "I'm so excited! Are you excited?" Then your eyes would move to the 12 women in Edith's group huddled together listening intently to one another. The laughter on the stage would draw your attention to Linda's group of young women, enjoying each other. And then back down on the left side of the room where ATL Mitch gave his very first Introduction Class with conviction and passion to 23 men and women.

Only five people were absent from the previous week. And two others who had said then they were only visitors came back to be placed into a group. And one woman in this week's Introduction Class, after hearing Ted's teaching went to Class Coordinator Franklyn. "I need to change my card," she said. "I want to be a member!" Only one of the new people did not sign up. Franklyn said, "We'll hang onto her card. She may be back!"

One of the women in Linda's group lost her lesson after doing part of it. It took that member until the morning of class to reach Linda. Associate Coordinator Avondale delivered her a new lesson. She came that night with lesson completed!

Enrollment was now 67 members! Still another female Discussion Leader was needed. Heather Henry, a woman with a great sense of humor and love for the Lord, answered the call.

We were thrilled the second week of class to have as guests Micki's sister and her husband, Louise and Chris Doherty. With the Antigua class well started, it was now time for us to begin the nearly 1,300-mile journey to Florida. We had agreed to meet up with Mickey and Ann Smith in West Palm Beach in late March to finalize the purchase of their Hallberg Rassy and put our Hunter sailboat on the market. Louise and Chris, both sailors, would help us sail as far north as Tortola, BVI.

The four of us were up at 6:15 a.m. Sunday morning, February 25. Chuck and Chris hauled the dinghy and outboard on deck. We cast off the lines, motored out to the middle of the bay and hoisted the mainsail. How great to have extra hands on deck! We were leaving historic Nelson's Dockyard—used by a number of British admirals during the Napoleonic Wars as a West Indies homeport—and sailing out of the bay with Fort Berkley overlooking us on our starboard side. Built in 1704, Berkley was the original British garrison. But this kind of history was not on our minds. Grateful for God's faithfulness, we were focused on the historic first of a CBSI class in the Eastern Caribbean on February 17, 2001 in Antigua! *"Lord,...all that we have accomplished You have done for us." (Isaiah 26:12)*

The sun was bright, the sky was blue, and with 80 degree temperatures winds were mild, from 6 to 13 knots, and seas calm as we began our 55-mile passage west to St. Kitts. Micki soon sighted a turtle! About 30 miles out, the winds kicked up to 18 knots, the seas built to six to eight feet and we were on a broad reach making seven to eight knots. As we approached the channel between the islands of St. Kitts and Nevis, the land blocked the wind, funneling and shifting it to northeasterly, accelerating it to over 20 knots on our starboard beam and heeling us to port (left), putting our rail in the water! We anchored in Majors Bay on the south coast, enjoyed snorkeling and walked the beach. Then as we dinghied back to the boat, a stingray leapt from the water!

The next morning we sailed north to the picturesque little French island of St. Barts, a playground for rich and sophisticated mostly French vacationers. Surprised, we arrived in time for the pre-Lent Carnival! Although we spent two days exploring the island, we avoided the partying, drinking, lewd dancing and other associated bacchanalian activities.

From St. Barts we motor-sailed the 14 miles west to Phillipsburg, St. Martin where we fueled up and spent the day touring, shopping, and enjoying French cuisine.

The Dutch island of Saba lies southwest of St. Martin. We had the calm weather needed to moor there so we sailed the 28 miles southwest, arriving just past noon. Saba is a five square mile volcanic mountain top. Its cliffs rise straight out of the water to the peak of Mount Scenery, elevation 2,854 feet. There are no sandy beaches, but the breathtaking views of the sea and the friendly people make up for the lack of sand. Hiring "Uncle Joe" for a quick taxi tour, Micki made sure we stopped at the studio of Jobean Designs, a working glass studio where we watched Jo create beautiful glass beads.

We departed Saba at 6:30 p.m. for the 14 hour overnight sail to Tortola. Louise and Chris took first watch while we slept for three hours. It was an uneventful sail under a blanket of stars, arriving early morning into Sir Francis Drake Channel and were greeted to the British Virgin Islands by a pod of dolphins playing in our bow wake!

Since Louise and Chris would be flying home the next day, we moored in Trellis Bay on Beef Island, near the airport. Our plan was to stay in Tortola about 10 days, hoping to be present when Rev and Nath's twins were born. During that time our spiritual daughter, Heidi Lynn Holz, would again join us, this time as crew for the sail to Florida.

Early Sunday, March 4, 2001, we dinghied Louise and Chris ashore where they walked the short distance to the terminal. We took pictures and waved good-bye as they boarded their flight. Eager to see Nath, we sailed around Beef Island to Road Harbour, Tortola and anchored. Nath was hospitalized in Road Town, awaiting the twins' birth.

During our Monday evening visit, the doctor scheduled her for a C-section at 9 a.m. the next day, due to the size and weight of the twins. She was in her 38th week, and the babies had no interest as yet in making their debut. We were with Rev in the waiting room when Nath gave birth. We wish you could have seen the Rev's face when they announced he had two sons! He and Nath had been praying for children for more than eight years. The firstborn, Charles Evanston Joshua Browne, was 43 centimeters long and weighed six pounds, six ounces. Brenstan Nathan Rene Browne was 43 centimeters long and weighed five pounds, fourteen ounces. Nurses wheeled the boys by us as they took them to be bathed and dressed. They were not identical twins, but they sure were identical to their parents! Charles has lighter curly hair and the fair-skinned features of Nath, while Brenstan has his father's dark-skinned features.

Nath asked that we be part of a prayer dedication a couple hours after the births. So we hung around, and the nurses invited us with Charlesworth to watch as they washed and dressed the babies. Then came the touching moment when a nurse handed Brenstan to his father to hold and feed him for the very first time!

Heidi arrived a couple days later, so the first order of business was for her to meet the twins and have time with the family. She had already met Rev and Nath since she was part of our Caribbean 2000 Adventure in BVI. But then we said our good-byes.

At 6:29 a.m. on Sunday, March 11, 2001, we motor-sailed the short distance to Cruz Bay, St. John's, where we docked *coram Deo* at Customs and Immigration, cleared into the USA and were on our way in 20 minutes. On our seven hour sail west to Vieques, a Spanish Virgin Island, Chuck caught a 40-inch kingfish! Anchoring for the night in Escanada Honda inside a reef all by ourselves, we enjoyed a tasty kingfish dinner! From there we sailed 55 miles west to Salinas on the southern coast of Puerto Rico and then onto Ponce for provisioning. We anchored and waited for high winds to die down so we could get the dinghy off the foredeck! Finally, at dusk, we dinghied to shore. As we pulled up to a dock, a man approached saying this was a fishing club and that the gate is locked at dark. Offering to drive us to a supermarket, he showed us a hole in the fence where we could get back in and instructed us to ask the store manager to call a taxi to bring us back. It was a great store with low U.S. prices and the trunk of an old Buick taxi was filled with provisions! Fortunately, the fishing club yard was open, and we somehow loaded all the groceries plus ourselves into the dinghy. We would certainly eat well on this voyage! From there we spent a night on the Puerto Rican west coast at Boqueron before the real sailing began!

Friday, March 16, 2001, we sailed northwest, crossing the dreaded Mona Passage. This can be a rough stretch of water and sailors have waited days or weeks for a good weather window. But God provided calm and enjoyable conditions as we headed north of the Dominican Republic, sailing day and night for three days. We scheduled night watches and kept up with weather reports. Twenty-five knot winds were reported heading our way so we planned a course to Sapidilla Bay, Providenciales Island, Turks and Caicos. In the early morning of the third day, we motored through the Caicos Bank with the most beautiful crystal clear waters! We were grateful for the clarity because of the number of coral heads sticking up in the shallow waters. After rolling starboard to port all night in the Sapidilla Bay anchorage, we called ahead and moved to Turtle Cove Marina on the island's north coast to wait out the windy weather.

After laying five days in the marina, we sailed through the Exuma Sound and Bahama Banks, anchoring one night on each of these places with no land in sight—just water as far as the eye could see and a magnificent star-lit sky! The waters in these banks are unlike any we had seen—clear turquoise, beautiful greens, and dark azure. Heidi tried to count the colorful pink, purple, and orange star-fish we could see on the bottom, but with so many, she gave up! One day we motored through nine sharks that were lazily swimming in the entrance of a marina where we made a quick diesel stop. With calm conditions, we spent our time on deck sunning, reading, and watching the water.

On Tuesday night, March 27, 2001, we anchored at Cat Cay, Grand Bahama Bank, poised to cross the Gulf Stream to Fort Lauderdale, Florida. Sailors have waited 10 days or more for good weather for the Gulf Stream crossing. If the winds are northerly, the seas can be dangerously rough. At 6:45 a.m. the next day, we set sail in 10- to 15-knot mostly easterly winds! Although we had 8- to 10-foot seas for a few hours and had to divert course to avoid a collision with a cruise ship, we safely sailed into the Intercoastal Waterway by late afternoon.

After 3 weeks and sailing 1,138 miles from Tortola, we docked at Bahia Mar Yacht Club, Fort Lauderdale. With God's help, we made it! We rested, saw Heidi off on a flight back to Michigan and did boat maintenance for about a week before moving to North Palm Beach to finalize the purchase of sailing vessel Discovery, renamed as our new *coram Deo*. It would be mid May before we sailed back down island. In the meantime, we flew back to Michigan to celebrate Easter and Micki's mom's 80th birthday and take care of personal business before returning to Florida to move aboard the new *coram Deo*.

During this time we stayed in touch with Ted Martin to encourage, advise and receive up-to-date prayer requests. Discussion had been ongoing with Ted about videotaping a Leaders Council and CBSI class to use as an introduction and training tool. Andy Brown from Anguilla was a videographer and agreed to do the project with a friend.

On May 3, 2001, Chuck flew from Florida to Antigua to begin the production. The Antigua class was into its second six-week study, the Epistle to the Galatians. Forty-six new people had signed up, bringing the membership to more than 100. Because of the class growth, Ted had expanded the leadership team and class was meeting at the Boy's Grammar School. After observing the Leaders Council and the class, Chuck was convinced that Ted was anointed by God to teach His Word. It was a vibrant class with people from all walks of life. Lives were being changed week after week. From the prayer requests for protection from enemy attacks, we knew the class was being effective. One leader was missing Leaders Council because of stress, another because of a heavy work schedule. Yet another had issues with a teenage daughter, and a fourth faced serious financial problems. *"The One who is in you is greater than the one who is in the world" (1 John 4:4)* is what we told them, and we prayed for them.

Eager to get back to Antigua, the new *coram Deo* set sail from West Palm Beach, Florida at 1:30 p.m. on May 15, 2001, with five crew aboard. We were joined by our brother-in-law Chris, his son Gered and a captain named Tom who was hired to help us learn the more complicated systems aboard the Hallberg Rassy. This time we would ocean sail directly to St. Thomas, U.S. Virgin Islands and the two of us would sail from there to Antigua.

Within an hour of departure, the boat was surrounded by a dozen dolphins, adults and juveniles, playing in our bow wake. About an hour later we came within 30 feet of a huge moss-and-barnacle-covered loggerhead turtle. Not too much later, a little black bird with orange markings flew next to us for a bit and then landed on deck. We gave it water and it stayed, entertaining us for hours before flying away. It was both a challenging and, at times, enjoyable nine-day sail to St. Thomas. It was great to arrive in placid waters where the sole (floor) and bed were flat for the first time in nine days! We docked at Crown Bay Marina where Captain Tom left for the airport. Chuck hoisted Chris up the 65-foot mast so he could repair a navigation light while Gered worked with Micki in the hot sun swabbing the deck. From there we sailed to Tortola where after a couple of days, Chris and Gered flew home. We would miss our helpful and fun crew, but we had made memories for a lifetime.

At that point we were itching to sail for Anguilla to check on Andy's progress with the *CBSI Live!* video, but strong winds and high seas weathered us into Tortola—an opportunity for precious time with Rev, Nath and godsons Charles and Brenstan! We stayed in contact with Ted in Antigua, who had all positive news. Class attendance was averaging about 80 and the school provided an additional classroom for use by two new discussion groups. Their Testimony and Honors night, concluding the Galatians study and introducing the James study, was to be videotaped by the national television station, Antigua Broadcasting System, to do a special report on the class. "Isn't dat jus like da Fada?!" Ted said excitedly in his Antiguan dialect. Translated "Isn't that just like the Father," it is a colloquialism Ted uses to point to the faithful character of God.

When the weather calmed down, finally, we sailed to Anguilla. Andy Brown who had done an effective job taping and editing the *CBSI Live!* video promised to have copies ready by July. For background music, he used a CD made by an Anguillan worship leader, Chris Richardson. It was dynamite! Andy called Chris' wife, and the two personally delivered CDs to us. Chris gave us permission to use "Sing Unto the Lord" and "The Islands Give You Glory" without cost for the video. This humble and talented couple blessed us even further by having a time of prayer before they left.

Our visit to Anguilla was way too quick! And if its encouragement was not enough, our overnight sail was awe-inspiring, passing St. Martin and continuing south to Antigua. Most of the night we traveled on a near to beam reach with 15- to 16-knot winds and two- to four-foot seas - fast and comfortable - and the sky was filled with stars! *"He determines the number of the stars and calls them each by name." (Psalm 147:4)* We had a great view of the planet Mars rising off our port (left) bow. It was the closest to earth that it would be for 17 years! Wow! Just think of the blessings God gives to His children!

The boat performed well, though we were still getting to know this much larger yacht and her systems. Arriving in English Harbour, Antigua, we were excited to attend CBSI for the first lesson in James, the third study of this class. We were not disappointed! We spent nearly two weeks encouraging the leaders, coaching where needed and observing both Leaders Council and the class in operation. We also met with pastors, making them aware of the class and its goals. Pastor Paul Andrews, Christian Fellowship Assembly, supported the work, and the pointers he gave us for working within the Eastern Caribbean culture were invaluable.

Before leaving Antigua we invited the leadership team aboard *coram Deo* at anchor for an afternoon of fun, fellowship and snacks. There was much laughter and sharing the joys of serving our Lord together in CBSI. Though we did not realize it then, open doors on other islands would limit our time with these beloved leaders in the years ahead.

On Wednesday, June 27, 2001, we sailed out of English Harbour filled to overflowing with what God was doing in the lives of precious, loving people in Antigua. While we stayed in contact with Ted Martin, it was October before we flew back for a short visit. After observing both the Leaders Council and the class then, we were encouraged by the strong commitment of the leadership. Ted, suffering from serious back pain, had tears in his eyes as he taught on the miracle at Cana. His aim was to cause the members to trust Jesus in everything, and he was living out the teaching! Though class attendance had slipped to about 60, the group was still vibrant.

When class numbers drop, it is usually because the Discussion Leaders are not actively shepherding group members with weekly contacts for encouragement and prayer. We suggested that Ted schedule a "leadership development" time during Leaders Council to focus on this weakness, and we created a week-by-week syllabus in this area for him to follow.

Shortly after this visit, we attended a CBS Teaching Directors Conference, where we learned that CBSI classes in European countries typically break 30-week studies into shorter segments. A light dawned! Antigua was doing the 30-week study of the Gospel of John. Such a commitment would typically be a huge undertaking for West Indians. We contacted Ted suggesting that he break the remainder of the John study into six-week segments with Testimony and Honors nights between them. This would reduce the members' commitments to only six weeks at a time.

Our goal was to visit Antigua no less than twice a year. We stayed in regular contact with Ted to encourage and support him and the team, and we and our prayer partners prayed regularly for them. While training leadership in Tortola in April of 2002, we took a weekend to fly to Antigua to attend a John study Testimony and Honors night. When Ted invited people to share, Eltonia came to the podium saying it was a joy for her to do the lessons each week and hear God speak to her through His Word—and, she said enthusiastically, "I get to share it!"

Eugene approached the podium saying that though he had a good thing going with his wife, "CBSI has enhanced our relationship." He also spoke of how he had been humbled. Thinking his answers were "right," he would attend discussion group and hear others express different views, some of them paralleling his wife's and he had to admit that these answers were valid as well. He said CBSI had also enhanced his ministry with teens by taking what he was learning and sharing it with them, guiding them to get into the Word.

Another class member said CBSI lessons make the Bible plain, helping him gain understanding. He mentioned specific verses and told of lessons he learned. Another man said he was immediately humbled as he entered the discussion group and found that his leader was a young man he had taught in school! Then James came forward and led the class in song, "God has brought me too far to leave me now." A relatively new class member said this was her first time back in three weeks. She had returned in response to the "constant calls" of her Discussion Leader. Another woman said her husband was so excited that she was coming to the class that he laid out her clothes! The final sweet moment came when the only 11-year-old class member (placed in a women's discussion group) went forward and sang, "Blessed, We Are Blessed."

That night we experienced what Paul speaks of in 1 Thessalonians 2:19, *"For what is our hope, our joy, or the crown in which we will glory in the presence of our Lord Jesus when He comes? Is it not you?"*

After the tremendous start, the exciting testimonies and the growth through 2002, the numbers began to decrease year by year. When class members asked for more discussion time and less teaching, the leadership team accommodated them. At a visit in 2004, we saw the discussion group time exceeding an hour and a half. Also one Discussion Leader brought a book from an outside class he was taking and used it to "teach" his men. In other groups discussions became heated because the Discussion Leaders were not keeping group members on the questions and in the passage. Ted and the leadership team seemed to turn a deaf ear when we advised that they return to the time-tested format. Later, at the 2006 CBSI Caribbean Conference, Ted acknowledged publically that they thought they had a "better idea" until their class dwindled to as low as 25 members.

In preparing to sail from Antigua after visiting the class briefly in October of 2007, we felt discouraged. The leadership team and class had lost their vitality. They were going through the motions without passion or personal application. Most importantly, we did not see or feel love being demonstrated. Deeply concerned, we asked God for guidance. Then, before sailing out, we met with Ted and shared our hearts. We reinforced what we said at that meeting with an email bathed in prayer, expressing our love but exhorted Ted and his team to love one another and become the shepherds God had called them to be!

Unbeknownst to us, Ted humbly went to his knees. He then persisted in prayer and began to shepherd his leaders. His leaders joined him on their knees for the class. Thirteen months later, on the Monday before Thanksgiving of 2008, we sailed into Antigua, walked into Nelson's Dockyard and were warmly welcomed by several friends who worked there. Wendell, a young, cheerful guy, asked if we would be coming to CBSI on Saturday. There was an unusual degree of joy among others we knew. Then, at the Leaders Council meeting, all leaders were there with completed lessons, and each was involved in every aspect of the meeting. The vitality and depth of the caring they showed for each other were remarkable! This was a model Leaders Council!

At class on Saturday night we realized that Ted and the leaders had withheld news from us, wanting us to see it with our own eyes. For the first time in seven years, CBSI had become a "family affair" for Ted Martin. His wife, Ann Marie, teenage son TJ and our pre-teen god-daughter Alexia were members! Also more than 50 people were in attendance! The discussions were vibrant with 98 percent lesson completion. Ted's teaching was focused and Spirit-empowered!

And this was not all. Before dismissing the class, Ted explained that three young girls who came to class with their parents were asking him weekly, "Where is my class?" That night an 11-year-old girl came to him, opened her purse, took out an Eastern Caribbean dollar coin and handed it to him saying, "This is to help start my class." The children were asking for CBSI Children & Youth Ministry! Ted told the class that he had been praying for children's leaders, and he appealed to the class for four people, men and women, to step forward so training could be scheduled. That was November of 2008. Six months later, God answered that prayer. Five women—Gail, Holly, Mavreen, Katherlyn and Junie—and two men, Bruce and Boris, stepped forward to be trained as Children's Leaders. The training that took place in Antigua was led by Jacqui Bridge from Trinidad, the Children & Youth Coordinator for CBSI Caribbean Inc.

In October of 2009, the Children & Youth Ministry welcomed nearly 30 children in two separate classes—the primary and junior groups. That one dollar investment of one child is paying enormous eternal dividends!

Back in May of 2008 we had passed the baton of CBSI leadership to the people of the English-speaking Caribbean with the formation of CBSI Caribbean, Inc., an entity recognized at a national level in CBSI. Each CBSI island nation is represented in this organization by its National Coordinator. Boris Teague, Associate Teaching Leader, was appointed National Coordinator responsible for maintaining and growing the work of CBSI on Antigua.

So the work, well established, goes on in Antigua. *"LORD,...all that we have accomplished You have done for us." (Isaiah 26:12)* To God be the Glory!

First Antigua leadership team (l to r)
front row: Bernie, Linda, Heather, Edith;
back row: (Micki), Avondale, Holly, ATL Boris Teague,
TL Ted Martin, CC Franklyn.

Men's discussion group led by Boris (left rear).

Chuck's brother Bob and wife Donna on deck of new
***coram Deo* in Florida in May 2001.**

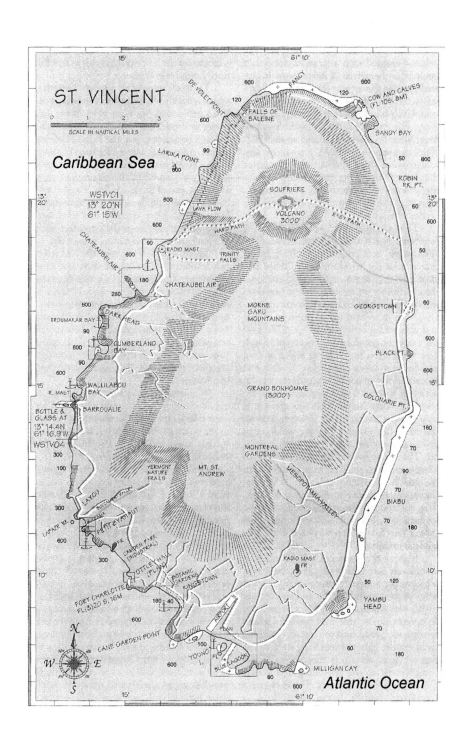

ST. VINCENT

SCALE IN NAUTICAL MILES
0   1   2   3

Caribbean Sea

WSTV01
13° 20'N
61° 15'W

DE VOLET POINT

FANCY

600   600

120   120   COW AND CALVES
                  (FL 10S, 8M)

FALLS OF
BALEINE   SANDY BAY

600

LARIKA POINT   ROBIN
                               RK. PT.
600
         90   50   600

              SOUFRIERE

13°
20'   13°
                                              20'
WSTV01   60
13° 20'N   LAVA FLOW   VOLCANO   600
61° 15'W   3000'   EASY PATH

600   HARD PATH   50

CHATEAUBELAIR I.   90
                RADIO MAST
600   TRINITY
          180   FALLS
          280
         CHATEAUBELAIR

500   DARK HEAD   MORNE   GEORGETOWN   60
                            GARU
TROUMAKAR BAY   MOUNTAINS
          90
600   CUMBERLAND   600
          BAY
          90   BLACK PT.
600
         WALLILABOU   600
R. MAST   BAY
15'   GRAND BONHOMME   15'
                            (3000')   COLONARIE PT.
BOTTLE & BARROUALIE
GLASS AT   180
13° 14.4N
61° 16.9W   70
WSTV04   MONTREAL
300   GARDENS   90
100   VERMONT
          NATURE   MT. ST.   70
          TRAILS   ANDREW   MESOPOTAMIA VALLEY
                                              70   BIABU
300   LAYOU   70   180
         LA PAZE RD. PETIT BYAHAUT
600   CAMPEN PARK
300   (INDUSTRIAL)   RADIO MAST
                      OTTLE HALL
                      (PLAN)
FORT CHARLOTTE   BOTANIC
FL(3)20 S,16M   GARDENS   50   120   10'
10'   KINGSTOWN
                  180 40   YAMBU
         600   HEAD
                     AIRPORT
                     PLAN   70
N   CANE GARDEN POINT
                      100
W   E   600   YOUNG I. FL   80   180
                  BLUE LAGOON
S   80 MILLIGAN CAY
                              600   Atlantic Ocean

4

St. Vincent and the Grenadines

"Therefore, my dear brothers, stand firm.
Let nothing move you. Always give yourselves fully to the
work of the LORD, because you know that your labor
in the LORD is not in vain."
(1 Corinthians 15:58)

CBS International was born in St. Vincent and the Grenadines (SVG) through the Kingstown interdenominational class on October 15, 2001.

SVG consists of the main island of St. Vincent and the northern two-thirds of the Grenadines, a chain of smaller islands stretching south from St. Vincent Island to Grenada. The area is densely populated with a weak, mostly agrarian economy and high unemployment. The language spoken is English, but the dialect is "Vincy twang," one more difficult for us to understand than that of Antigua.

On Wednesday, June 27, 2001, we sailed out of Antigua after observing the growing, vibrant CBSI class in its third six-week study. We were on a spiritual high as we sailed to St. Vincent to participate in the Layou Conference. Unlike Antigua, the Lesser Antilles islands to its south are generally volcanic, mountainous and usually lush and green as a result of the rainfall the mountains attract from the easterly trade winds. While we enjoyed a leisurely "sailing vacation," soaking in the beauty of the islands and the sea, our thoughts, prayers and conversation continually turned to the conference.

Originally our intent in visiting SVG was to receive our new mainsail from Sunsail, but God had a greater purpose. At the invitation of Pastor Verrol Blake, we would be introducing CBSI at the 14th annual St. Vincent Christian Leadership Conference. Scheduled for July 15-20, this gathering had the potential of opening many doors for CBSI. From our presentations on Tortola, Anguilla and Antigua, it had become clear that the CBSI process was significantly different from any Bible study our Caribbean contacts had experienced. The *CBSI Live!* video would help leaders grasp CBSI's study method and its benefits versus their traditional mid-week Bible study format.

In the months after Verrol's invitation, we learned of his need for conference speakers and suggested our friend, Dr. Bruce Fong, the president of Michigan Theological Seminary. With Verrol's full encouragement we recruited Bruce and his lovely, spirited wife Yvonne. They accepted the speaking engagement and our invitation to stay aboard *coram Deo* during the conference.

Upon our arrival in SVG on July 10, 2001, we rounded the southern coast and moored in Young Island Cut, between the mainland and Young Island, a small resort island. The land around us was covered with lush green vegetation and trees full of ripe yellow, orange and red mangos falling to the ground everywhere. The whole landscape was accented with red-flowering flamboyant trees. In this beautiful and quiet anchorage protected from any ocean swells, we and the Fongs would surely be secure and comfortably well rested, though we would have a 45-minute drive each way to Layou.

Even in that idyllic setting with a gently rocking boat, as soon as Dr. Fong came aboard, he practically turned green from sea sickness! He and Yvonne arrived on Saturday, the day before the conference began. Bruce was committed to preach at Pastor Blake's church on Sunday morning as well as speak several times during the conference. Despite the many crackers he ate to help settle his stomach, he said the church never stopped moving during his sermon! Declining our offer to house him at a hotel, he valiantly carried out his speaking schedule, despite continued queasiness.

We emailed our prayer partners a long list of prayer requests for Dr. Fong, us and the conference and once more we experienced the reality of James 5:16, *"...The prayer of a righteous man is powerful and effective."*

Every morning at 7 a.m. we dinghied ashore, driving the coast road to the leeward side (west) and Layou. The drive was quite intense as the narrow mountain roads had no shoulder or guard rails and long stretches were under construction with a trench down the middle, making it a thrill when large oncoming trucks had to squeeze by. Driving became even more interesting at night with bright lights blinding Chuck. And, in this formerly British colony, people drive on the left hand side!

When we arrived at the conference in the morning, we quickly forgot the drive. Praise and worship—led by the Blakes' sons, Nigel and Allister, their wives Ruth and Debbie and others—opened and closed the sessions. The West Indians sing with such joy and with their whole bodies. There is no standing still! And what happy hands they have! We visitors had to learn the different styles of clapping. Yvonne Fong was not clapping, so energetic Mauricia went behind her, put her hands over Yvonne's and taught her to clap. The hardest part was clapping and dancing at the same time!

The conference was attended by 50-plus pastors and leaders from SVG, the British and U.S. Virgin Islands and Trinidad. In addition to Pastor Blake and Dr. Fong, the speakers included Pastor Gary Hamrick and Pastor Andy Wagner from Cornerstone Chapel in Leesburg, Virginia, Pastor Vickram Hajaree from Point Fortin Open Bible Standard Church in Trinidad and ourselves.

Our time slots were the first two evenings, Monday and Tuesday from 7 to 9 p.m. It was absolutely amazing how God sovereignly guided the teaching of all four speakers on both mornings. Each one, in turn, spoke on the great need for in-depth study of the Word. God had clearly set up CBSI as the answer to each teaching! How faithful He was to His calling on our lives. As Ted Martin would say... *"Isn't that just like the Father!"*

After presenting a brief background on CBSI, we showed the newly produced *CBSI Live!* video of the Antigua class. Those viewing it sang with the praise singing, prayed along and listened intently to Ted's lecture. Wow! The video was indeed an effective tool. We handed out a lesson for all to do in the next day's breaks so they could participate as we modeled a CBSI class the next evening. What a heartwarming sight it was during free time on Tuesday to walk around the grounds, watching men and women diligently doing the lesson, some under the shade of trees, others in their dorm rooms. And they were not only doing the lesson but discussing their answers with one another.

After a short time of praise and worship on Tuesday evening, Micki led the discussion group, and Chuck followed with a simple but compelling teaching. Many from SVG wanted to get CBSI started—and not in just one place but around the entire country!

The fact that we lived on a yacht was fascinating to many. So during the last morning session, we slipped out early and sailed *coram Deo* into Layou Bay for an "open house." After lunch about 20 to 30 people came aboard, some swimming out and others were dinghied out by Chuck. Brenford Millington, a young man attending the conference and familiar with Layou, arranged a watchman for the boat so we could attend the closing events of the conference.

After the conference Bruce got his sea legs, and we all had a great five days of rest and recuperation enjoying the sailing, snorkeling and fishing around the Grenadines. Once the Fongs went home, our work on St. Vincent began!

It was suggested at the conference that we hold a seminar in SVG for interested pastors, using the presentation we gave at the conference. So we planned a Pastors CBSI Information Dinner for Friday, August 10, at the Paradise Inn overlooking Young Island Cut where *coram Deo* remained moored. Shirley Jones, a Christian and the proprietress of the inn, became an encouraging friend and enthusiastic supporter of CBSI. We sent out more than one hundred invitations to pastors and Christian leaders, hoping to reach most of them.

In addition to Shirley and Verrol's guidance and assistance, God provided some special help for that important event in Tony and Beth (Thompson) Nagle. Beth was part of the prayer group that resulted in the young adult Bible study we taught for eight years in the States. When Tony became a leader, they met, fell in love, got married and were now joining us for a vacation. They arrived one week before the Pastors Information Dinner. We dinghied them to the boat and as Beth was climbing aboard, Tony started telling Chuck how moody and crabby Beth had become, particularly in the mornings. Micki overheard and looked as if she was about to knock Tony into the water when Beth started laughing! Then we got it. Beth was pregnant! What a blessed start to a great week together! We played hard and worked hard.

On Sunday after church we were joined by Nigel & Ruth Blake aboard *coram Deo* for a sail to Mustique, one of the Grenadine Islands known as a place for the rich and famous. Since Ruth's sister worked there, we got an up close and personal tour. After sandwiching in a three-day sailing trip, it was back to the St. Vincent mainland and preparations for the Pastors Information Dinner.

When we were not sailing, Chuck spent much of his time on his local cell phone calling all the pastors who had been invited. That is how we learned that the postal system was unreliable. Only a few people actually received their invitations, even though we mailed them at the post office where most had postal boxes. We were learning the ways of the Caribbean! If it is important, either personal delivery or a phone call, or both, are required. Even an email usually requires a phone follow-up to insure that the person got the message.

Despite the problem with the invitations, more than fifty pastors and spouses attended. Beth made nametags and distributed information packets while Tony set up and ran the audio equipment and took photos. We can still picture Beth making nametags, laughing and greeting all as they entered the Paradise Inn. We were proud and deeply touched to have these two serving by our side once again in God's work! Their help freed us to greet, mingle and get acquainted with our guests.

Verrol Blake was the Master of Ceremonies praying at mealtime and introducing us afterward. We gave a brief history of CBSI and talked about God's call on our lives before showing *CBSI Live!* Again, the people sang, prayed along and were "Amen-ing" Ted's teaching! We discussed the uniqueness and benefits of CBSI, answered questions and encouraged people to contact us with names of potential leaders so we could schedule the training sessions.

Nineteen potential leaders from several denominations attended a CBSI introduction meeting on August 27, 2001 at the large Methodist meeting hall in Kingstown, the capital city. Micki presented our background and told how God had combined our love for sailing and devotion to His Word to bring CBSI to the Eastern Caribbean. She gave a brief history of CBSI and talked about the sole mission of disciple-making and the unique five features of the ministry's approach to Bible study before showing the video. Chuck wrapped up the evening with an overview teaching on 1 John, issuing a final challenge: "Who will join God in changing SVG through leadership in CBSI?" Heads were nodding, and people were declaring that they wanted to be trained.

Training began the following Monday, September 3, 2001, and went for six weeks with class start-up targeted for October 15. Six men and five women faithfully and enthusiastically attended the weekly training sessions as we went through CBSI's 1 John course. We began every session with praise singing and our three-part prayer followed by a 30-minute weekly training on the CBSI mission, process and leadership roles as well as discussion of their completed lessons. One of us modeled the Discussion Leader role and the other one modeled a brief teaching on the passage. In essence we followed the pattern of a Leaders Council meeting but with more training time and teaching.

A strong bond of fellowship quickly developed in this group of leaders, and after every session we would *lime*—the West Indian term for hanging out and enjoying refreshments with friends. Someone would bring tasty homemade petite triangular-cut cheese sandwiches, store bought peanut butter and crackers or cheese and crackers snack packs, or we would saunter to the ice cream wagon for homemade ice cream.

Half way through the training Roy Lewis answered God's call as Teaching Leader. A deep thinker who loves the Word of God, Roy was in training and challenged by the need for a Teaching Leader. He hesitated, however, because he wanted to support his church in its regular Monday night prayer meetings. During those first weeks of training, church leaders decided to combine their prayer meeting with Wednesday night Bible Study, freeing up Mondays for Roy. That clarified Roy's decision! Some call that coincidence. We say, *"Isn't that just like the Father!"*

Now with Roy as Teaching Leader, we approached the others in training, and the team came together. John Lewis, Roy's brother, former Youth for Christ leader and recent seminary graduate, accepted the call to be Associate Teaching Leader. Dependable, conscientious and highly organized Marcia (pronounced Mar see ah) Seales was clearly the Class Coordinator. The remaining leader-ship training sessions were completed as we interviewed men and women to be Discussion Leaders. Rohan Winsboro, Antonio Brazil and Norville Gardner stepped forward as men's Discussion Leaders while Annette Martin-Kennedy, Laurette Davis and Rosita Gardner accepted the call to be women's Discussion Leaders.

A central location for class meetings was vital for ease of access to bus transportation. Many do not own vehicles and rely heavily on public transportation. Pastor Fitzroy Sam, a school principal, put us in contact with Mrs. Laura Brown, the Chief Education Officer of the Ministry of Education, who was supportive and guided us in securing the use of the small auditorium at the Kingstown Girls High School. Perfect location!

Flyers announcing the CBSI class start-up were printed and dis-tributed to various churches. A crusade was being held in a small sta-dium in Kingstown, and we joined the leaders in passing out CBSI flyers while the people exited. One recipient of a flyer was a young man named Brian Burke, who took note and attended the new class.

On Monday, October 15, 2001, the first CBSI class in St. Vincent and the Grenadines began! A total of 29 persons were in attendance. Almost half of these were the leadership team. We had been praying for 100 because the trained leadership could have shepherded that number. *"We are... perplexed, but not in despair..."* *(2 Corinthians 4:8)*

The class began with dynamic praise singing powerfully led by Al Blake, singing and playing the keyboard. While the auditorium was not full of people, praise singing filled the room and spilled out onto the school campus! We gave an introduction of CBSI to the group, and Roy Lewis followed with an inviting overview of 1 John to whet people's appetites for the study.

Only two of the six Discussion Leaders were assigned group members. But we were still excited about those who did attend, three of which were pastors! Oneika, a young waitress to whom we had been witnessing, joined. She was there with a smile and hugs for us, saying she would return next week. She was a Christian about to be born!

The second class drew eight new members, reaching a total enrollment of 37, which Roy said was more than in his church! It was exciting to see the discussion groups meeting for the first time, with Rohan leading the men and Annette the women. Micki sat in the women's discussion group led by Annette, who has a joyful, loving way of making people feel comfortable. The discussion began slowly, but at the end all were laughing and sharing openly what God had shown them in home study. Annette took time to get as many as possible to share on a personal question, asking if they'd had a personal experience with the Word and, if so, would they describe it? After most volunteered their experiences, Annette looked at Oneika, who seemed to enjoy what she was hearing, asking if she would like to share. Oneika said she couldn't because she didn't have a personal experience. The next minute we were on holy ground. As if Annette was alone in the room with Oneika, she kindly and lovingly asked, "Would you like to?" Not seeming to be put on the spot, Oneika smiled and quietly said, "Yes." And right there in the midst of all the ladies now silently praying, Annette explained the gospel, introducing Oneika to her Savior Jesus Christ.

Teaching from 1 John 1:1-4, Roy delivered a wonderful message on the joy in knowing Jesus and in fellowshipping with His people. It was particularly encouraging to hear from a pastor in class the following week, saying that because of what he had learned in the prior week's lesson he had to come back for more!

God gave Chuck the sensitivity to intercept one young guest who seemed interested during the presentation but was abruptly leaving when it came time to enroll. In talking to him Chuck learned that the young man could not read, nor could his family. Rohan and Antonio immediately committed to meeting with this young man weekly to read the commentary and questions to him so he could be a part of the class. Coordinator Marcia noted that illiteracy might have been a reason for relatively low enrollment in class so far. The illiteracy rate in St. Vincent is high. In view of this we were ecstatic to see the lengths to which class leaders were willing to go to live out the lessons being learned in 1 John. We had stressed in training that every person who attended would be sent by the Lord for His purposes. "So allow God to love them through you," we said. "Be conduits of His love." These leaders got it and were living it out!

After four months in SVG and watching God faithfully bring about a CBSI class, we prepared to depart on November 7, 2001. Roy Lewis seemed to be in awe of God's calling, even as he considered God's will for him in his impending retirement. In every week we had met and worked with him, we saw God further equipping him. His two teachings before we left the island were answered by applause from the class! The excellence of the teaching and the surplus of leaders prompted us to think of beginning a second class. So CBSI-Kingstown was well started and primed for growth.

Before we sailed out, however, the leaders had a farewell barbeque on the beach at the Paradise Inn. Rosita, a cook, guided the preparation of appetizers of chicken kabobs and our favorite cheese sandwiches, followed by the traditional Caribbean main course of huge barbequed chicken legs and thighs, roasted breadfruit (yum!), carrot salad and piles of rice and beans. It was not long before the dominoes were being slammed on the table. It was a beautiful expression of God's love.

At 6:10 the next morning, we dropped the mooring line and motored west into the Bequia Channel, past the E.T. Joshua Airport, Kingstown harbor, around the southwest corner of the mainland and north along the leeward coast. Pleasant memories came to mind as we passed Buccament Bay, where Verrol's church was, and then Layou Bay, where so much of the SVG work began. We continued motoring, enjoying the incredible beauty and majesty of St. Vincent's lush green mountains with their volcanic and deeply cut ravines. As we reached the northern tip of the island and entered the St. Vincent Channel, the winds came up. As always Chuck was quick to raise sails and kill the engine, and it was not long before *coram Deo* was making eight knots for St. Lucia with the 15- to 20-knot easterly winds.

In coming weeks we stayed in contact with Teaching Leader Roy Lewis. The CBSI Kingstown class completed the 1 John study and held a Testimony and Honors night. Every member testified about what CBSI meant to them, and those with 90 percent participation received a Certificate of Achievement suitable for framing. When we called Roy asking about that night and how he was doing, he said, "I'm so excited!" He was already reading Galatians, the subject of the next study due to start January 14.

Another huge demonstration of God's faithfulness in SVG was a divine appointment between Al Blake and Dr. Bruce Fong during the Layou conference. For more than a year Al and Debbie had been praying for an opportunity to further their education to better help their Vincentian people. In God's sovereignty Al shared his prayer with Dr. Fong at Layou. God prompted Dr. Fong to discuss Al's situation with his colleague, Dr. Joe Stowell, the president of Moody Bible Institute in Chicago. Al received his admission to Moody for the spring semester in 2002, just before we left SVG. When he and Debbie flew to the States, they stayed with us in our home. Our Faithful Friends Adult Fellowship Group (AFG) at Woodside Bible Church helped them with much of what they needed to set up housekeeping, prayed for them and had them back to Michigan for breaks. Both Al and Debbie graduated from Moody and went on to Michigan

Theological Seminary, where Al interned with Harvest Bible Chapel. In 2010 Al and Debbie returned to SVG with their master's degrees. Al planted and now pastors Harvest Bible Chapel of SVG, with Debbie providing administrative and counseling support.

From personal experience we knew the opposition that effective Bible teachers would likely encounter and their need for encouragement and a sounding board. When Chuck spoke with Roy in January of 2002, Roy was overwhelmed with personal issues. His brother John, the Associate Teaching Leader, quit, and Roy had eye problems requiring surgery, and he was opening a pharmacy in Georgetown, a two-hour drive from Kingstown. Class start-up would have to be postponed. For some reason class members were not notified of the postponement. So on January 14, when some members went to Girls High School with guests, they found no class. Some returned the next Monday to find the same situation. Finally, after a four-week delay, the class began on February 11. Most members were still not notified, so only 15 of the 38 pre-registered attended. Roy was deeply discouraged.

Knowing of this, we left *coram Deo* at anchor in Sopers Hole, Tortola, and flew to St. Vincent on February 28. We then spent six days encouraging the four committed leaders to persevere. We attended Leaders Council and class, speaking with class members to discern how best to help. What we learned was that communication had broken down in the leadership team as well as between Discussion Leaders and their group members. Leaders were not kept informed about when class would resume, and when they were informed, they did not take it upon themselves to contact all pre-registered members.

In CBSI leadership training we say with emphasis that making disciples is what we do and shepherding is how we do it. Communication—showing you care by investing time with a phone call or a visit to a member—is the simple key to shepherding.

The Discussion Leaders had limited funds for phone calls. So, to jump start the shepherding, we purchased pre-paid phone cards for them, suggesting that in the future some class contribution money could be used for phone cards - a legitimate expense to help facilitate effective shepherding. We encouraged Roy to lead by example by communicating regularly with his leaders. *"Let us not become weary in doing good, for at the proper time we will reap a harvest if we do not give up." (Galatians 6:9)* We exhorted them to finish, not just somehow, but victoriously! Then they could get off to a strong start mid-April with the study of James.

Sadly, after completing the Galatians study, Roy left CBSI with no attempt to have his good work carried forward. In June of 2002, during a short visit to Michigan, we received a phone call from Class Coordinator Marcia Seales and Discussion Leader Annette Martin-Kennedy, saying they needed help in getting the class started again. People were calling and wanting the CBSI study. They said we needed to come back to St. Vincent. Not sure what to do, we said we would get back to them. At that time we had no intention of returning to restart that work. We felt we had poured out our all!

Shortly after those calls Chuck stood before the Faithful Friends AFG at our home church, confessing our stubborn attitudes and saying he felt like Jonah. He did not want to go back to St. Vincent! We had invested four intense months in SVG, thinking we were witnessing God putting the CBSI class together in October, only to see it fall apart the following March. During that rebellious time we asked our prayer partners to pray for God to reveal the next place He would open the door for CBSI. We wanted to go anywhere but SVG! However, not wanting to experience a devastating storm aboard *coram Deo* or be washed overboard and swallowed by a whale, Chuck submitted to what he and Micki knew in their hearts was the Lord's will - return to SVG and trust God for new leadership. Micki said she would go back but for only two weeks! We asked for prayer from our Faithful Friends and our full prayer support team. God changed our hearts and attitudes even before we arrived in SVG at the beginning of August of 2002, and we stayed there for two exciting months!

Within one week following our return, God identified six men as potential Teaching Leaders or Associate Teaching Leaders! Four had been in the class, and the other two were business professionals with solid reputations as lay Bible teachers. We met with them one by one and challenged each to pray for God's will about CBSI leadership. Then we waited and prayed as He worked in their hearts and ours.

God started eliminating them. One had already applied at Open Bible College in Trinidad and was accepted. Another had a busy law practice and felt Bible teaching would have to wait a couple years until his retirement. A third lost interest, and then God sovereignly pared the choice down to two school teachers, Brian Burke and Rev. Chiefton Charles. We met with them a number of times to discern their leadership positions since both were willing to fill whatever role God revealed.

God called Brian Burke to be the Teaching Leader. We interviewed him because of his perfect attendance in the previous two studies and at the recommendation of two of the leaders. From the very first of three interviews Brian indicated that he was on board. "We need CBSI in every village in SVG," he said. "I'll do whatever you need to keep it going." He had made a decision to follow the Lord and was not turning back! While only 31, he had 14 years of teaching experience in social studies and religion as well as coaching the school's cricket team and the national volleyball team. He was a leader in Youth for Christ and had an ongoing video evangelism program in the villages. Our only hesitation, especially in Micki, was Brian's quiet demeanor. So we prayed and waited for God to make His intentions clear. We would not make such a decision until we were in agreement.

As we sat before the Lord one morning in our personal Bible study, Chuck said, "Here it is! Here's our answer!" He pointed out Judges 6:14, where God responds to Gideon's questions, saying, ***"Go in the strength you have… Am I not sending you?"*** The strength we had was a young man committed wholeheartedly to the Lord. We agreed this was God's direction.

God also made the Associate Teaching Leader choice clear with Rev. Chiefton Charles. While 20 years older, he and Brian had taught at the same school and were friends. As we interviewed Chiefton, God made His presence felt and His wisdom known. He had provided a mature pastor to support, encourage and mentor the younger Teaching Leader. *Isn't that just like the Father!*

We trained Brian and Chiefton using a small meeting room at the Paradise Inn, having meals together and getting to know one another. Meanwhile, Marcia and Annette were getting out the word that the CBSI study on James would begin on September 23, 2002. Or so we thought it would!

All was in readiness on Monday, September 23, when Tropical Storm Lili passed over Barbados, 90 miles east of SVG. This storm was packing winds of 60 to 75 mph and heading straight for us! We had been so focused on CBSI that we had not been keeping up with weather reports. There was no time to sail *coram Deo* to a hurricane hole either north or south. Charley Tango, from whom we rented our mooring in Young Island Cut and who had become our friend, helped us tie multiple lines to his five ton mooring. We dropped two additional anchors, removed all canvas, wrapped all sails with lines and lashed our dinghy to the davits. Shirley Jones called, pleading with us not to stay on board but to spend the night at the inn. A room was ready for us. With the winds howling over 35 knots and the seas kicking up wildly, Charley picked us up in his dinghy. When we reached the dinghy dock, we were walking on water, in a manner of speaking, because the dock was already submerged from the storm surge. We moved into a room on the second floor of the inn, hearing the winds whistling outside. As they grew in intensity, the steel roof started shaking. Believing it was about to blow off, we prayed Ted Martin's hurricane prayer, "Lord, sit on it!" The roof stayed on, but many other roofs on the windward (east) side of the island were blown off. More troublesome, four people were killed, and 50 percent of the banana crop was destroyed.

We slept little that night, and at dawn Micki prayerfully rushed to the window to see *coram Deo* swinging safely on her mooring. Thank you, Lord! One local fishing boat had dragged anchor and was close to a reef. We discovered a hilarious thing that morning in a waterproof bag Micki had packed quickly with our important papers. In her panic the night before, she had put our Volvo engine manual in the bag and left the very important boat registration and passports on *coram Deo*!

Lili caused us to postpone the first class meeting for a week. The leaders continued spreading the word of class start-up to former members, to churches and even through a local radio interview. On Monday, September 30, 2002, after a spirited time of praise and worship, Associate Teaching Leader Chiefton Charles gave a creative introduction to CBSI for the newcomers. Teaching Leader Brian Burke gave an excellent overview of James, challenging all with the truth that Christianity must not only be believed, but lived. Among the 15 in attendance was a young lady we met and invited while grocery shopping, and Keith Joseph, who heard the radio interview. Afterward Keith encouraged Chuck by saying, "I don't care if there are just a few in class. I want to study the Bible!" ***"Who despises the day of small things? Men will rejoice when they see the plumb line in the hand of Zerubbabel." (Zechariah 4:10)*** For Keith, a building contractor, the plumb line of life was not a string. It was the Word of God. Within a short time, and not surprising to us, he was called to be a men's Discussion Leader.

While we were accustomed to U.S. classes with several hundred members, God continued to teach us that He is interested in individuals who desire to know and follow Him. ***"...and you, O Israelites, will be gathered up one by one..." (Isaiah 27:12)***

Twenty-one people attended the second class meeting. Annette was an excellent example for other leaders who needed deeper commitment and growth in leadership skills to make everyone feel comfortable, cared for and able to grow in confidence in studying God's Word. So with the love and passion for God's Word and His people shared by Brian, Chiefton and Annette, the Lord was laying a foundation upon which CBSI would be built in SVG.

As Brian learned the importance of shepherding and saw the leaders' resistance to contacting their group members regularly, he began texting all the class members. Weekly he sent prayer requests, thoughts from the lesson, encouragements and exhortations to do their lessons daily.

Praising God for His faithfulness and knowing we would return soon, it was time for us to leave and let these leaders take ownership. Verrol Blake had introduced us to the Evangelical Association of the Caribbean (EAC) and its Congress of Evangelicals in the Caribbean, or CONECAR. This Congress was to be held in Barbados October 20 to 24, and Verrol strongly encouraged us to attend. This was another door opener, so we registered and prepared to sail to Barbados and return to SVG afterwards.

After two months at anchor, we were looking forward to a time of sailing. On Tuesday, October 8, 2002, after the encouraging second class meeting, we began our sail to Barbados, which is 90 miles upwind to the east of SVG. We dropped the mooring line in Young Island Cut at 6:27 a.m. and enjoyed a great sail north to Rodney Bay, St. Lucia. With a full main, a reefed jib and a full staysail, we raced across the St. Vincent Channel at speeds of seven to nine and a half knots with over 20-knot winds and minimal seas. From St. Lucia we sailed northeast to St. Anne, Martinique, from where we would make the sail southeast to Barbados. Late in the afternoon on Saturday, October 12, we motor-sailed overnight, arriving Bridgetown, Barbados, at noon on Sunday.

CONECAR was another step forward for CBSI in the Caribbean. We had had a CBSI Caribbean display built, and we set this up in the exhibit tent. Here, before and after sessions and during breaks, we made contacts and entered into relationships with leaders from 11 Caribbean countries. Pastor Vickram Hajaree, whom we had met at the Layou conference, came to our display and invited us to join him shortly after CONECAR at a "Deeper Life" conference in Tobago, 118 miles southwest of Barbados. We had hoped to sail there afterward for a short rest, but maybe God had a different plan!

As anticipated, there was interest on the part of pastors and Christian leaders in Barbados. So with help from Dr. Nigel Taylor, President of the Barbados Evangelical Association, we planned a

CBSI introduction meeting following CONECAR. Fifty-five potential leaders attended! We prayed about how to handle this outpouring of interest in view of the fact that our tight schedule did not allow us to train leadership. As they say in Barbados, we would have to "big it up." That is, we needed to mature in our way of establishing and developing CBSI in the interested island nations.

Earlier that year at the CBS Teaching Directors Conference, we had learned about the eight-week CBSI introductory course called If You Will Pray. The purpose of this is to introduce interested persons to the CBSI prayer pattern, give them a brief Bible study on leadership from portions of the book of Nehemiah, introduce them to the leadership roles needed for a CBSI class and provide specific prayer concerns weekly for God to identify persons of His choosing for the specific leadership roles. Unlike a CBSI class, there is no teaching time in an If You Will Pray study, and rotation of leadership is encouraged as a way of discerning the gifts of persons in the group and how they might best be used in leadership. If enough leaders are identified in the course of eight weeks, leadership training is the next step. We later discovered the confusion this study can cause for those unfamiliar with CBSI, particularly if they do not have experienced local guidance.

So, rather than let the Barbados interest cool off until we could return six months later, we offered this course. We had the group divide into six prayer groups according to where they lived and identify a leader. The leaders were given a copy of If You Will Pray to photocopy for their weekly meetings, and they were asked to stay in contact with the other prayer group leaders. We tried to monitor their progress by telephone. Only two groups actually did the study. Sadly, this approach failed to result in any classes—even though we returned and held CBSI leadership training in April of 2003 for them and leaders from other islands.

After contacting all the new prayer group leaders to encourage them, we set sail south to the vacation island of Tobago, part of the Republic of Trinidad and Tobago, to meet with Pastor Hajaree. We made landfall in beautiful Man of War Bay on the northwest coast. The bay was teaming with fish life. The surrounding mountains were covered with forests of bamboo and flamboyant trees with beautiful red or yellow flowers. We caught up with Pastor Hajaree and his team but too late for the conference. He introduced us to his colleagues from Trinidad, Tobago and Grenada. We introduced CBSI to each and gave them the If You Will Pray study. In addition, he invited us to introduce CBSI at the Open Bible Caribbean Missions Conference in Point Fortin, Trinidad, in February of 2003.

It was a quick three-day visit in Tobago. We would have loved to stay longer, even just for the weekend, but we wanted to be in SVG for CBSI on Monday. The weather forecast was threatening large northerly swells expected to arrive on Saturday, with seas building to eight feet on Sunday. So we set sail north to SVG late Friday afternoon, November 8, 2002, to miss the weather. But the weather report was wrong. The swells came shortly after we left Tobago, and they did not build to eight-footers—they started at that size! Not only were we bucking into high seas, an unreported tropical wave hit with winds up to 30 knots. Yikes! But we praised the Lord for our strong, seaworthy *coram Deo* as she provided safety in the tough 20-hour overnight sail! Thankfully the winds and seas finally settled down the last five hours. Since we did not have to be in St. Vincent until Monday, we stopped to rest in Bequia, the northernmost Grenadine Island.

On Monday morning we sailed the eight miles across the Bequia Channel to Young Island Cut, arriving in plenty of time to attend the Monday evening CBSI Kingstown class. What an encouraging short visit! Although only 20 people were in attendance, we saw much potential. Keith was leading the men's group, and Mauricia George was a Discussion Leader in training, supporting Annette with the women.

Even at this early stage, Annette was sensing God's call to start a class in her neighborhood. In addition, we met leaders from the rural villages of Sandy Bay and Carriere who wanted CBSI classes in their churches. We gave them the If You Will Pray study to seek God's will in determining leadership.

On November 16, 2002, we set sail north for Antigua with brief layovers in St. Lucia and Martinique. A week later we sailed into Antigua, where *coram Deo* was stored in Jolly Harbour Boatyard while we flew home to spend Christmas with family and attend the January CBS Teaching Directors Conference.

When we returned to Antigua at the end of January of 2003, we would have *coram Deo* refitted, converting a bunkroom into an office for our CBSI work. That would keep us in Antigua at least into mid March. While at home we brainstormed how best to "big up" our CBSI training to cover more islands at one time. We decided, rather than training the whole leadership team, to train just Teaching Leaders and Associate Teaching Leaders but instruct them in all the leadership roles, much as CBS and BSF do. The Teaching Leaders and Associate Teaching Leaders would return to their homelands and train others on their leadership teams. After looking at the location of those we needed to train from four islands, we felt Barbados offered the most convenient airline access. So we scheduled and announced a Teaching Leader/Associate Teaching Leader Training Seminar for April 2-5, 2003, in Barbados.

On March 13, 2003, after the completion of the office refit on *coram Deo,* we set sail for Barbados to prepare for the Training Seminar. This time we were joined by Micki's sister Louise and husband Chris. They had not been south of Antigua, so we island hopped, stopping in Guadeloupe for French baguettes and pastries, then further south to Isle de Saintes, where we toured one island on motor scooters, and then sailed to the place that became their favorite spot, peaceful and quiet St. Anne, Martinique. We relaxed there before making the overnight sail to Barbados from where our crew returned home. It was so great to share these islands and our life aboard with family!

We then had eight days to finish preparing for the Training Seminar and finalize arrangements. All existing Teaching Leaders (TLs) and Associate Teaching Leaders (ATLs) were invited as well as those who would be starting new CBSI classes. Our thinking was that this training would be a refresher for existing Teaching Leaders, and they would be a help and encouragement to the new leaders. The ten men and women representing four islands who attended were TL Ian Macintyre from Tortola, ATL Boris Teague from Antigua, TL Brian Burke as well as Olford Walters, Beverly Warren, Annette Martin-Kennedy, Stedroy Dean and Winston Lavia from SVG and Eileen Rowe and David Kirton from Barbados. As a result, three new CBSI classes were started in April and May of 2003 in SVG. Newly trained Teaching Leader Annette Martin-Kennedy started a CBSI interdenominational group in her home in Kingstown Park upon her return from training.

The CBSI Carriere class, led by Teaching Leader Alwyn Joseph, started on May 7, 2003. Although Alwyn was not able to attend the training, newly trained Discussion Leaders Olford Walters and Beverly Warren took their knowledge and training materials back to help Alwyn begin the class with Brian Burke's assistance. Prior to using CBSI as their mid-week Bible study, they would have 10 to 15 people show up. More than 40 people attended the first CBSI class night, and it grew from there.

The CBSI Sandy Bay class, led by Teaching Leader Stedroy Deane with Brian's help, started on May 27, 2003, with more than 20 in attendance. These two classes—Carriere and Sandy Bay— were the first in the Eastern Caribbean to be held in churches and to provide an enhanced church based mid-week Bible study. Because the entire leadership teams were from these churches, the classes were not interdenominational, although a few people from the community did attend the Carriere class. Because of the high denominational walls, CBSI classes held in churches usually have few members from the outside. Even so, church-based classes which meet consistently and follow the CBSI process produce transformative growth in the members and develop leaders for the church.

CBSI's Children & Youth Ministry became part of the Carriere class in 2006. Children's Supervisor Ingrid Cambridge sent out buses to transport the children to and from class. She was a passionate leader, and soon there were large numbers in the Primary, Junior and Youth groups.

The Youth group was led by Toni Warren, whose mother Beverly spent the last months of her life helping to establish CBSI at the Carriere church. It was a couple of days into the training in Barbados before Beverly revealed that she was suffering from stomach cancer. That was the reason she could not eat and often would need to rest, but she made every session! A petite, bubbly and godly saint serving those God brings around her, Toni is made of the same stuff as her mom! Prior to visiting the Carriere class in November of 2008, we learned that Toni had just been diagnosed with CML, a rare form of leukemia. While there was a chronic shortage of Children's Leaders in this class, we certainly did not expect to see Toni. But in a room jammed full of young teens laughing and sharing what they had learned in their Bible study, there was Toni, lovingly leading them and laughing with them. In talking with her after class, we learned that a potentially life-saving medication, Glivec, was available. At $4,000 per month it was extremely expensive — more than three times her monthly income as a government computer systems analyst! For her to have it would require a miracle. But Toni was holding unswervingly to the hope she professes in her faithful Father. So we, along with all the CBSI Caribbean leadership and our prayer team back home, joined in praying for our faithful God to provide for Toni.

One day Chuck had the thought of calling our nephew, Larry Lyons, who we knew was somehow involved in administering clinical trials of drugs for FDA approval. Toni hoped she could be part of such a research program. Larry, in his previous position, *just so happened* to have been a lead player in the testing of Glivec, the gold standard treatment for CML! He called some of his old contacts, worked his way into the bureaucracy and made a plea to help Toni. Three months later Toni wrote that she had gone to St. Lucia and received a two-month supply of Glivec free! She was later enrolled in the Glivec Patient Assistance Program through an administrator who eight months earlier could not help her. This was the miracle for which we prayed! God chose to use Larry Lyons, who persistently brought Toni's need to the attention of those who could help.

Providentially God sent us 3,000 miles south to introduce CBSI to St. Vincent and its neighbors—and, by the way, to meet Toni Warren and introduce her to our nephew by marriage, a man we did not even know when we answered God's calling to the Caribbean. Larry married our niece five years later in 2005, and cared enough to persist to fight through a bureaucracy to get life saving help for a young woman he had never met. *Isn't that just like the Father!*

In 2007 CBSI Area Director Brian Burke labored with Chuck, CBSI Area Director Ian Macintyre and Trinidad Teaching Leader Joe Caterson on the steering committee whose work resulted in the formation of CBSI Caribbean Incorporated. On May 8, 2008, CBSI Caribbean Inc. was founded as a non-profit corporation in SVG, affiliated with CBSI, but self directed, self determined and self funded. Brian became the first Caribbean Director and Rev. Chiefton Charles became the National Coordinator for SVG.

God's faithfulness to those He called to the CBSI ministry in SVG is abundantly manifest—from taking us to a different church during our 2000 CBSI training to learn of Verrol Blake, to stopping to pick up a mainsail, to an invitation to the Layou conference, to Andy Brown's video *CBSI Live!,* to the SVG information dinner, to Al & Debbie's meeting Dr. Fong and the subsequent invitation to Moody, to Roy Lewis' stepping forward as the first SVG CBSI Teaching Leader, then backing out, opening the door for Brian's calling as Teaching Leader, to classes starting on many of the islands of the Eastern Caribbean, to the vibrant Children & Youth Ministry, to Brian Burke's calling in 2008 to lead CBSI in the Caribbean as Director of CBSI Caribbean Inc. *Isn't that just like the Father!*

"LORD,…all that we have accomplished You have done for us." (Isaiah 26:12) To God be the glory!

SVG leadership team that restarted the class, (l to r) Mauricia, Marcia, (Micki), Annette, ATL Chiefton Charles, TL Brian Burke.

Kingstown, St. Vincent Girls High School; meeting place of first SVG CBSI class.

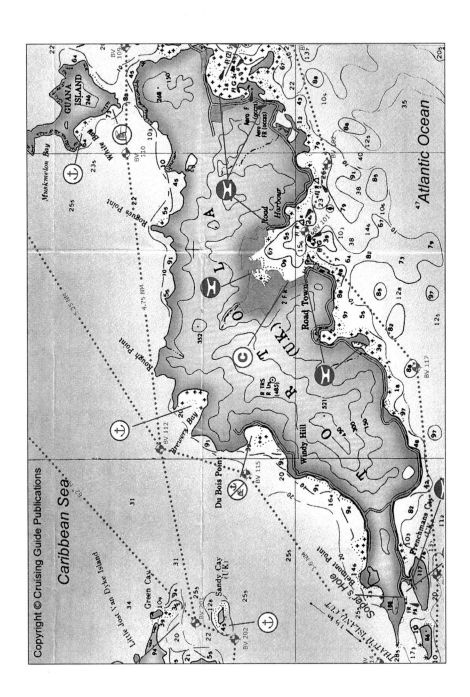

5

Tortola

"Who despises the day of small things?"
(Zechariah 4:10)

The CBS International Tortola class was born on Tuesday, May 21, 2002, with 26 persons in attendance.

While it was a small beginning by U.S. standards, the population of the island was only about 23,000. Tortola, the largest and most populated of the British Virgin Islands (BVI), is a British territory thirteen and a half miles long and three miles wide. Financial services are the main source of income, and BVI residents are among the most affluent in the Eastern Caribbean. BVI has many small islands with beautiful beaches, wonderful snorkeling and great sailing.

In our *coram Deo* online for December 8, 2001, we wrote, "And now we are trusting in Christ's faithfulness to raise up a class in Tortola in the spring of 2002. We will be going there totally by faith." The potential Teaching Leader bailed out, expressing serious reservations about taking on the commitment. So we enlisted our prayer partners to pray with us for God to lift up His leaders for the training and the start-up of CBSI Tortola. ***"Trust in the Lord with all your heart and lean not on your own understanding; in all your*** *ways acknowledge Him, and He will make your paths straight."* *(Proverbs 3:5-6)* We were trusting, not leaning!

When we enlisted the prayer support, we were in Antigua, where we stored *coram Deo* in Jolly Harbour Boatyard and flew back to Michigan for Christmas. After returning to Antigua in January of 2002, we were joined again by Les Posey, who would help us with the sail to Tortola. But first we would put him to work in the ministry! Les had been a leader with Chuck in the BSF men's class in Michigan.

We had prepared a Leaders Workshop for the Antigua leaders to get them off to a good start after the Christmas break, assigning one of the sessions to Les. He enjoyed the assignment and the leaders were very receptive to him.

On Sunday morning the three of us attended church with the Martins, and then set sail at dusk for St. Martin before going on to Tortola. Les, a seasoned Great Lakes sailor, had a taste of the Christmas winds with six to eight foot seas in high winds of 20 to 27 knots! After a couple days of scuba diving, enjoying the French cuisine and provisioning in St. Martin, we sailed overnight to Soper's Hole, Tortola. On arrival Les encouraged us to do our clearance with Customs and Immigration while he stayed onboard. When we returned, he had washed the salt off the entire boat! He was a pleasure to have aboard and an excellent deckhand, always looking for ways to serve. We were truly sorry to see him go.

We enjoyed "family time" with Rev and Nath, and our almost one year old godsons, even babysitting one Saturday evening! With Rev's help we mailed letters of introduction to all the church leaders in BVI in hopes of organizing a CBSI information meeting. With the letters in the mail, we flew to St. Vincent for five days to support the struggling work there. Immediately upon our return to Tortola, we welcomed Micki's sister Louise, husband Chris and adult children Shannon and Gered for 10 days of family vacation aboard *coram Deo*. We enjoyed sailing, swimming, snorkeling and the beauty of BVI and St. John's USVI. One night six sea turtles and a huge tarpon fish entertained us while bats circled the boat.

Refreshed by relaxing with family, it was time to see what God had done. Chuck began telephoning the church leaders. In one day's contacts ten pastors were interested. The letter had worked! We scheduled a CBSI information meeting for Thursday, March 21, at 7:30 p.m. and emailed our prayer partners to pray for good attendance and an effective presentation. Fifteen pastors and Christian lay leaders from six denominations gathered for the presentation. The climate was friendly. The people were receptive to us and CBSI. This ecumenical group committed to fully support the formation of a CBSI class by sending a dozen potential leaders for six-weeks of leadership training scheduled to begin April 2. Class start-up was targeted for the week of May 19, 2002.

On the day of the meeting, we realized that we had no contact for Anglicans so they had not been invited, at least not by us. Our meeting was held in a large, air-conditioned and carpeted conference room above the KMarks grocery store. Upon arrival we were introduced to Michael Georges, an executive with the firm, who was to lock up when we finished. After being present for much of the meeting, he expressed interest and asked for a couple information packets. He *just so happened* to be in the leadership of the Anglican Church! The Anglicans were indeed represented! The next morning we received a telephone call from the Anglican office asking for a dozen information packets to distribute to their leaders. *Isn't that just like the Father!*

The following week we met with Mr. Elmore Stoutt, the principal of BVI High School, who graciously approved our use of an air conditioned multi-level hall for the CBSI training and class with excellent quality desks and capacity for about 100 people. On Tuesday, April 2, the first Leadership Training session was held with nine persons in attendance in that big hall. We were elated! The six male and three female potential leaders included a pastor, lay preachers and persons working in various professions. Three more would join the following week. We would be training "12 disciples" in the hope of giving life to a CBSI class. Mike Georges, from the Anglican Church, and his wife Celia were two of the 12! Celia *just so happened* to be chairman of the English Department of BVI High School. For the second week of training she invited us to use her departmental teacher's lounge for a more intimate setting. She also stored the CBSI materials in her office, photocopied the lessons and maintained a great working relationship with Principal Stoutt.

The leadership training pattern was the same as in Antigua and SVG using the CBSI 1 John course. We began with praise singing and the three-part prayer followed by a 30-minute weekly training on the CBSI mission, process and leadership roles, discussion of their completed lessons with one of us modeling the Discussion Leader role and the other doing a brief sample teaching on the passage.

We had a special blessing the day after the first training when we sailed three hours to Charlotte Amalie, St. Thomas. Chuck's brother Richard, with wife Mary and daughter Debbie Olinger with husband Skip and two younger kids, Zach and Jasmin, were making a port call there aboard the cruise ship SS Norway. It took us awhile, but we found them on the waterfront, dinghied them to *coram Deo* and sailed to nearby Honeymoon Bay, Water Island. That was where we participated in a business conference with Richard and Mary and older brother Bob and wife Donna on our first trip to the Caribbean 15 years earlier. We had a whirlwind of fun with a great sail, fun swimming, lunch aboard and a fast return to the dock. After they left, it was back to Tortola to continue the training.

We modeled a Discussion Leader's shepherding responsibility by making contact with each of the 12 trainees at some time between sessions to encourage their preparation, get better acquainted and find out how we could pray for them. By the fourth training session, we were on a spiritual high! Between the third and fourth sessions we had flown to Antigua to attend the Testimony and Honors night for that class, which was totally encouraging, and among the ten committed leaders in Tortola we were seeing the lights go on as they began to understand the process and share their excitement in studying God's Word. Start-up time was fast approaching, but we did not see a potential for the Teaching Leader. We knew God's timing is perfect, but class was only three weeks away! We were starting to stress, but God's Word is clear. ***"Do not be anxious about anything, but in everything, by prayer and petition, with thanksgiving, present your requests to God."*** *(Philippians 4:6)*

Just as in Antigua and SVG, as we neared the target date for the new class, our plates were overflowing! Arrangements had to be made to move our Hunter sailboat in the States to a better sales location. Each of the leaders-in-training was interviewed about specific leadership positions. We spoke at and participated in the BVI Interdenominational Day of Prayer. Our interview on local TV was broadcast on several TV programs. In the midst of all this, Chuck received a call from Ian Macintyre from the hospitality committee of New Life Baptist Church. He was calling to welcome us to the church and invite us to his home for dinner the next Sunday. Ian was intrigued when he read our guest card, noting our affiliation with CBSI. He had the impression that CBSI was already meeting on island, so when we were at his home after church he expressed further interest in our Bible study.

God had sovereignly brought Ian (an attorney) and Denyse (a gynecologist) to Tortola in May 2000 from their homeland of Trinidad and Tobago. Ian was a legislative draftsman for the BVI government. When they first attended New Life Baptist, they saw from personal experience the need for a hospitality ministry. So with the pastor's permission they organized a team to call visitors, particularly foreigners, and invite them into their homes for a meal and fellowship.

At their home we talked some about New Life, but Ian was genuinely interested in Bible study and wanted to know about CBSI. As we explained our work, he was very supportive and expressed a desire to get involved. We learned from Denyse that Ian has the spiritual gift of teaching. Furthermore, he had spoken at youth camps on several occasions, taught Sunday school and Bible studies, and organized a chapter of Intervarsity Christian Fellowship at his law school. We saw the potential, got excited, and invited the two back to *coram Deo* to learn more.

After viewing *CBSI Live!* and perusing a lesson, they knew that God had brought us together! It was then Denyse shared her prayer from service that very morning, as she silently cried out to God, "I want to know you, Lord! I want to be obedient, but I need to know more about you!" They both saw CBSI as an answer to their prayers. So we gave them the leadership packet including the three back lessons already completed by the trainees, plus the current fourth lesson and invited them to join the leadership team. They would need to do the next lesson before training, only two days away. They did the next lesson, and Ian did all the back lessons as well!

In only two weeks their leadership qualities were apparent, not just to us but to the other leaders. We met them for dinner the Friday before the last training session. Micki challenged Ian to pray about becoming the Teaching Leader, which he did and in so doing accepted God's call.

Ian's call to leadership was confirmed by Celia Georges. Celia, as a professional educator, had the tools to be the Teaching Leader, but God was not leading us to her. The day after Ian gave us his decision, Micki tentatively asked Celia to pray about becoming the Class Coordinator. She laughed out loud, saying she had told Mike at breakfast that she saw Ian as Teaching Leader and herself as Coordinator. God had gone before Micki! Ian had 100 percent support.

Ian's training was done on a Saturday ten days before class. He was a quick study, easily grasping his responsibilities to lead the leaders and class and to teach using homiletics in preparation.

The week before class start-up, the entire leadership team was in place. Mrs. Esmie Potter, better known as Sister Esmie, had been at the CBSI informational meeting, stayed in touch with us and was very supportive. She was not in leadership training because she was leading a Tuesday evening Bible study. A mature, godly woman, she was the pastor of a small congregation on the east end of Tortola. We approached her for the Associate Teaching Leader position. She accepted, saying she would find others to lead her Tuesday night Bible study. We drove to meet her in East End where Micki trained her the Thursday before class. With more than 41 years as a pastor and much enthusiasm for the CBSI process, she too was a quick study! Micki also trained Celia as the Class Coordinator on Thursday, then helped her photocopy lessons and enrollment cards for the first class.

Mackel Chalwell, a quiet, devout man, and Robert "Storm" Wright, an aggressive, high-spirited young man, accepted God's call to be men's Discussion Leaders. Carolin Romney, an industrious, organized single, Gloria Wheatley, an enthusiastic and fun-loving mom, and Denyse Macintyre accepted God's call to be Discussion Leaders for the women. Even the timing of this class was direct answer to prayer. Our prayer team had been praying for a class to begin in spring 2002. God who calls is faithful, and He had done it! *Isn't that just like the Father!*

Twenty-six persons came on Tuesday, May 21, 2002, for CBSI Tortola's first night. Guitarist Freddie Clyne accompanied Ian, an excellent singer, in leading praise and worship. We introduced the CBSI process, passed out the first lesson, gave some tips in lesson completion and encouraged everyone's enrollment. After introducing his leadership team, Ian gave a well thought out, Spirit-driven overview of 1 John. Afterward he fielded questions from the class, including one on whether there are apostles today. His answers confirmed his firm grasp of and commitment to the truth of Scripture. Many commented on his clarity.

As we had warned, the enemy attacked this leadership team and class members with flu, schedule conflicts, car breakdowns, diabetes and other distractions. We called out for prayer protection from our U.S. prayer warriors and the leadership teams from Antigua and SVG. The Tortola team stayed strong! On the first Testimony and Honors night a few weeks later, the membership had grown to 30, and seven guests were in attendance to hear the testimonies, share in the "swallowship" (food and fellowship!)—and, hopefully, return for the next study.

That night some talked of being skeptical of CBSI, hearing about it from friends, over radio, on television or from newspaper articles, but they were happy they checked it out. One said she came "testing the spirits" because she didn't want to be drawn away from the truth, and she found Ian to be a man filled with God's Spirit. Many praised Ian for his humility and skill in clarifying Scripture. One kiddingly said, "Can you believe we're being taught truth by a lawyer!" All praised the program for its adherence to teaching the Bible alone. One gentleman said, "Never once did I hear about this church or that church, but the Word, the Word, the Word!" A young woman said she spent half an hour on the phone with her sister in New York discussing one of her home study questions. Fran spoke of how the study of 1 John made a difference in her interactions with people every day. After more than an hour of constant testimonies, Romeo sang a song about the message of love from John's epistle.

We often refer to Isaiah 55:11, ***"so is my word that goes out from my mouth: It will not return to me empty, but will accomplish what I desire and achieve the purpose for which I sent it."*** The "so" that begins this verse refers to the preceding verse, which speaks of rain watering the earth and making it bud and flourish. The water will have this flourishing effect only if it is drawn up into the plant. Likewise, God's Word must be drawn into our minds through diligent study and into our hearts through meditation, not just reading. The wonderful testimonies by the Tortola class members were made by men and women who had soaked up the Word and applied it to their lives. This class has maintained a membership of 20 to 30 through the years. What an enormous privilege it is to be a small part of God's life transforming work!

In 2008 Ian became the Tortola National Coordinator, responsible for maintaining and growing the work of CBSI in the Virgin Islands. He was instrumental in the formation of CBSI Caribbean Inc., voluntarily drafting the by-laws. When officers were elected, Ian was unanimously voted president.

In December 2009, Ian, Denyse and their toddler son Yonathan moved back "home" to Trinidad. Ian started a CBSI group there at West Side Community Church, their home church and the church we attend when visiting Trinidad. Kendolph Bobb, a long time class member and detective with the BVI police, answered God's call as Tortola Teaching Leader, replacing Ian. Brother Bobb, single and from the island of St. Vincent, is a humble 40-year-old man of God. We got to know his heart when he flew to St. Martin for further Teaching Leader training in May 2010. It is a difficult assignment to replace a beloved founding Teaching Leader after eight years. But the One who called Brother Bobb is faithful, and He will do it.

God's work of CBSI continues in Tortola. ***"Lᴏʀᴅ,...all that we have accomplished You have done for us."*** *(Isaiah 26:12)* To God be the glory!

Tortola team with ATL Esmie Potter wearing hat in back row, TL Ian Macintyre at her right in back row.

Tortola class opening with praise and worship.

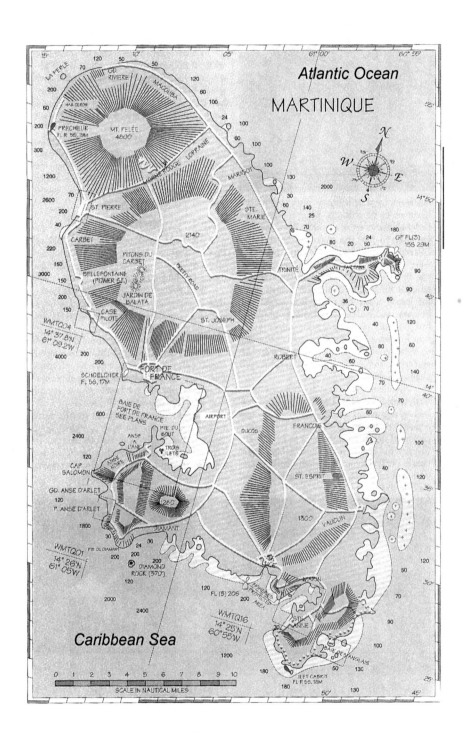

6

Martinique

"I planted the seed, Apollos watered it, but God made it grow. So neither he who plants nor he who waters is anything, but only God who makes things grow."
(1 Corinthians 3:6-7)

The CBS International Martinique-Fort de France class was born on Friday, September 19, 2003, becoming the weekly Bible study of Eglise Evangelique de la Saintete.

Martinique is largest of the Windward Islands with a population of 400,000 and, apart from a few short spells under the British, has been French since it was colonized. Fort de France is a city bustling with shoppers and cars. It is European in culture with excellent roads and a thriving economy. There are large supermarkets and open air markets for fresh fruits and produce. Boulangerie/patisseries are everywhere selling the wonderful French baguettes, pastries and coffee. The people of Martinique boast that they introduced coffee into the Americas and that the sun shines on all but five days per year on average! Though we loved to pass through Martinique as cruisers and enjoy all it had to offer, we do not speak French. So it was not on our CBSI radar screen—that is, not until God set a divine appointment for us in Antigua, an English speaking island!

After celebrating Christmas in Michigan and attending the January CBS Teaching Directors conference, we returned to Antigua. Arriving on January 30, 2003, we spent one night in the Jolly Beach Resort, within walking distance of the shipyard where *coram Deo* was stored. As we walked through the resort lobby the next morning, we heard a familiar voice call our names. It was Sister Esmie, CBSI Associate Teaching Leader from Tortola! She was there to attend the Caribbean-wide Church of God of Prophecy Conference. While talking to her, Bishop Edward Payne was hustling through the lobby, saw us and greeted us warmly. We had gotten well acquainted the previous year during and after the CONECAR meeting in Barbados, his home. He was head of the Church of God of Prophecy denomination for the Windward Islands. Bishop invited us to stop by the conference to greet others we would know. When we did, the leadership invited us to set up our display in the conference lobby. They were thinking of the display we used at CONECAR, but *it just so happened* that we had in our luggage a brand new customized CBSI table top display! Once they saw this, we were asked to speak to the entire assembly of 300 pastors and leaders. As a result, interest was expressed by leaders from nearby Montserrat, St. Kitts and Nevis to as far away as French Guiana and Curacao (in or near South America), and as far north as Haiti and the Cayman Islands. Bishop Payne introduced Felix Alexander, a delegate from Martinique, who asked if we were working in his country. Chuck said we would love to work in the French islands but we were handicapped in not speaking French.

Felix smiled and quickly responded, "I am your mouth. I will be your Aaron. I will speak for you." Clearly, this was a God ordained appointment so CBSI could reach the people of the French West Indies! ***"Now to Him who is able to do immeasurably more than all we ask or imagine..."*** *(Ephesians 3:20)*

While Chuck manned the display, spoke at the conference and experienced the faithfulness of God, Micki was at the boatyard preparing *coram Deo* for her launch.

It was June before we were able to sail to Martinique because of boat work and the ministry ramping up. In February and March we were in Antigua refitting the boat's forward bunkroom into an office for a more efficient CBSI work station. In April we sailed to Barbados for the Teaching Leader/Associate Teaching Leader Training seminar; from there to Tobago to follow up with the pastors we had met at CONECAR and the Open Bible Missions Conference in Trinidad; and from there north to St. Vincent to visit classes. In May we sailed back north to visit the Antigua class, left the boat at the dock and flew to Michigan for family graduations and weddings before returning mid June to Antigua. Whew!

On June 21, 2003, we set sail for Deshaies on Guadeloupe's northwest coast. The next afternoon we hauled anchor to make the overnight passage from Deshaies south to Martinique. While motor-sailing away from the Guadeloupe coast, Chuck noticed smoke coming from the engine room. It was the belt on our engine driven refrigeration compressor. This was not a huge problem, he just tripped the breaker. Since we have a backup 110-volt refrigeration compressor, we could wait for repairs. However, while in the engine room Chuck noticed that our new filled-to-the-brim 10-gallon upright hot water heater was lying on its side against the wires of the generator. We turned back to Guadeloupe, anchored, emptied the tank, tied it upright and padded it. There was no time to sail back to Antigua, as we had a schedule to keep. Proper installation would have to wait until we returned there in August. Meanwhile cold showers would be refreshing!

The next afternoon we again left Guadeloupe, heading south to Martinique, and we were blessed with great weather! A couple hours into our sail, seven dolphins played in our bow wake and were jumping three to four feet out of the water, entertaining us, taking our minds off our problems. *Isn't that just like the Father!*

Our next visitors, however, were not so entertaining! Sailing about five miles off the coast of Guadeloupe, the French Navy zoomed out in their large inflatable, hovered at our stern questioning us on the VHF, and then informed us they were boarding *coram Deo*. Micki sent up an arrow prayer for protection, since we had heard stories of damage to boat interiors during "routine" boardings. After instructing us to stop making headway, three armed French Navy sailors came aboard. They spoke little English, and we speak no French, but we calmly showed them around—we had nothing to hide. We knew they were looking for drugs since drug traffickers had begun to use sailboats, not just go-fast boats, for transporting their goods in the islands.

After this short encounter, we thanked God for the safety and were on our way. Winds started to pick up, and the rest of our 20-hour sail was uneventful. Due to reports of dinghy thievery and the amount of ferry traffic in the Fort de France anchorage, we chose to anchor directly across the five-mile wide bay at Anse Mitan. With only four to five hours of sleep during the passage, there was no time to rest before we caught the ferry to the commercial area of Fort de France. Felix Alexander met us at the ferry dock, welcoming us with the French greeting of a kiss on both cheeks. He was visibly elated to meet us again. Felix was born in St. Lucia, grew up in French Guiana and as an adult moved to Martinique. Therefore, he speaks fluent French and English. As we walked the few blocks to the church, Eglise Evangelique de la Saintete, Felix related details about this mostly Haitian congregation and their pastor, Henri Doyen, a former building contractor who had been called by God to minister to his Haitian brethren in Fort de France. We arrived at the church, a small white concrete building on a narrow side street, and entered a tiled sanctuary with worn wooden pews that could hold maybe 100 people. Felix led us to the front, up the tattered stairs and across the carpeted platform to the pastor's small office behind the platform curtain. Pastor eagerly jumped out of his chair and enthusiastically greeted us with the kisses and made us feel very welcome.

With Felix translating, we spent more than an hour explaining the CBSI process. We told him about the studies that have been translated into French and shared a sample of the study of 1 John. Pastor Doyen was immediately interested. Though this was Tuesday and our presentation to his congregation was scheduled for Thursday, he said, "You are here now. We'll have the meeting tomorrow night!" OK! There would be no catching up on sleep!

Fortunately we had faxed ahead, and Felix had completed the translation of CBSI introduction materials for the overhead transparencies. Wednesday was spent printing out other French materials provided by the CBSI Western Europe Regional Director, Gilles Cailleaux, including the If You Will Pray course.

With fear and trepidation we made our first CBSI presentation through a translator to about 40 people. They were smiling, nodding and very receptive. Many came up afterwards to greet or thank us. God's love within these people transcended the language barrier. We could not wait to work with them!

Pastor Doyen, totally excited about the CBSI process and materials, decided that since some of the people invited to Thursday night could not change their schedule, we would do another presentation the next night, and the prayer group would start on Friday with If You Will Pray. Wow! He let no grass grow under his feet!

Thursday morning was spent refining our presentation and scouting out a photocopy place. More than 30 people attended that night's presentation, which went more smoothly. Pastor Doyen wanted us to model the leading of a prayer group the next evening, so we spent Friday preparing and photocopying more materials.

Friday night 52 men and women joined the prayer group. We modeled the format for the weekly meetings Pastor Doyen would lead, but he would need to choose four persons as small group discussion leaders. He and Felix were beside themselves with excitement and could not stop praising God for the blessing of CBSI in Martinique. We can still hear Felix shouting, "Hallelujah! Hallelujah!" over and over again.

With all that had happened in four days, we needed to share the blessings with our prayer partners. We wrote a *coram Deo* online saying we had asked for wisdom and clarity in our words as we worked with a translator for the first time. God answered, as the people were receptive and eager to start. We asked for sailing safety. God answered with protection through our mechanical failures, the hot water heater falling over, the boarding by the French Navy and good sailing weather. *"The prayer of a righteous man is powerful and effective." (James 5:16)*

It was an exhilarating four days, but we were exhausted from the pace, so we took the weekend to rest and do maintenance on the boat. Felix invited us to attend a picnic on Sunday with six French families. Good thing we had our Aaron! Although the young people took English in school and loved to practice it, we struggled with the language barrier. Eight year old Ocean (O see an) took it upon herself, patiently, to try to teach us some French, accomplishing two phrases, *de la mer* (by the sea) and `a demain` (see you tomorrow). What a great experience! We were so well received by the families as they proudly shared their potluck. There was an interesting assortment of food: blood sausage (you sucked the meat out of the pigskin), fish cakes, couscous with vegetables, guinea fowl, stewed and BBQ chicken and cold rice salad with palm hearts. Their home-made passion fruit and local cherry juices were wonderful!

After ten days on the island and a promise to return in September, we hauled anchor July 9 for the 26-hour sail north to Antigua, where we stopped for the delayed repairs on our hot water heater and refrigeration compressor. From there we continued north, making the 28-hour sail to Tortola to participate in a Church of God of Prophecy Conference. This was the beginning of a heavy schedule of sailing and coaching six CBSI classes on three islands and prayer groups on the two islands of Barbados and Martinique. *"If I rise on the wings of the dawn, if I settle on the far side of the sea, even there Your hand will guide me, Your right hand will hold me fast." (Psalm 139:9-10)*

As promised, we sailed back into Martinique on Saturday, September 6, 2003. The Fort de France group had completed If You Will Pray. Leadership training was set to begin the following Monday evening, the first of four sessions scheduled throughout the week. Preparation for this training was unlike any we had done. Not only would it take place through an interpreter, but we were dealing with a European mindset rather than Caribbean thinking. Between training sessions we had materials translated, typed and photocopied. This time we anchored in the south of Martinique, at St. Anne, where we had an hour's commute each way. It was a calmer anchorage, and because it is a popular yachting center, more people speak English there than in other areas. Felix was at his job and unavailable during the day, so we could take care of getting typing and photocopying done on our own just a dinghy ride away in Marin.

God gave us an interesting acquaintance in the anchorage, Ed Hamilton, another cruiser. We have a ministry of the Spirit, and he had a ministry of spirits! His business is called the "ministry of rum," and he was working on importing French rum into the States. Since he had been in the islands twelve years, he was a fount of information from translation to internet cafes to rental cars to cultural differences. His father had been a Presbyterian minister, and though Ed had no interest in things of God, he sure was helpful and friendly to us. God has creative ways of providing!

Leadership training, intense through a translator, took about twice the time it normally would, but we felt it went well, and all were ready for God to finish equipping them as they stepped out in faith. Pastor Henri Doyen was the Teaching Leader. Many French pastors feel the need to be the teacher of their flock, so we were surprised and delighted when Pastor Doyen asked Felix to assume the role of Associate Teaching Leader. While Felix worshipped at the church, his background was in the Church of God of Prophecy, which had no churches in Martinique. The Class Coordinator, Janvier, was a joyful, humble young man and a picture of organization and efficiency. With their four male and five female Discussion Leaders trained, they were prepared for a large class.

Friday, September 19, 2003, arrived, and what a night it was! Fifty-nine persons attended the first CBSI class in Martinique. There was a sense of awe and privilege among the 12 men and women on the leadership team. Pastor Doyen asked Chuck to introduce him officially to the class as the Teaching Leader and present him with his name badge. After introducing Pastor Doyen to the class, Chuck took the Teaching Leader name badge and hung it around his neck. Pastor Doyen, in turn, individually introduced and hung the name badge on each leader. As the leadership team stood together at the front of the sanctuary, Henri Doyen asked the class to pray for them. A chorus of prayers was raised on their behalf. What a beautiful commissioning service!

Felix gave a passionate CBSI introduction, with one of the young men, James, interpreting for us. Pastor Doyen followed with a thorough overview of 1 John, challenging the class members to commit and be involved by doing their lessons and participating on class night. This was one of the best run first class nights we had experienced. We thought this was a confirmation that we had communicated well in training.

The second Leaders Council meeting, however, was a disaster! The concept of class night was understood, but Leaders Council was fully misunderstood. We had covered this in detail in leadership training, but apparently we missed the mark. During the If You Will Pray study they had only one meeting per week, where they would come together and discuss the questions and pray. We had led the first Leaders Council at Pastor Doyen's request, to model the format. Since the first Leaders Council takes place before the lessons are distributed, we led them in conversational three-part prayer, reviewed the responsibilities of leading the discussion and shepherding the members, and discussed how the introduction class would flow — but, of course, there was no lesson to discuss. Pastor Doyen may not have understood that the lesson was to be completed beforehand, so he and most of the leaders came to the second Leaders Council without their lessons completed. Rather than have this promising class get off on the wrong foot, we did a rewind, had them prepare their lessons and met briefly before class to go over the questions. Also, our travel plans were altered to remain in Martinique for at least another week. The leadership team was very open to training, and Pastor Doyen acknowledged that they had much to learn. In French, he said "Theory is one thing, but putting it into practice is a whole other thing!" The idea of preparing your leaders before class night was foreign to them, and this was just the first of the French classes where we encountered the problem. The third Leaders Council led by Pastor Doyen went much better. We set aside time to coach him prior to the meeting, making sure he understood not just the format but the reasoning behind each component. We also created both a Leaders Council and Class Night agenda to leave with him to follow.

The postponement of our departure allowed us to assist the Nazareen Church in Godissard, Martinique, with its second meeting of If You Will Pray (*Prions!* in French). In our preparation time before the meeting, it became obvious that the leader for that night's discussion did not understand his role. So Chuck, with translator Felix by his side and the leader sitting in, modeled leading the discussion. They all had fun, and the leader caught on. Toward the end of group time, with no prompting from Chuck, the leader took over!

Feeling comfortable with the class and the Godissard prayer group, we promised to return in mid November. We then set sail October 3, 2003, heading south to Trinidad with a layover in SVG. We visited the four Vincy classes and then sailed on to Trinidad for two CBSI introductions in Laventille and Couva. Meanwhile, reports of spiritual and numerical growth were coming in from all classes in SVG and Tortola. Antigua, however, was struggling with a decline in membership.

Five and a half weeks later we were back, anchored in St. Anne, Martinique. The Godissard Nazareen Prayer Group concluded *Prions!* prior to our arrival, and training was scheduled to begin the next evening. Nine men and women were trained in the four sessions totaling 16 hours of instruction. The CBSI-Godissard Class would begin on December 9, 2003, under the direction of Teaching Leader Pastor Fabien Descas.

Between training sessions we visited the CBSI Fort de France Leaders Council and class and were greatly encouraged! They held a very organized Leaders Council and had initiated adding assistant Discussion Leaders to the groups for growth and leadership consistency. That was a great idea! The class had grown to more than 70 adults with at least a dozen children in attendance with their parents. While Felix could only be with one of us to translate, we each sat in groups observing animated discussions, much laughter and a general maturing of the leadership. They were listening more and not talking as much.

With our schedule not allowing us to stay around for the Godissard Nazareen Class start-up and needing someone on island to coach and encourage the classes, we approached Felix to be the "key CBSI person for the French West Indies." In this way he could coach and shepherd the leadership teams which, because of the language barrier, we could not do. And he could spread the word and follow up on the growing interest in Martinique, informing us when training would be needed.

On November 25, with the CBSI work in Martinique in the hands of Felix, we set sail north to Antigua to store *coram Deo* while we returned to Michigan for the Christmas season and attend the yearly CBS Teaching Directors Conference in January.

Upon returning to the Caribbean in January of 2004, we remained in contact with Felix, knowing we could not return to Martinique until May. We spent February through April visiting the six classes meeting in Tortola, Antigua and SVG as well as training leadership teams and starting classes in Trinidad. As we were passing by Martinique, we squeezed in a day visit in February and again in March to encourage him and catch up on the progress of the two classes there.

On May 10, 2004 we sailed into Martinique for a whirlwind five-day visit. We attended both CBSI-Fort de France and CBSI-Godissard Leaders Councils and classes—four meetings on four consecutive nights! Both classes made excellent progress towards implementing the five features of the CBSI process. Both were vibrant and enthusiastic. The Fort de France class was averaging 60 in attendance, and the new Godissard Class about 30. With Felix interpreting, participants in both classes lovingly thanked us for the blessing of CBSI. But what impacted us most about the Fort de France class was the good number that arrived early—and not for chit-chat. When you walked into the sanctuary before class, you heard a chorus of prayer from the people on their knees on the tile floor at their seats. What a scene of humility and love!

About two weeks prior to our arrival in Martinique, we received an email from Felix requesting prayer for a class to be formed in the French island of Guadeloupe, 80 miles to the north. We began praying. Two days before our arrival in Martinique, CBSI's Western Europe Regional Director, Gilles Cailleaux, emailed the contact information for Alice Ossard, who had been a Discussion Leader in a CBSI class in Paris, France. Gilles said that his region could provide materials and some kind of shepherding over the phone, but he was concerned about training and follow-up. Could we help? To what extent could we get involved? Chuck explained that, while we did not speak a word of French, Felix could and was interpreting for us, enabling us to train French speakers. With Gilles' authorization we advised Felix that his prayer had been answered. We learned that Roger, Alice's husband, had recently retired from his career as Captain of the Gendarmes in Paris and that they had moved back home to Guadeloupe. Both were evangelical Christians, and hoped to bring the life transforming CBSI process to their hometown of Sainte Rose in northwestern Guadeloupe. Wow! *Isn't that just like the Father!* We emailed the information to Felix, who ran with it.

Roger Ossard and Bertrand Maricel flew in from Guadeloupe, were chauffeured by Pastor Henri Doyen to the training and to housing he had arranged. Our training sessions were graciously hosted by Teaching Leader Fabien Descas at the Godissard Nazareen Church on May 14 and 15. The ownership shown by the current Martinique leadership teams was so encouraging for us!

Along with Roger and Bertrand, Martinique Pastor Denis Ponchteau from the Morne Vente Nazareen Church was trained as a Teaching Leader. The already trained Martinique Teaching Leaders and Associate Teaching Leaders came to the sessions for a review. The plan was for a class to be established in the Evangelical Church in Sainte Rose in northwestern Guadeloupe on May 30. A third Martinique class was to get under way at the Nazareen Church in Morne Vente. Jesus says: ***"You may ask Me for anything in My name, and I will do it."*** *(John 14:14)* We asked, and He did it!

The Guadeloupe classes never got off the ground due to opposition from the Evangelical Church leadership at Sainte Rose. The Martinique-Morne Vente class, under the leadership of Teaching

Leader Denis Ponchtreau, did start as planned on July 8. Within a few months he was moved to another church on island, and Pastor Solitude, who had been trained by us, took over leadership. Sad to say, within two years both the Morne Vente and Godissard Nazareen church classes went inactive. The long breaks for church programs broke the habit of regular Bible study, and people lost interest. The church leadership, other than the pastor, never got involved or supported CBSI.

The Fort de France class remained alive and vibrant until September of 2006. The church had grown and moved into a newly refurbished building in October, so they put CBSI on hold until the following January while holding crusades. We sailed to Martinique in November, meeting with Pastor Doyen and Felix to encourage class start-up as soon as possible in January to continue building their legacy with CBSI in Martinique. An encouraging sight awaited us when we sailed there in June of 2007 and found the Fort de France class meeting in the new church facility under the leadership of Felix Alexander with more than 40 class members.

In April of 2008 Pastor Henri Doyen invested three weeks in his homeland of Haiti, helping Caleb Lidovick Pierre train new CBSI leadership teams and coach existing CBSI leaders. This was his second trip to help train leadership in Haiti. Pastor Doyen had said from the outset that he wanted to spread CBSI to other islands, as we were doing.

In May of 2008 when CBSI Caribbean Inc. was formed and we handed the baton to the Caribbean leaders, Felix Alexander was appointed National Coordinator for the French West Indies. His responsibilities are to maintain and grow the work of CBSI in the French West Indies of Martinique and Guadeloupe. French Guiana, while known as part of the French West Indies, is part of the CBSI South America region.

When we stopped in Martinique in November of 2008, Felix told us of the longing of the Fort de France class to have the Children & Youth Ministry. A major stumbling block was the need to translate children's materials. In our *coram Deo* online of January 2009, we appealed for prayer and for the $5,000 needed to translate the Gospel of John children's materials. God faithfully provided the funds from His people. The translation was completed and available for the children of Fort de France and for French-speaking children and youth classes worldwide. *"And my God will meet all your needs according to His glorious riches in Christ Jesus."* *(Philippians 4:19)* Children's Leaders were trained for the Fort de France class July 7-11, 2009, and about 30 children began meeting on Sunday mornings to study the Gospel of John.

After the glorious beginning, the joy, the growth and the Children & Youth Ministry, during the writing of this book in March of 2011 we received the extremely sad news that the Fort de France class has gone inactive. Why? We have not been able to get any definitive answer. Because neither we nor CBSI Director Brian Burke speak the language and cannot communicate heart to heart with Pastor Henri Doyen, we can only speculate. But it breaks our hearts. Shepherding is the key to the work in CBSI, and that is why we believe if a bilingual (French/English) Caleb couple could work in the French West Indies, there may be hope for the future.

"Be still, and know that I am God." *(Psalm 46:10)* When we don't understand, we rest totally on the Word of God—because we know that *"As the rain and snow come down from heaven, and do not return to it without watering the earth and making it bud and flourish, so that it yields seed for the sower and bread for the eater, so is My word that goes out from My mouth: It will not return to Me empty, but will accomplish what I desire and achieve the purpose for which I sent it."* *(Isaiah 55:10-11)*

We were faithful to what we believed was God's direction. *"I planted the seed, Apollos watered it, but God made it grow. So neither he who plants nor he who waters is anything, but only God who makes things grow."* *(1 Corinthians 3:6-7)*

"Lord,...all that we have accomplished You have done for us." *(Isaiah 26:12)* To God be the glory!

**Fort de France, Martinique, leadership team with
ATL Felix Alexander kneeling on right.**

**Chuck presenting Fort de France TL Pastor Doyen
with his nametag, with Felix translating.**

Fort de France women's discussion group.

**The future of the church, children of Fort de France class
members, attended long before Children & Youth
Ministry began.**

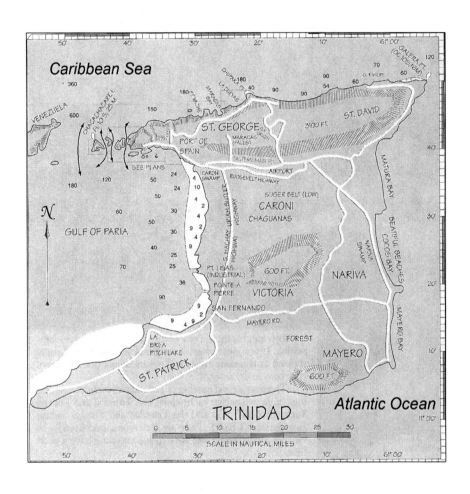

Caribbean Sea

Venezuela

Atlantic Ocean

TRINIDAD

GULF OF PARIA

N

SCALE IN NAUTICAL MILES

7

Trinidad

*"For God has not given us a spirit of fear,
but of power and of love and of a sound mind."*
(2 Timothy 1:7 NKJV)

CBS International was born in Trinidad through the Belmont interdenominational class on April 7, 2004. More classes throughout the island would soon follow!

It is the larger of the twin island Republic of Trinidad and Tobago in the southern Caribbean, northeast of Venezuela. Unlike its quiet and serene island neighbors to the north, Trinidad is a huge, bustling, traffic snarled, industrial place with an area of 1,980 square miles, a population of 1.3 million and vast amounts of natural gas which supply much LNG to New England and the East Coast of the U.S.A. Naturally, its largest industry is petroleum production, refining and petrochemical manufacturing. Its location takes one out of the hurricane belt, so many cruisers spend hurricane season here. Thus, many yacht services are available. While it has beautiful mountains, abundant sea and bird life, our favorite howler monkeys and nice beaches, its waters are not the turquoise of the Caribbean. They are brackish and somewhat green due to the outflow of Venezuela's massive Orinoco River into the Gulf of Paria.

At the invitation of Pastor Vickram Hajaree, we flew into Trinidad in February of 2003 to introduce CBSI at the Open Bible Standard Missions Conference in his church in Point Fortin. The denomination had an advanced and apparently effective Bible study program. Since most of the attendees were from that denomination, while they appreciated what CBSI was doing, they had no immediate need. But God had another plan.

In the summer of 2003, CBSI Caleb Director Gordon Spaugh forwarded us the name of June Taklalsingh, a native of Trinidad living in the Toronto, Ontario, Canada area. She had heard about CBSI as a CBS class member. Also, she was doing Alpha facilitation in Trinidad and saw CBSI as the next step for new believers from the Alpha program. Though we were buried in preparation for the August CBSI Caribbean Leaders Workshop, we contacted June explaining our schedule constraints. Because of her eagerness to follow up Alpha with CBSI, she asked to meet us by attending the workshop in Antigua. We thought it would give her a good picture of the work in the Caribbean and what leadership in CBSI required, so we included her. After the workshop and despite our already full schedule, we reluctantly agreed to squeeze in a CBSI Introduction in Trinidad. Dates were set for October 24 and 25, 2003. June agreed to help organize it.

Trinidad had not been on Micki's radar screen up to that point! She was skeptical of sailing into Trinidad because of the widespread crime and violence reported by other cruisers. A clincher was the attack on a cruising couple who were accosted by a local as they got out of a bus (small van) after grocery shopping. As the woman was stepping out the van door, a young man leaned out of the bus slicing her leg with a knife!

Because of her fear Micki would agree only to fly to Trinidad and for just the days needed. "I'm not taking my boat there!" she said. Chuck, on the other hand, wanted to sail. It was pretty tense whenever Trinidad was brought up. Micki finally agreed to pray about sailing there, saying that if this was God's will, He would have to take away her fear and give her a peace. As late as our October 4 *coram Deo* online sent from St. Lucia, Micki requested prayer "to work in some rest while in St. Vincent before flying to Trinidad for the introduction meetings." During our time in SVG visiting classes, God did just what she asked. He gave her His peace. ***"Do not be anxious about anything, but in everything, by prayer and petition, with thanksgiving, present your requests to God. And the peace of God, which transcends all understanding, will guard your hearts and your minds in Christ Jesus."*** *(Philippians 4:6-7)* Not all fear was gone, but God had given her a peace that she could trust Him as He sends us there for His purposes.

Before our departure from SVG, we made a reservation at Crews Inn Marina in Chaguaramas, Trinidad, on the advice of Mickey Smith and others. We were told it was a safe marina with 24-hour security. On Friday, October 17, we sailed from SVG to Tyrrel Bay, Carriacou, one of our favorite peaceful places, anchoring for the night. The next morning we sailed to Mt. Hartman Bay, Grenada, another comfortable anchorage where we caught up with friends before departure day. Late Monday afternoon we motor-sailed out the channel, weaving through the reefs, and sailed south overnight to Chaguaramas. Admitting her fear and trepidation, Micki leaned on a favorite Scripture verse. ***"For God has not given us a spirit of fear, but of power and of love and of a sound mind."*** *(2 Timothy 1:7 NKJV)*

This was our first time using an oil rig as a landmark! It was 25 miles north of the western tip of Trinidad and was lit up like a Christmas tree at night. The Trinidad coast was actually inviting, with its lush, green northern mountain range and channels between the islands to the west. We arrived mid-morning at the Bocademonos (Boca), the channel between westernmost mainland and Monos Island. As advised by cruiser friends, there was a strong current against us as the tide was flowing north out of the gulf. We powered our way through the current and, once through the channel, turned left, motoring between Gasparillo and Gaspar Grande Islands into the protection of busy Chaguaramas Bay, which is full of oil field service and supply docks as well as a half dozen marinas. As we approached Crews Inn Marina, we spotted the nearby Customs dock where we were to make clearance. Since another boat was on the dock, we circled, waiting for more than an hour. Then we heard *"coram Deo"* hailed over our VHF radio by the Crews Inn office, instructing us to come straight to our assigned slip. Two dockhands were waiting to take our lines. We asked Elvis, a dockhand with Rastafarian-like dreadlocks, "How are you doing?" He looked us in the eyes, smiling and said, "Blessed and highly favored." This, we would learn, was a common response of Trini (Trinidadian) Christians. That was only the beginning of God removing Micki's fears.

Within the hour we heard a knock on the hull of *coram Deo*. On the dock stood a short, smiling woman in business attire. "Hi, I'm Maria Wyke, Ian's sister." Ian was the CBSI Tortola Teaching Leader! We invited Maria on board, and she said Ian had called to remind her we would be arriving, probably also telling her of Micki's fears of Trinidad! She worked nearby and came on her lunch hour to find the people she said Ian spoke so highly of! She asked about our schedule of meetings. We told her when and where and then asked if we should take a taxi or rent a car since we had no clue where these places were or how far. She hesitated a moment, then said she and her husband Gordon would transport us. Wow! More of that sweet Trini hospitality we had experienced from Ian and Denyse as well as at the Point Fortin Missions Conference in February.

On Friday, October 24, Maria and Gordon picked us up at the marina and drove us through the grid-lock traffic of the capital, Port of Spain, to the Open Bible Standard College in Laventille, where we were graciously received by Mrs. Charmaine Alexis, president of the college. We had met her at the Open Bible Standard Missions Conference in February, and she recognized the potential of CBSI. She had hoped to organize one CBSI class with all the churches in the Laventille neighborhood. So, remembering Charmaine's interest, Chuck called her. Without hesitation she arranged for the use of the largest classroom at the college for an introduction meeting. We felt the location near Port of Spain would be perfect since the other introduction would be over an hour's drive to the south.

Even while setting up, people began arriving. Soon the room was filled with more than 40 people, mostly women, listening intently to our introduction. After presenting the life transforming CBSI process of Bible study, Chuck challenged the group to pray for God's will about forming a class. They all sat looking at us and saying nothing! Chuck had noticed during the presentation that Jean Thomas and her friend Marilyn Phillips were really tracking with us. So with a little nudging from Chuck, they agreed to start a prayer group. Jean expressed her determination to do God's work but later would tease Chuck about his insistence that she was the one to start!

On the ride home that afternoon, we found out why Maria and Gordon so willingly offered to transport us. Maria did not want to frighten Micki but said Laventille was one of the most violent areas in Trinidad! We then understood a comment made that morning to the group by June Taklalsingh about "what good could come from Laventille!" Micki realized that God had given her a peace because He had His people in place to provide and protect. This would not be the last time we would experience God's protection in Trinidad or on other islands!

On Saturday morning Maria and Gordon again drove us through the traffic of Port of Spain, then an hour south to Couva for the second introduction held at Credo House, a Catholic retreat center. Nearly forty men and women, Catholic and Protestant, were attentive and enthusiastic, and as a result a number of prayer groups were formed. As we did with Jean Thomas in Laventille, we gave a copy of the If You Will Pray study to those leading the prayer groups to photo-copy and use. We took their contact information, and June offered to follow up on their progress. We tentatively planned to provide train-ing in March of 2004 for leaders raised up through If You Will Pray.

With the presentations done, we stayed on to take advantage of the Chaguaramas yachting services and learn more about Trinidad. It is a great place for boat repairs and maintenance, having large chandleries (boating equipment stores), woodworkers, sail lofts and a plethora of fabric stores with reasonable prices for upholstery, cushions, canvas, etc.

Maria and Gordon introduced us to some of the unique culture. Trinidad has an ethnically mixed population due to the slaves and indentured servants brought in during colonial times. We regularly came in contact with people whose ancestry was Indian, African, Amerindian, European and Oriental. Because of this ethnicity, there is a diversity of religious and cultural practices. Trinidad takes pride in its diversity, with one consequence being many government-recognized religious holidays celebrating the holy days of the Christian, Muslim, Hindu and others. There must be more holidays in Trinidad than anywhere in the world!

We were there in October for Diwali, the biggest Hindu festival. Though celebrated for five days, the third day is the Festival of Lights, where candles are lit all around peoples' homes. Though Christian, Maria invited us to their home for some typical Diwali foods. The traditional Dawali meal is meatless, with lots of curried vegetables and fruit such as pumpkin, bodi (about a foot long skinny bean), chataigne (chestnut), green mango and ripe mango, which are wrapped with various roti skins (very thin bread). She also stretched the menu for us Americans with some delicious curried chicken legs prepared by their son Ethan. After dinner Maria, accompanied by teenage daughter Hilary and pre-teen sons Ethan and Matthew, drove us to a local park and through Hindu neighborhoods where thousands of Diwali candles were burning. What an interesting but quick 'taste' of the diverse Trini culture!

Time was approaching, however, for a scheduled leadership training in Martinique, more than 200 miles to the north. With June committed to work with the prayer groups, we said our good-byes to Maria and her family and on November 2, 2003, sailed north to Martinique. As Trinidad's coast faded in the distance, Micki realized that God had replaced her fear of Trinidad with His love for the blessed and highly favored people we met. *"For God has not given us a spirit of fear, but of power and of love and of a sound mind."* *(2 Timothy 1:7 NKJV)* Now, *isn't that just like the Father!*

After leadership training in Martinique, we headed north to Antigua to store *coram Deo* for our usual trip home for Christmas.

Soon after the Christmas season June emailed us that the prayer groups were following through with If You Will Pray and asking to schedule leadership training. She again committed to help organize the venue and details.

With this training in mind, we began planning our 2004 schedule: return to Antigua January 30; take a flight from there to Tortola February 1-4 to visit Leaders Council and class; stay in Antigua for Leaders Council and class February 5-7; sail to Martinique to visit Leaders Councils and classes February 11-19; sail to St. Vincent to visit Leaders Councils and classes February 22-29; sail to Trinidad for Leadership Training and coaching class start-ups March 9-May 1.

How's that for a schedule! We are tired just writing about it! In 2004 we visited every CBSI class, logging more than 1,500 nautical miles. There were then 15 classes on six islands. By God's provision and strength, we were able to keep this schedule fairly well. Weather delayed our planned arrival in Trinidad, but that was only one of many obstacles we overcame.

In our March 17, 2004, *coram Deo* online we wrote: "Trinidad was named by Christopher Columbus after the Trinity (Trinidad in Spanish) because of its three mountain ranges. In spite of this wonderful Christian name, Christianity has much opposition in this fair land. God's enemy has a firm foothold and doesn't want to give up his ground. We witnessed this by our weather delayed arrival from Bequia, the distractions caused by many equipment breakdowns aboard *coram Deo*, by Chuck's brother Richard suffering a mild stroke two days before the training, and then, it was almost laughable when our rental car had a dead battery the morning of the first day of leadership training! Due to the car problem we were more than half an hour late starting the seminar. To us these blatant attacks were proof that great things were going to happen!"

One of the greatest blessings was that for the first time in any leadership training, we were joined by Teaching Leaders Brian Burke and Alwyn Joseph from St. Vincent and Associate Teaching Leader Felix Alexander from Martinique. We had recently identified Brian and Felix as CBSI Key Persons and were training them to do leadership training in the future.

With our late arrival on Friday, we began by praying for God to make the clock stand still as He did with the sun and moon in Joshua 10:12-13. *"On the day the Lord gave the Amorites over to Israel, Joshua said to the Lord in the presence of Israel: 'O sun, stand still over Gibeon, O moon, over the Valley of Aijalon. So the sun stood still, and the moon stopped, till the nation avenged itself on its enemies."* By the end of that day, we had made up the lost time and covered a session scheduled for the next day! Not only that, but all of the training was completed an hour ahead of schedule Saturday. God gave us more than that hour! Sunday was our backup day. He gave us His day as a day of rest.

Twenty-one Teaching Leaders and Associate Teaching Leaders were trained that weekend in Couva, along with a number of Coordinators and Discussion Leaders. As a result, we anticipated two to four classes to begin before Easter and the potential of another four to six classes to follow.

But sadly, toward the end of training, an influential person at the seminar refused to follow the CBSI five-fold approach to Bible study. He wanted to use CBSI materials but follow the If You Will Pray format with rotating leaders and enfold this into his denomination's weekly prayer meeting. We patiently explained that CBSI is a process, not just Bible study materials. The excellent materials are only one component of the process to achieve our mission of making disciples of Jesus Christ through in-depth Bible study. Without the whole process—especially without shepherding by committed leadership—CBSI loses its distinctive effectiveness. Regrettably, this man could not agree, so we contacted our authority, CBSI Executive Director Damon Martinez. Damon confirmed our understanding that CBSI is not a materials providing organization and that the process must be followed. Later we met with this person, encouraging him to continue Bible study and suggesting other widely available Bible study materials he could adapt for his format.

During the next few weeks we worked with four leadership teams, helping with publicity and assisting with the details for class start-ups. In the midst of the preparation and for the week prior to Easter, dear friends Sue and Ben Kohns from Michigan joined us aboard *coram Deo*. Like Beth Nagle, Sue was part of the prayer group that resulted in the young adult Bible study we taught for eight years. Also, in that same week our much loved CBSI Tortola leaders Ian and Denyse Macintyre were visiting their families while on vacation in Trinidad. They introduced us to some great Trinidad entertainment such as the Marionettes, a chorale in which they had once performed. One night the six of us attended a magnificent Marionettes classical concert in Queens Hall. The Trinis have such beautiful voices that we are convinced Trini babies sing at birth rather than cry! Another night we visited the Trinidad All Stars Steel Orchestra "pan yard" and listened to them practicing outdoors. What a fantastic night of free music!

Ian drove the six of us to Trinidad's northeast coast, where we spent a night in a rustic beach hotel. All three couples were in one room with mosquito nets over our beds. At about two in the morning we were awakened to head out onto the beach. We grabbed our flashlights and observed huge leatherback turtles coming out of the surf, walking up the beach, digging three foot deep holes in the sand and laying their eggs. They then used their flippers to bury the eggs and hide their tracks as they returned to the sea. It was such a laborious task we had to fight the urge to help!

As exciting as leatherback turtle egg-laying was, it paled compared to the birth of the first Trinidad CBSI group on April 7, 2004! The Wednesday night before Easter we were blessed and highly favored as we joined in the excitement of the first meeting of the CBSI Belmont interdenominational class. Belmont is a rough neighborhood of Port of Spain bordering Laventille. Three women, however, trusted God to provide and protect, believing the CBSI motto, "Everyone in the world...in the Word." Teaching Leader Jean Thomas, Discussion Leader Marva Joefield and Class Coordinator

Glenda Culzac stood at the iron entrance gate to the small private chapel where the class would meet, laughing and hugging each of the 12 persons who came. Jean expressed her excitement and gratefulness to God for each one before giving an encouraging overview of 1 John. "What good could come from Laventille?" The birth of CBSI in Trinidad!

This class faithfully continued in Belmont until 2008. Then Jean and Marva moved it to a school in Carenage, closer to Jean's home. We had the privilege of visiting one class meeting after the move. The potent testimonies of this small group of women from all walks of life, including one former convict, spoke of the transforming power of God's Word!

The CBSI Marabella Anglican Church group began on April 19, 2004. Marabella is in southeast Trinidad. Teaching Leader (and pastor) Tony Mowlah-Baksh suffered a mild heart attack one week before class start-up. Associate Teaching Leader Allison George stepped in, started the class and continued during his recovery. But Tony is not one to be held down. He was released from the hospital at 3 p.m. the first day of class. Visiting him at his home that day, he insisted on coming with us to observe the first class meeting! Sixteen men and women began the study of 1 John.

Tony, who pastors three small Anglican congregations and was secretary of the Steel Workers Union, taught at times but never assumed leadership of the group. Quiet and determined Allison George, an Anglican lay minister and grief counselor at a nearby hospital, remained as Teaching Leader. She trained Deana Callender, a government pharmacist and also a lay minister, as Discussion Leader. In time they moved the group to nearby Gasparillo, where a majority of the small membership lived. This group continued through the summer of 2006 before going inactive.

The CBSI Trinity interdenominational class began on April 20, 2004, meeting in Trinity Primary School near the Trinity Mall. We attended the exciting first Leaders Council in the home of Teaching Leader Marlene Thomas. Though a professor at Trinidad

Teachers College, Marlene was nervous about teaching the first night of class. Earlier in the week she called Micki to see if she would do the initial teaching. Micki encouraged her that she could do it. We prayed and saw God answer. Marlene is a clear and gifted teacher of God's Word!

God raised up a loyal and committed support team for Marlene including Associate Teaching Leader Lucille Williams, Class Coordinator Veronica Fongyit and Discussion Leader Phyllis Motley. Leaders Council was a great night of prayer, encouragement and preparation for what lay ahead. For class, the team was there early for set-up and pre-class prayer, and then the people trickled in. Only seven persons attended that night! Disappointed but committed, they prayed and made phone calls, and the next week their numbers grew to 21.

As with all classes we visited Trincity whenever possible. But traffic in Trinidad can be daunting. Within one month we attempted two visits to Gasparillo and one to Trincity, only to turn back because of traffic jams. We allowed three hours to drive to each of these classes, which were 20 to 30 miles from where we were docked in Chaguaramas. Each time the congestion was so bad that our arrival would have been after the class or Leaders Council was finished!

On another night on the way to a Trincity Leaders Council, our rental car died just as it was getting dark. Our Trini friends and colleagues had warned that the worst thing to happen was a car breakdown after dark because the only ones who would stop were the bad guys! But if it does happen, do not turn on your interior lights or get out of the car. This particular night as we approached the major N-S and E-W intersection, the car began sputtering. As Chuck pulled off onto the shoulder, the car died right behind a parked police car! The traffic signals were out at the intersection so police were directing traffic. Patrol cars were on all four sides of the intersection. We were saying, *"Isn't that just like the Father!"* Now both Ronnie Heerah, then pastor at Westside Community Church where we worshipped, and Jessie James, our regular taxi driver and friend, had given us their phone numbers, insisting that we call if we ever broke down. But we were driving a rental car, so we called the company emergency number. The driver with the replacement car was caught in the same traffic, so we sat in the dark car a couple of hours before he arrived. Once he came with the rental car, we continued on our way to the Leaders Council, though by the time we arrived it was about over. We had called Marlene about our situation, and they were praying. We were praising God for His protective hand through the police! Then we learned that the police were not known to be helpful in situations like ours. Some were as crooked as the thieves! We had done all we could to protect ourselves by renting the best car available, which was more costly and had a local license plate rather then a rental plate. God protected us that night from all the thieves and bad guys! *"for He guards the course of the just and protects the way of His faithful ones." (Proverbs 2:8)*

And talk about God's protection! The Trincity leadership experienced it big time during a routine Leaders Council meeting in Marlene Thomas' home. A burglar, running from would be victims, climbed over her five to six foot high concrete fence, jumped over her three and a half foot verandah wall and crashed through the front door while Marlene was leading the meeting! The women scattered, locking themselves in the bathroom and bedrooms and called the police. Fortunately, her neighbors were hot on the crook's tail and caught up with him in Marlene's living room where they thrashed him severely. Then the police arrived and carried the scoundrel off to jail. Trusting in the Lord and carrying out His work, class met as usual the next evening.

The CBSI Trincity interdenominational class continues to meet under the excellent leadership of Marlene Thomas. When CBSI Caribbean Inc. was formed in 2008, Marlene Thomas accepted the additional position of Caribbean Training Coordinator on the Caribbean Servants Team.

The CBSI Diego Martin class began in May of 2004 at the home of Teaching Leader Kimlin Philip, with a small group of about eight persons. Kimlin, a director of Intervarsity in Trinidad, is motivated and serious about the study of God's Word. She wanted to minister to the men and women in her neighborhood, but after about three years the group dwindled and became inactive.

The CBSI St. Augustine Class met first on February 26, 2005. Twenty eight members enrolled for the pilot class on 1 John. We were thrilled to meet the leadership team and visit the class at their Testimony and Honors meeting on April 23 at the end of that first study and the day after we sailed into Trinidad. We were warmly greeted by leaders and given a 5x7 handout with the program for the morning on one side. On the flip side there was a brief explanation of the upcoming course in Galatians, followed by a list of dates for class meetings and a recap of the five-featured approach of CBSI. Were we ever impressed! Brian Burke, who had trained the leaders, flew in for this meeting and presented Teaching Leader Joe Caterson with a Certificate of Achievement, just as Joe had presented certificates to many of his class members.

This class struggles with attendance. Because of the threat of violence, Trinis do not like to come out at night for activities, and that is why this class meets on Saturday mornings. Though small, it is still strong and vibrant. In 2006 the CBSI Children & Youth Ministry was added to the class. Creative and loving Jacqui Bridge, a transplanted Jamaican and engineering professor at University of West Indies, was trained at the 2006 Caribbean Leaders Conference as the Children's Supervisor. Due to the small number of children in the class, she has served as the Children's Leader along with Violet Caterson.

In 2008 when CBSI Caribbean Inc. was formed, Joe Caterson was appointed Trinidad National Coordinator and elected Secretary of the Board of Directors. Jacqui Bridge accepted a position on the Servants Team as the Caribbean Children & Youth Coordinator. She provides shepherding and training for all CBSI Children & Youth Supervisors and Leaders in the Caribbean.

The CBSI Trincity Family Church class began in June of 2006 under the leadership of Teaching Leader (pastor) Julien Rullow. Ian Macintyre, then CBSI Key Person for the Leeward and Virgin Islands, trained this leadership team on one of his trips to Trinidad to visit family. Trincity Family Church is in the middle of a sprawling neighborhood. Pastor Julien Rullow is a sincere and compassionate leader who longs to reach this entire area with the life transforming

Word through CBSI. Thus the class continues today and is praying for leaders to start the Children & Youth Ministry.

As we look back now, we realize that God sovereignly brought us to Trinidad for this specific time in our ministry. The time was right for CBSI to get started, but there were many more reasons God had us in Trinidad for extended times in 2004 and 2005. It was here we spent those two hurricane seasons (June into October) just as the Eastern Caribbean experienced an increase in hurricanes. Because of the yacht services, we were able to make some small and some major improvements on *coram Deo*. Of course, God also knew we would need the availability of easy airline transportation and the services and caring support of the Trinis through much ministry development and life challenges. There are daily direct flights from Trinidad's Piarco International Airport to Miami, as well as many daily flights to the other islands in the Caribbean. In early August of 2004 the three-day Acts in August Conference for Teaching Leaders and Associate Teaching Leaders was held at Anapausis, a private conference center owned by friends Subesh and Debbie Ramjattan, not far from the airport. Twenty-eight leaders flew in from five other islands for refresher training and preparation for their next study.

In early September of 2004, Hurricane Ivan just missed Trinidad before devastating Grenada and the boats of a number of our cruising friends with a direct hit at 165 mph. We had wanted to spend the 2004 hurricane season in Grenada, but the Acts in August Conference brought us to Trinidad! Then from Trinidad we were able to join other cruisers and the Trini people and churches in a great outpouring of aid and assistance to the cruisers and the people of Grenada. Our dear friends and fellow cruisers Gary and Sharon, whom we followed to Venezuela in 2000, were unfortunately in Grenada in 2004. After Ivan passed, they found their 36-foot Catalina, Elusive, in a tree at the head of Mt. Hartman Bay!

One month later, on October 20, the very morning we planned to sail out of Trinidad, we received an 8 a.m. phone call from Micki's sister, indicating that her father, Roman Mroz, was dying. This is when the Trini love poured in from the marina staff and taxi driver/ friend Jesse James. Our time on the dock was indefinitely extended, and the marina manager assured us of *coram Deo's* care. Jesse told us to pack and not to worry about anything—he would take care of the travel details. By noon we were in Jesse's taxi on the way to the airport. Though Micki's dad entered eternity before our arrival, we were there to help with funeral arrangements and mourn with family, especially Micki's mother.

After experiencing such sweet Trini hospitality, we returned for the 2005 hurricane season. With the yacht services available we contracted to replace *coram Deo's* old, leaking windshield with one shipped from the manufacturer in Sweden. When the new windshield was installed, workmen discovered that the old protective hard dodger, which was to be attached atop the windshield, was rotten. With the services of David Morand of Ships Carpenter, we designed and built a lighter, larger, dryer hardtop, giving us good protection from rain, sun and sea spray. They did the work while we visited and encouraged the Trini leaders and classes.

But the greatest blessing of our time in 2005 was meeting Donna Gilbert, a former CBS Children's Supervisor temporarily living in Trinidad and looking to be used of God in a ministry there. God had prepared Donna and had her in Trinidad as one of His instruments to begin the CBSI Children & Youth Ministry in the Eastern Caribbean. *"...and He determined the times set for them and the exact places where they should live."* (Acts 17:26)

The work on the hardtop continued into October, taking weeks longer than anticipated. We figured God wanted us to spend more time with the Trini leaders and classes, which we happily did. But come October, for the second year in a row, we found ourselves flying back to Michigan for another funeral. Chuck's 68 year old brother, Richard Harding, went to be with the Lord on October 3, 2005, after a long struggle with Lewy Body Disease. And again the Trini love poured in from the marina staff and taxi driver/friend Jesse James.

"For God has not given us a spirit of fear, but of power and of love and of a sound mind." (2 Timothy 1:7 NKJV) Knowing, praying and trusting in God's Word brought us to Trinidad for His purposes. He continues to bear much fruit in the blessed and highly

favored people of Trinidad through the CBSI process of in-depth Bible study.

"Lᴏʀᴅ,....all that we have accomplished You have done for us." *(Isaiah 26:12)* To God be the glory!

Belmont, Trinidad, TL Jean Thomas introducing leadership team at first class.

**St. Augustine, Trinidad, TL Joe Caterson teaching
with outline displayed.**

2005 Trinidad annual leadership workshop.

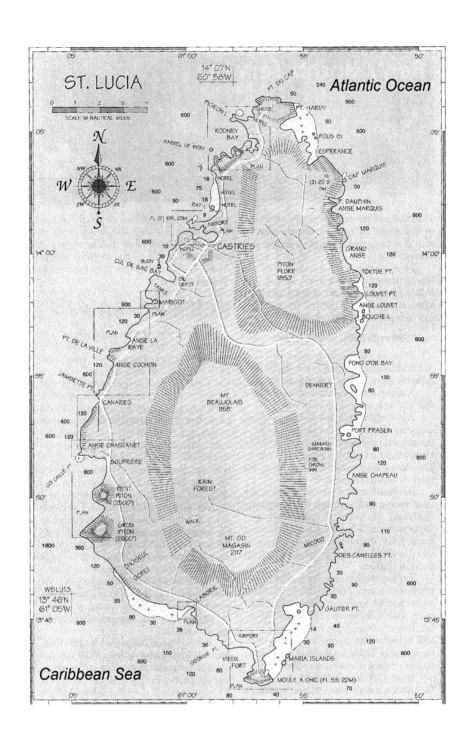

ST. LUCIA

SCALE IN NAUTICAL MILES

14° 07'N
60° 58'W

Atlantic Ocean

Caribbean Sea

WSLU13
13° 46'N
61° 05'W

8

St. Lucia

*"There is a time for everything,
and a season for every activity under heaven..."*
(Ecclesiastes 3:1)

CBS International was born in St. Lucia February 8, 2005, at the Rhema Pentecostal Church in Dennery, becoming its weekly Bible study. A number of other classes sprang up thereafter throughout the island.

Located near the northern end of the Windward Islands, St. Lucia is volcanic, mountainous and lush green with fertile valleys and plentiful rain. It has the largest English speaking population of the Lesser Antilles, at approximately 160,000. Its main industries are agriculture, with bananas the principal crop, and tourism. There are many hotels and resorts, visiting cruise ships and a dynamic yachting sector centered in Rodney Bay in the north. With its large protected anchorage, full service marina and convenient shopping with a large chandlery, hardware store and supermarkets within dingy or walking distance, this is one of our favorite layovers. St. Lucia is also popular for destination weddings, and we're sure *coram Deo* is in the background of many beach wedding photos!

While we were working in SVG shortly after the disastrous 9.11 attacks in the U.S., we received an email message from CBSI Headquarters providing us with a contact in St. Lucia, John Robert (JR) Lee. He was a newspaper writer and elder at Calvary Baptist Church in Gros Islet, near Rodney Bay. Don and Jean Peterson from New Jersey had touched lives in St. Lucia when they came as short term missionaries. Tragically, they were aboard American Airlines flight 93, which crashed into a Pennsylvania hillside on 9.11. Mr. Lee, having known the Petersons through their work with Calvary Baptist, was writing a memorial to honor them. During his research he learned that Don Peterson was a CBS Teaching Director, so he contacted the CBS office, where he learned of CBSI. Because of the Petersons' strong testimony, JR expressed further interest in CBSI. Chuck called JR, explaining the CBSI ministry, mission and process, and at his request, an introduction meeting was scheduled for the night of November 9, 2001, at the Gros Islet church. So would God bring new life to St. Lucia, extending the spiritual legacy of two saints who died tragically along with others on 9.11? Was He opening the door to the study of His life giving Word using the CBSI process?

If the door was opening, we were ready to step through it! With CBSI SVG under way, we planned to sail north to Antigua to store *coram Deo* for our return to Michigan for Christmas. St. Lucia was on the way, so we set sail to Rodney Bay to introduce CBSI at nearby Calvary Baptist.

We were surprised and encouraged when nearly 50 people turned out for the presentation. With this kind of interest, a class could have started on the spot if only we had time for training! The *CBSI Live!* video was played, and as usual was well received, sparking a lot of interest. While the people at Calvary Baptist liked the effective CBSI process and saw the need to help believers become true disciples of Jesus Christ, the leadership wanted a program to bring people into the church from the community. JR was under the impression that CBSI was an evangelism outreach course because of its name, Community Bible Study International. Chuck explained that while evangelism is a certain outcome of the CBSI disciple making process, it is secondary to our mission of making disciples of our Lord Jesus Christ. The most effective evangelism tool is the transformed life of a reproducing disciple. CBSI's mission of disciple making goes to the very core of the Great Commission. *"Therefore go and make disciples of all nations, baptizing them in the name of the Father and of the Son and of the Holy Spirit, and teaching them to obey everything I have commanded you."* *(Matthew 28:19-20)* While Calvary leadership chose not to commit to CBSI, we remained in contact with JR.

The following August of 2002 as we island-hopped from Antigua to SVG to revitalize the Kingstown class, we made a four-day stop in St. Lucia. Finding no further interest in developing CBSI at Calvary Baptist, Chuck contacted Sherwin Griffith, chairman of the St. Lucia Fellowship of Gospel Preaching Churches. Pastor Griffith led the Wesleyan Holiness Church in Castries, the capital, as well as lectured at Sir Arthur Lewis Community College. On Sunday morning we hopped the local bus (an eight-seat van into which they squeeze up to 12 people!) to Castries to worship at Pastor Griffith's church. When we experienced his homiletical style preaching/teaching, we were encouraged. He'd be a perfect CBSI Teaching Leader! After service he invited us to his home for dinner. After a truly enjoyable dinner and time visiting with his vivacious family, he led us into his home office, where we viewed *CBSI Live!* A skilled teacher himself, Pastor Griffith recognized and embraced CBSI's five-fold approach as the key to learning retention. He encouraged us, suggesting a presentation at a meeting later in the month. However, it was not God's timing. We had committed to Annette and Marcia in SVG, and more importantly to the Lord, to return to help restart the Kingstown class. While this appeared to be another open door, God had something even better in store!

More than a year later, in late 2003, Augustine St. Fort, an evangelist based in St. Lucia, was introduced to CBSI through a Discussion Leader in the Fort de France class. Augustine presented CBSI to his support team, and one person committed to organize an introductory meeting in St. Lucia with the support of Pastor Griffith. We checked back several times, even meeting Augustine for breakfast at the Bread Basket in November of 2003 on our way north to Martinique, but nothing developed. While this was disappointing, we recognized that it still was not God's timing.

Another year passed. On November 2, 2004, upon returning to Trinidad from the funeral of Micki's father, we had a full plate. Our return flight to Michigan for Christmas was booked for December 7 out of Antigua, some 400 miles north. Keep in mind that we average less than seven mph with *coram Deo*! Also, on the sail north we planned class and Leaders Council visits involving four SVG classes, three Martinique classes and one or two in Guadeloupe. Would you believe this was God's timing for St. Lucia? *"In his heart a man plans his course, but the Lord determines his steps." (Proverbs 16:9)*

While we were in SVG, Brian Burke gave us the name and phone number of his Vincentian friends, Pastor Elroy (Roy) Martin and his wife Tashia. Roy had wanted Brian to introduce CBSI to his small church in Bequia, northernmost island of the Grenadines. Before arrangements could be made, Roy was transferred to Rhema Pentecostal Church in Dennery, a fishing village on the windward coast of St. Lucia. Another Vincy friend recommended we contact Josephine Romaine, a volunteer with Intervarsity Christian Fellowship in St. Lucia.

It is written in Matthew 14:17 that Jesus took five loaves and two fish, gave thanks to the Father and fed thousands. So we thanked God for these two Lucian contacts and in *coram Deo* online asked for prayer for them. Wow! Did God multiply what we had! Arriving in St. Lucia on Wednesday evening, November 17, 2004, after a ten-hour sail from SVG, we anchored in comfortable Rodney Bay, looking forward to picking up our new dock lines, ordered from Island Water World. That was our main purpose for this stop. Though we were on a tight schedule, we planned to follow up on our two contacts. On Thursday morning God took over! *It just so happened* that when Chuck contacted Felix Alexander in Martinique to apprise him of our late arrival there, Felix informed him that the Martinique classes were on break for Christmas. We could relax in lovely St. Lucia! Or so we thought.

Chuck next called Roy and Tashia Martin who *just so happened* to be on their way across the island to Castries. They agreed to meet us for a late lunch. It was then we learned that Tashia had briefly attended the CBSI-Carriere class in SVG before her marriage and relocation. She recalled how much she enjoyed the small group discussion and the blessing of hearing many different perspectives. Pastor Roy requested we introduce CBSI to his congregation the following Tuesday night at their Bible study.

After lunch and our time with the Martins, Chuck called Pastor Griffith just to touch base. During the friendly conversation, the pastor asked how he could help CBSI, and Chuck suggested organizing a meeting of Christian leaders. Pastor Griffith, now past chairman of the Fellowship of Gospel Preaching Churches, said he would make some calls to get us on the agenda at the end of the fellowship's executive board meeting the following Tuesday morning. When confirmed, he gave us phone numbers for all the members of the executive board. Chuck called each one, briefly introducing ourselves and CBSI, and invited them to stay for the CBSI introduction followed by lunch at the restaurant of the beautiful Bay Garden Inn where the meeting was to be held. And *it just so happened* that the fellowship's annual nationwide service was on Sunday, two days before the meeting. Pastor Griffith strongly encouraged us to attend.

Chuck then contacted Josephine Romaine who was very friendly and interested in meeting us. She mentioned the ecumenical service on Sunday and offered to transport us there. When we arrived at the sports arena in Castries with Josephine, we followed the people into the bleachers section. Before we could sit down, Pastor Griffith saw us and had us brought into the dignitaries' tent with the leading pastors and the Governor General of St. Lucia. We were astounded by this honor! But that wasn't all. Not once but twice we were introduced from the podium and asked to stand! This was God's provision for us to be recognized by those around us. Afterward we had the opportunity to meet each fellowship board member in person and present him with the written invitation we had prepared. *Isn't that just like the Father!*

Twelve pastors and members of the executive committee from various denominations attended the CBSI presentation Tuesday morning and responded enthusiastically. Ready and eager, they wanted to know the next step. We committed to return to St. Lucia in mid January of 2005 to train leadership and assist in starting classes. The potential was island-wide. With God's provision of leadership, St. Lucia could become the sixth CBSI Eastern Caribbean country. In the next *coram Deo* online we reported God's miraculous multiplying of our "five loaves and two fishes" and asked our prayer team to pray for God to raise up committed men and women, eager for leadership training in January.

Think about this: We arrived Wednesday evening, made contacts and meeting arrangements Thursday through Saturday, were introduced to the entire St. Lucia Evangelical community on Sunday, introduced CBSI to the Executive Board of the Fellowship of Gospel Preaching Churches on Tuesday morning and to Rhema Pentecostal Church on Tuesday evening, where the response was enthusiastic and they were on board. Then we sailed to Martinique Wednesday afternoon. After several fruitless attempts on our time schedule, this six-day visit was God's perfect timing! What had taken us months in other islands, He did in six days in St. Lucia! *Isn't that just like the Father!*

Even with our brief stop in St. Lucia, *coram Deo* sailed into Antigua in plenty of time for our December 7 flight to Michigan. We flew back to Antigua on December 31, in time to bring in the 2005 New Year by enjoying the fireworks display at Jolly Harbour Marina. Though we were anxious to get under way to St. Lucia, we were weathered in by what is known as "the Christmas Winds." Rather than complain, we spent time building memories with the Ted Martin family and with the Rev's family, who had relocated to his homeland of Antigua. After also visiting and being encouraged by the Antigua CBSI leadership and class, we saw a weather window open on Monday, January 10, for the 200-mile sail south to St. Lucia. We sailed during the day, anchoring at night, and arrived in Rodney Bay on Thursday afternoon. Though we were in a "weather window," there was some rough sailing with high winds and seas! It was a good shakedown cruise to begin 2005, enabling us to make needed minor repairs each night after anchoring. Sailing in the lee (side away from the wind) of the islands, we had calm waters, allowing us to make enough water to fill our tank as well as relax and recuperate from the hard sailing. Rough seas followed by calm waters, then rough seas again, was a foretaste of what lay ahead.

After washing down salt encrusted *coram Deo* on Thursday, we prepared for the Leadership Training Seminars. Chuck began calling and meeting with interested church leaders, getting names and numbers of those who would attend. Brian Burke was enlisted to fly in and make a presentation at each seminar, including a sample homiletical teaching. Through this we hoped that the St. Lucians would recognize Brian as their Key Leader in the Windward Islands and a source of guidance and support. Micki revised the lengthy PowerPoint presentations for the training to have lasting power and effectiveness. It was enhanced so that each element would be driven and empowered by the Word. We printed and bound the CBSI Caribbean leadership training manual with added attendance forms, sample agendas, sample certificate of achievement and other helpful tools for each participant. But a persistent cough hampered Micki's ability to communicate. Knowing that in Jesus all things are possible, we communicated with our prayer team, asking them to pray that trainees would hunger for the Word and adopt a shepherding spirit to help others, that God would use His Word as the dominant training tool, and that He would preserve our health overall and heal Micki's persistent cough.

By Monday, four days later, we had commitments from several pastors to send leadership teams to the seminars held on the next two Saturdays, January 22 and 29, at Castries Nazarene Church. God was about to take back enemy territory through the study of His life transforming Word with CBSI. But Satan would not give up without a fight. The battle for St. Lucia began! Pastor Roy Martin from Dennery called to inform us that over the weekend a man murdered his girlfriend, decapitating her. The man and the woman had relatives in his church, Rhema Pentecostal, the first church to commit to begin CBSI in St. Lucia! The funeral was scheduled for the following Saturday, which would keep all his leaders from attending that first training seminar. We immediately prayed with Roy and then agreed to drive to Dennery during the week to hold a separate seminar for his team so they could overcome Satan's attack. His leadership team would then be ready for the seminar to be held the following Saturday.

Through our years in Bible study God has faithfully taught us to recognize Satan's tactics and respond with prayer. The devil knows that the study of God's Word can release the transforming power of the Holy Spirit in a person's life, thus breaking his hold. Bible study makes the believer spiritually armed and dangerous to the devil! To keep his power over that person, Satan will attack with lies, trickery and discouragement. To combat these attacks, CBSI has shepherding as a core element in every leader's responsibilities. The Teaching Leader and Associate Teaching Leader shepherd all the other leaders. The Discussion Leaders shepherd their group members. When under attack, a leader's personal contacts, availability and prayer can help the class member gain victory over the devil by keeping that person in the Word.

At that time in St. Lucia, however, no CBSI shepherding prayer was in place. So on January 19, through *coram Deo* online, we called on our prayer warriors to pray for the protection of all these new St. Lucia CBSI leaders—that their commitment would be strong and that they would recognize and resist enemy attacks.

God faithfully answered both prayers! Sixty men and women attended the first six-hour seminar on Saturday, January 22, the training for all leadership roles. On the following Saturday thirty of those leaders returned for training as Teaching Leaders and Associate Teaching Leaders. Micki had no cough. Scripture drove home every element. The trainees were hungry to learn, eager to put CBSI to work and attentive in both seminars. The homiletics interaction showed that the Teaching Leader and Associate Teaching Leader candidates wanted to handle the Word properly. And the Dennery team for whom we held that separate first seminar were fully trained and started the first CBSI class in St. Lucia on February 8, 2005. Take that, devil!

Through this seminar Brian Burke had shown his readiness to train CBSI leaders—and God provided the opportunity! Shortly after this seminar Joe Caterson in Trinidad contacted us, asking for training of a leadership team at St. Augustine Evangelical Church. He wanted to start a class as soon as possible. We had more on our plate in St. Lucia than we could say grace over and needed to stay focused. After working with us in St. Lucia, Brian had the complete seminar on PowerPoint and leadership training manuals in hand. He now had experience as well. In His perfect timing God had prepared Brian. For the first time an Eastern Caribbean CBSI leadership team would be trained by a West Indian! Brian flew to Trinidad in mid-February and with the support of local leaders did an excellent job of training the team at St. Augustine Evangelical Church. From there he flew to the Bahamas to represent CBSI Caribbean at CONECAR. What a privilege it was to watch God faithfully put the pieces of His plan together for the leadership of CBSI Caribbean! His timing is always perfect.

While God used Brian elsewhere, we employed a blitz strategy—a concentrated effort to start several classes in a short time frame. Within three weeks after the St. Lucia training, three CBSI classes were meeting. It was a privilege for us to attend the first class meeting of CBSI Dennery as well as its second meeting, in which God's hand moved in a powerful way. During the discussion a woman named Vern, who attended church regularly, asked members of her group to pray for her. In answering a question in the first lesson of the 1 John study, she realized she had never committed her life to Christ. Before that evening's lecture began she stood boldly before the entire class and joyfully announced her new relationship with Jesus Christ! This was a powerful affirmation for a leadership team that had faced and overcome enemy attacks. *Isn't that just like the Father!*

With the next two class start-ups on two consecutive nights the following week in Laborie and Soufriere on the south end of the island, we weren't relishing the long drives. So we sailed *coram Deo* to Soufriere Bay, a marine park with fixed moorings in the shadow of the majestic towering twin volcanic Pitons. Here we would be a short walk to the Soufriere class and less than an hour's drive from

Laborie, rather than the two- hour drive each way from Rodney Bay to either class. The only available mooring, however, was in an area of the bay with unsettled seas and prone to thievery! But God provided. Harmony Beach Restaurant was located nearby on a surging, rocky and isolated section of the waterfront, picturesque but hard to reach. Benny, the owner, provided transportation to and from yachts to shore so cruisers could patronize his restaurant. For us he also arranged on-board security for *coram Deo* while we were away at classes after dark. This sounded good, but there was a challenging price to pay! Leaving our dinghy locked on *coram Deo,* we were picked up in Benny's large wooden pirogue style boat and dropped off in crashing surf at the ruin of a concrete dock. Benny watched the surge carefully, and when he shouted "OK!" we scrambled over the gunnels, jumped onto the wet, slippery dock and ran ashore. Meanwhile, the driver slammed the engine into reverse, backing away to keep the boat off the rocks before the next wave hit. And Micki did this all in a dress!

On Wednesday night, February 16, 2005, CBSI began in Laborie under the leadership of Teaching Leader Robert James. Laborie is a south coast fishing village east of Soufriere. We were picked up from Harmony Beach Restaurant by Laborie Associate Teaching Leader Greg Laurent, a friendly and busy local bus driver. The church was packed out with 78 people, about a third of them children. The group was planning to split into two classes, cooperating with a sister church in the nearby mountain village of Banse, and they later did this. Robert James, a quiet and unassuming lay pastor and metal fabricator by profession, was fighting laryngitis, but God, in answer to prayer, provided the strength and voice for him to give his first teaching. Because of the large turnout, they ran out of enrollment forms and lessons but promised delivery the next day to all who did not receive their materials. With all the children, they wanted to organize something, but what they really needed was a CBSI children's program. Robert's young adult daughter, Joni, took it upon herself to provide a class for the children on the small front porch of the church. Her step of obedience for these children would soon be honored by God to impact the world through CBSI!

After the Laborie class and by the time we returned to the dock at Harmony Beach, the worsened sea conditions made getting back aboard *coram Deo* even more treacherous, but we hardly noticed! We were so blessed by God's faithfulness that we felt we could have walked on water back to *coram Deo*! Thankfully, the next morning a mooring opened up on the calm, safer side of the bay. Also, as part of the protected marine park, the mooring offered incredible snorkeling right off the boat!

On the following night, Thursday, February 17, 2005, the CBSI Soufriere class began at Christ is the Answer Church under the leadership of Teaching Leader Kendall Nicholas. Twenty-one men and women attended. While this was a relatively small start, we felt there was good potential. The leadership team was four strong, vibrant young men focused on outreach into their village, and Kendall was a gifted, enthusiastic teacher.

The next three classes would be established in March, giving us a week's break. Pumped up from the exciting expansion in St. Lucia and not wanting to waste time, we sailed the 25 miles north to Martinique with enough time to visit the three classes and Leaders Councils there and help Felix Alexander make a CBSI introduction to two Christian leaders before sailing back to St. Lucia.

The CBSI Castries Streams of Power class started on Tuesday, March 1, 2005, directed by Teaching Leader Darrius Garraway. Fifty to sixty people turned out for the CBSI introduction. At 22 years of age, Darrius was the youngest Teaching Leader in the Eastern Caribbean, and we were concerned. We can still see him on that first class night, dressed in jeans and a grey t-shirt, leaning on the lectern with his legs crossed, at times rambling, not quite knowing what to say. But his pastor, Tim Robinson, knew his character and potential and supported him wholeheartedly. A native of Trinidad and a steel pan player and music teacher, he had moved to St. Lucia to teach. He was awed and overwhelmed by the responsibility of teaching this large class and leading its experienced leadership team, which included Pastor Robinson's wife, Marilyn, and his sister Dawn. At Darrius' request we initially spent much time with him to talk through his teaching preparation. *"Do your best to present yourself to God as one approved, a workman who does not need to be ashamed and who correctly handles the word of truth." (2 Timothy 2:15)* This verse was the desire of Darrius' heart, and he was willing to put in the time and effort it took to prepare well. Most of the people in the class were older than he, but week by week, as they watched God increase his understanding of Scripture and empower his words, they grew to respect him and his teachings. When we would visit the class, we usually drove Darrius home since he lived on the way back to Rodney Bay. He would climb into the back seat and say, "OK. Sock it to me!" He was so teachable and craved our honest critique of what he was doing well and where he could improve. God used His powerful Word, our coaching, his pastor Tim Robinson's input and encouragement and the 2006 Leadership Conference to mature Darrius into an effective teacher as well as a more confident and organized leader.

Fast forwarding to March of 2007, Darrius was 24 and had two years of CBSI teaching experience. Wearing a dress shirt and dress pants, he stood calmly at the podium with his teaching outline digitally projected on a screen overhead, giving a powerful, confident and anointed message on Exodus Chapter 20—the Ten Commandments, the covenant and the Sabbath. At one point he came into the audience and took the arm of a male class member who then stood and walked arm and arm with him down the aisle while Darrius talked and illustrated a biblical truth. This was a natural and comfortable way of maintaining people's engagement in the Word. We sat in awe of how God's Spirit had grown this young man. With great clarity he taught, applied and illustrated truths of the Word to help class members understand who they were as covenant people and how God's law applied to them. We were nailed to our seats by God's faithfulness in His calling on Darrius' life! *Isn't that just like the Father!*

Pastor Sherwin Griffith, a friend, a strong CBSI supporter and a seasoned teacher, opened his church to a CBSI class on March 2, 2005. The CBSI Castries Wesleyan Holiness class was directed by

Teaching Leader Randolph Campbell. Pastor Griffith joined him in introducing CBSI to about twenty middle-aged men and women from their congregation. This was the fifth class to start in St. Lucia in five weeks. CBSI was like a wild fire spreading throughout St. Lucia!

We then had commitments in the States, so we docked *coram Deo* at Rodney Bay Marina and flew to Florida. Micki vacationed with her mom in Tampa while Chuck continued on to Michigan for business meetings. God gifted Micki and her mom, Cecilia Mroz, with special time together after the passing of Micki's dad just five months earlier. While in Michigan, Chuck was invited by Teaching Director and friend Mike Wendland to give a ministry update to the large CBS class that meets in our home church. Chuck talked of God's perfect timing in the starting of classes in St. Lucia, and he challenged the CBS class to support formation of a CBSI children's program on the island. The response was the catalyst for a chain of communication that God ultimately used to launch the long prayed for CBSI Children & Youth Ministry, blessing Laborie, the Eastern Caribbean and the world. *Isn't that just like the Father!*

We both returned to St. Lucia for the start-up of the sixth class, CBSI Castries Nazarene, on March 23, 2005, under the leadership of Lynette Ragnanan. About twenty persons attended and enrolled. Many class members and leaders worked in the tourism industry and consistent attendance was an ongoing problem. But this first St. Lucia female Teaching Leader, diminutive and spunky, was not afraid of challenges. She is by vocation a school teacher and an interesting and thorough Bible teacher. Her Associate Teaching Leader and pastor, Rev. George Leonce, gave consistent support and provided the church building for CBSI training whenever possible.

As we continued to observe these six new classes, we saw that some Teaching Leaders didn't grasp homiletics well enough to use in their teaching preparation. With our sailing departure two weeks away, we realized that a refresher for them and their Associate Teaching Leaders was needed. It could improve their effectiveness in helping members grasp how each passage applied to their everyday lives and encouraged appropriate life changes. So on Saturday, April 2, these leaders gathered at the Castries Nazarene Church for an interactive refresher workshop. A special bonus was the attendance of CBSI four-year veteran SVG Associate Teaching Leader Chiefton Charles, a Nazarene pastor who *just so happened* to be there on district business. He brought helpful and encouraging insights from his background in using homiletics in his preparation for teaching the CBSI Kingstown class—even showing PowerPoint slides with outlines, central ideas and applications.

Three days after the workshop, on April 5, 2005, the CBSI Castries Bethel Tabernacle class began with Priscilla James as its Teaching Leader. Experienced and committed, Priscilla is a vibrant teacher of the Word. The CBSI introduction was given to nearly 70 persons of all ages. Priscilla's pastor, Bishop Emmanuel McLoren, then chairman of the Fellowship, had played a key role in the establishment of CBSI in St. Lucia.

With seven classes established in less than four months in St. Lucia, we set sail to visit and share the awesome news of God's faithfulness with the classes in SVG and Trinidad before storing *coram Deo* in Peake's Boatyard in Trinidad for hurricane season.

As we sailed, we thought back on all God had done in bringing CBSI to St. Lucia. God's faithfulness...God's timing...God's provision. What an awesome privilege He had given us to help people grow in Christ through the CBSI process of Bible study! We were humbled by the prayers expressed for us by the St. Lucia leaders and class members. They were grateful for CBSI, many seeing it as answer to long-time prayers. And we were tired! There were so many details involved in starting all those classes, requiring constant focus, time and energy. We thanked God for His provision of all that we needed. When we thought we had not one more word of encouragement or one more ounce of energy to train one more leadership team or attend one more Leaders Council or one more class or make one more phone call, He provided. *"My grace is sufficient for you, for my power is made perfect in weakness...For when I am weak, then I am strong."* (*2 Corinthians 12:9-10*) Amen!

Back in Trinidad after hurricane season with several delays including finishing our new hardtop, we sailed back to St. Lucia, dropping the anchor in Rodney Bay on November 1, 2005. The hardtop, with its increased visibility and clear plastic side windows, provided a dry ride despite a tropical wave with many squalls packing winds up to 38 knots. After nearly seven months we were eager to observe the classes! What more had God done? What more did these leaders and classes need?

With growth we were well aware of the additional need for organization and planning. There were 23 classes on seven island nations. Shepherding would be essential to sustain the classes and support further growth. As a result we identified three key leaders as Area Directors: Brian Burke for the Windward Islands and Trinidad, Felix Alexander for the French West Indies and Ian Macintyre for the Virgin and Leeward Islands. Our new Regional Director, Dr. Glenn Collard, arranged for these three Area Directors to meet him and us in St. Lucia for a weekend strategic planning meeting. This process caused us to recall and record what God had done through CBSI in the West Indies, the leadership and other assets He had identified and obstacles that needed to be overcome. Also, we sought God's vision for the future and inquired how He would have it fulfilled. This culminated in the future formation of CBSI Caribbean Inc.

After that fruitful, thought-provoking weekend, we again turned our faces to observe and coach the St. Lucia classes. We were able to fit in only four of the Leaders Councils and class meetings before setting sail November 23 for Antigua. As usual, we stored *coram Deo* in Jolly Harbour before flying home for Christmas.

Upon our return to Michigan, we found Micki's mom suffering from extreme neck and hip pain. After the Christmas season we delayed our return to the Caribbean to seek diagnoses and treatment. The biggest disappointment was that we had airline tickets for Micki's 85-year-old mom to fly to Antigua in January to see and come aboard *coram Deo* for the first time as well as meet our Antiguan friends and CBSI family. Those in Antigua were as disappointed as we were! Doctors were able to treat her neck pain, but hip replacement surgeries were planned for later in the year.

Finally, on January 19, 2006, we rejoined *coram Deo* and visited the Antigua class. Again facing "Christmas Winds," it was

February 5 before we sailed south to Dominica, where we expected to spend three to four weeks introducing CBSI and possibly training leadership teams. After ten days Micki was called to go home for a family emergency. We dropped anchor in Rodney Bay on February 20, 2006, and Micki caught a flight to Michigan.

Chuck stayed in St. Lucia shepherding classes. It had been one year since CBSI began there and more churches were expressing interest. Chuck helped prepare CBSI Castries Evangelical class for their start-up on March 12, 2006, under the leadership of Teaching Leader (pastor) Waltrude Dantes. This church was a five-minute walk from CBSI Castries Streams of Power. In the prior year the Streams of Power Church building had undergone major construction. Their neighbors in Castries Evangelical opened their facility as a temporary meeting place, including the CBSI class night. CBSI leadership invited the Evangelical congregation to the class, and some joined. Once construction was completed and Streams of Power moved back to its own facility, Pastor Dantes told Darrius they wanted to start CBSI. Darrius called us in Trinidad, saying, "What should we do?" Area Director Brian Burke flew to St. Lucia in October of 2005 and trained their leadership team, but by February of 2006 they had not launched the class. Chuck called Pastor Dantes and gave the team some refresher training, and the class became a reality. We initially suggested that the two churches join for CBSI and hold one class since they are in the same part of town. That would be a great testimony to their congregations and the watching world! But each church wanted its own class. Thus, with Castries Nazarene just up the street, Water Works Drive had three CBSI classes within minutes of each other.

Chuck was also busy providing CBSI introductions and leadership training for three more pilot classes in the south at Victory Tabernacle in Vieux Fort, Redeemed Christian Fellowship in Desruisseaux and New Life Pentecostal in Laborie. While these three pilots did not become classes, many leaders from the classes across St. Lucia participated in and were blessed by the 2006 CBSI Leadership Conference in August in Antigua.

In 2005 God blessed Laborie by choosing it to pilot the CBSI Children & Youth Ministry. Details of God's faithfulness there are in the next chapter. By April of 2008 there were six exciting Children

& Youth Ministries meeting in St. Lucia! About a month later, at the founding of CBSI Caribbean Inc., Robert James, the Teaching Leader of the Laborie class, became the National Coordinator for St. Lucia.

From 2008 to this writing in 2011, the worldwide economic downturn has hit the Caribbean tourism industry hard, particularly St. Lucia. Devastation from Hurricane Tomas in 2010 further impacted the economy. Sadly many leaders' work schedules were changed, keeping them from attending class and Leaders Council, resulting in all of the classes closing. Because they have experienced a life transforming ministry, we pray and trust the Lord to bring them back to CBSI in His perfect time, just as in His perfect time He brought CBSI to St. Lucia in 2005. The Word was studied. Lives were transformed. *"...so is My word that goes out from My mouth: It will not return to Me empty, but will accomplish what I desire and achieve the purpose for which I sent it."* (Isaiah 55:11)

"Lord,...all that we have accomplished You have done for us." (Isaiah 26:12) To God be the glory!

Laborie, St. Lucia, TL Robert James teaching; curtains separate discussion groups.

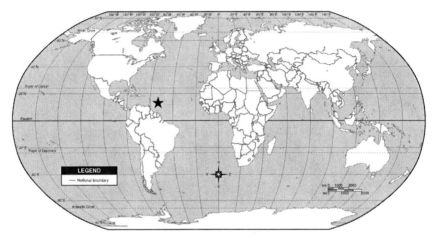

While the first CBSI Children & Youth class was established in St. Lucia, West Indies, the ministry has spread worldwide.

9

Children & Youth Ministry

Jesus said, "Let the little children come to Me,
and do not hinder them, for the kingdom of heaven
belongs to such as these."
(Matthew 19:14)

CBS International Children & Youth Ministry began its first pilot class in the world in Laborie, St. Lucia, on September 28, 2005.

This ministry had been in our prayers and those of our prayer warriors before the beginning of the CBSI Eastern Caribbean ministry. On a June night in 1999, when we sat in the Officer's Quarters at Nelson's Dockyard in Antigua after a powerful time of Bible study, we were asked, "How can we have this kind of Bible study here?" The question included the children. Malvaire, who asked the question, had her pre-teen daughter at the Bible study that night. When discussing in-depth Bible studies available in the States, we also mentioned associated children's programs, making clear that they were not babysitting services, even for toddlers, but were solid Bible studies. Not until our training did we learn that CBSI had no children's ministry. To have it, we were told, would require an international children's director. When God again impressed on us the need for children's ministry at the start-up of the Antigua class in 2001, we began praying specifically for a director.

As classes were established, there were usually children attending with their parents. (Caribbean parents rarely leave their children at home.) What really pulled at our heartstrings was the sight of twenty to thirty children overflowing the porch in the CBSI Laborie class in St. Lucia in February of 2005. These children came with their parents or grandparents or strolled in from the neighborhood and sat on the porch steps, the railing, little ones on the laps of bigger ones, wherever they could fit their little bottoms. Teaching Leader Robert James' young adult daughter, Joni, would gather the children on the small open front porch of the church, a space six feet by nine feet, where she led them with Bible stories, Scripture recitation and a craft. Because of her love for the children, every week she created a lesson on her own. We knew that children's materials were available through CBS, but we had no idea that God was already at work on this and would use Joni's simple commitment to impact CBSI around the world!

While in Michigan on business the next month (March 2005), Chuck was invited by our friend and CBS Teaching Director Mike Wendland to give an update on our ministry to the large class he leads in our home church. With Chuck's heart tenderized by God's faithfulness in St. Lucia, he shared passionately about God's perfect timing. He showed pictures of the new classes, including one of the many children on that tiny porch at Laborie. He talked of the obvious need for the children's ministry and an international children's director. He appealed to the class, "Could anyone help?" After class Mrs. Barb Michaels, a friend of Micki's and former leader with her in Bible Study Fellowship, approached Chuck, offering to do what she could.

Barb's step of faith encouraged Chuck to contact CBSI Field Director Gilles Cailleaux. Chuck emphasized the great need for children's ministry in St. Lucia and the possible availability of Barb Michaels. Although appreciating the need, Gilles expressed concern about starting such a ministry based on the cost of translating materials into many languages. Chuck suggested starting with a pilot program using the existing English lessons made available through CBS Children's Ministry. This pilot experience would provide the background needed to transition into other languages and cultures. At Gilles' request we wrote out our thoughts on a pilot project and submitted it to him on March 21, 2005. Of course, God was already in motion. In addition to making the need for children's ministry obvious to us in Laborie, He already had His person for director in process. Debbie Nilsen, a CBS Teaching Director in Rancho Santa Margarita, California, for four years, with five years of experience as a CBS Children's Director as well, was sensing God's call in the summer of 2003 to return to the children's ministry. She answered that call by announcing she would step down as Teaching Director after the 2003-2004 class and by continuing to seek God's will. She spent the next six months in God's waiting room. At the CBS Teaching Directors Conference in January of 2004, she had a chance meeting with CBSI Executive Director Damon Martinez. Naturally, children's ministry came up, with Damon indicating that an international director would need to be identified before children's ministry could begin. Debbie sensed that CBSI was where God would have her serve, but she heard nothing from CBSI and for another 18 months was back in God's waiting room! She was asked to pray about many different roles during that waiting time, but the Lord confirmed time after time that she was to wait on Him. So she obediently waited.

God had heard our prayers and those of others. Just as He had kept us waiting and praying for His open door for St. Lucia, He had kept Debbie in the wings for His perfect timing in beginning the ministry. While the CBSI leadership committee was resisting expansion into the children's ministry due to severe growing pains, God was clearly and irresistibly saying NOW, 2005 is My perfect time for the children! Gilles got the necessary support and approvals to move forward with the pilot in Laborie and brought Debbie Nilsen on board to take the helm as Director of Children's Ministry. God used the Laborie Class in a small fishing village in the far south of St. Lucia to pilot and begin the CBSI Children's Ministry, which would eventually bless the children of the world! *Isn't that just like the Father!*

It just so happened, in the providence of God, that in July of 2005 while we were in Michigan, Debbie's husband Fred had a business meeting in a nearby suburb. We met them at their hotel one afternoon. From the first moments of hugging and sharing the excitement of what God was doing, we could see why our Lord had chosen tenderhearted, passionate Debbie to champion the children for Him in the world through CBSI. What a blessing to come face to face with God's answer to our long time prayer!

Jesus said, *"You did not choose Me, but I chose you and appointed you [Debbie Nilsen] to go and bear fruit—fruit that will last. Then the Father will give you whatever you ask in My name."* *(John 15:16)* Debbie would definitely need help for this God-sized mission! But before she could even pray specifically for help in the Caribbean, God had His person in place.

On May 15, 2005, the Sunday before we stored *coram Deo* for hurricane season in Trinidad, we worshipped as usual at Westside Community Church in West Moorings. After the service Pastor Ronnie Heerah introduced us to a couple, Jeff and Donna Gilbert. Pastor Ronnie knew of our CBSI work, and he knew some of Donna's background. Jeff and Donna had moved from Connecticut to Trinidad a couple years earlier for an employment opportunity for Jeff. Or so they thought that was the only reason. We learned from Donna, a pretty, dark-haired and perky woman, that she had been a CBS Children's Director for 12 years in Connecticut and was looking for a ministry in Trinidad. It *just so happened* that the CBS International Children's Ministry in the Caribbean was about to be born. Did God have a ministry for Donna? Oh yes!

We contacted Debbie Nilsen when we reached the States. So before we met her in Michigan, she and Donna had talked, and plans were coming together to train a Children's Supervisor and Leaders to pilot the fledgling CBSI Children's Ministry in September in Laborie. Debbie would do the training with assistance from Donna during the St. Lucia pre-class workshop we would be leading for all CBSI leadership teams on August 27 in Castries. Donna could then continue coaching and shepherding the Children's Ministry leaders in the pilot and, Lord willing, across the Caribbean in the future.

God faithfully brought together His called ones from California and Connecticut, already prepared, to *"Let the little children come to Me"* in Laborie and in a short time around the world through CBSI Children's Ministry, which in time God would expand to CBSI Children & Youth Ministry! *Isn't that just like the Father! "Consecrate yourselves, for tomorrow the LORD will do amazing things among you." (Joshua 3:5)*

We returned to Trinidad in August, excited about flying to St. Lucia for the Saturday pre-class workshop but thrilled, most of all, about the training of CBSI's first Children's Ministry team in the world! Since the devil was about to lose some valuable territory in the hearts of the children of St. Lucia and beyond, he fought back. On the Tuesday before the workshop, when Debbie was scheduled to fly out of California, she was stricken with food poisoning. She postponed her flight until the next day. We sent out an emergency prayer request for Debbie to be well and able to travel on Wednesday and for the training for the Children's Leaders to take place as planned. Early Thursday morning (two days before the workshop), while Chuck, Micki and Donna were sitting in the LIAT departure lounge at Trinidad's Piarco Airport, Chuck received a call from Debbie's husband Fred. Debbie had collapsed on the way to the ticket counter at Los Angeles International Airport and would not be coming!

Though we were concerned and prayed for Debbie, there was not a moment of panic or anxiety. *"In his heart a man plans his course, but the LORD determines his steps." (Proverbs 16:9)* The Lord immediately gave us the wisdom to reorganize the workshop agenda. Donna was called into action by God, and He would provide all she needed to do the entire training for this new ministry. Area Director Brian Burke was also meeting us in St. Lucia, so he could take over Micki's adult sessions, freeing her to assist Donna. The Lord ordered our steps, even as we almost missed our flight! Chuck was on the phone alerting Brian of the situation. Donna and Micki were so engrossed in going through materials that not one of us heard the announcement for boarding or noticed people moving around us. When the waiting area was quiet and we looked up, the gate area was empty! As we rushed to board, the gate attendant laughed, saying they were about to announce our names over the PA system!

Fred Nilsen FedEx'd a box of the needed printed materials, which arrived in plenty of time. Debbie emailed, "I'm still pretty weak. I so wish I could be there right now! But, the Lord had even better plans. He planned for our precious Donna to be His mouthpiece." The Lord provided a clear, strong voice and loving demeanor for Donna as she taught for two and a half hours before lunch and another hour afterward, even though she was recovering from bronchitis. She had no voice the night before she left for St. Lucia. *Isn't that just like the Father!*

Bernadette Henry, a joyful, loving single woman, was trained as the Children's Supervisor, along with Children's Leaders Jacqueline Hunte, Judith Charlery and Joni James. They would pilot the Children's Ministry in Laborie. On September 28, 2005, CBSI's first children's class in the world opened with more than 20 kids! It soon grew to 50 children, ranging from pre-school to junior level. Because of the growth, the Laborie class divided between the church in Laborie and its sister church in Banse with the Children's Ministry in both locations.

While we were delayed in Trinidad much of October with the work on *coram Deo's* hardtop and the funeral of Chuck's brother in Michigan, God provided the opportunity for a three-day visit to Laborie to observe the class and specifically the Children's Ministry. Donna and Micki flew to St. Lucia, as did Debbie and Fred Nilsen. How exciting it was for Debbie to see with her own eyes what God was doing in the first CBSI children's pilot! Together Debbie and Donna encouraged, further trained and coached the leaders. Since Micki was familiar with the roads and area, she was chauffeur. Fred, an excellent photographer, recorded for posterity this groundbreaking pilot. One day on the main road between the guest house and Laborie, they were delayed by an accident—a van had hit and killed a cow. On their return trip the cow was still on the road on its side with legs sticking straight out. The people milling around were trying to decide who would get the meat! While the division of the Children's Ministry between Laborie and Banse was still in the planning stage at this time, Micki gave Fred, Debbie and Donna a real thrill by driving up the narrow, potholed, twisting mountain road and fording streams to show them the church at Banse. They were sure glad Micki was driving! During the rainy season this road can become impassable.

When the August 2006 Leadership Conference began, the Laborie and Banse pilots had a full year's experience and had matured into established classes. The CBSI Children & Youth Ministry was a reality! At the conference Children's Supervisors from three island nations were trained by Director Debbie Nilsen, assisted by Donna Gilbert and Linda Baber, a delightful newly recruited helper from California. Five newly trained Children's Supervisors were ready to begin the Children & Youth Ministry in the St. Augustine class in Trinidad, the Carriere class in SVG, and the Castries Streams of Power class, the Castries Evangelical class and the Dennery class in St. Lucia. The highlight of the meetings on Saturday afternoon was a very moving commissioning service where these trained Children's Supervisors knelt and were surrounded by more than 70 CBSI leaders and speakers in attendance. All laid hands on these called ones as Chuck prayed for them and their awesome responsibilities before God to teach and lead His little ones. Meanwhile, the now renamed CBSI Children & Youth Ministry (C&Y Ministry) was multiplying in the Caribbean and beginning to spread worldwide.

In November of 2006 we sailed to St. Lucia, anticipating the visits to classes with C&Y Ministry. Donna Gilbert flew in for three days as excited as we were to see how classes were doing. We visited Laborie and Banse classes and found the children more faithful than adults in completing their lessons and were eager to share their answers—hardly waiting for questions to be read! The Children's Leaders were helping the children not just answer questions but understand the meaning of biblical principles in their own little lives.

When we visited the new Dennery C&Y groups, which started in October with 20 children ages five through young teens, we had to move out of the entryway because the five- to seven-year-olds were running into the church, dropping their shoes at the foot of the platform, racing up the steps and disappearing behind the large pulpit where their class met. You could hear their excited little voices, but all you saw were little shoes scattered on the platform steps! These were the same little ones who had complained to their leader that the older children had homework and they did not! Afterward we met with Children's Supervisor Tashia Martin and Children's Leader Theo to discuss sending some kind of papers home with them.

From there we sailed to St. Vincent and journeyed to the mountain village of Carriere to observe the CBSI class there. It truly was a mountaintop experience for us to visit the C&Y groups! In September they started with more than 30 children in regular attendance. In the Youth group, the boys and girls verbally stomped on one another to answer the questions, learning and laughing together. Since they knew we were coming, the three levels combined and prepared a special song for us, assembling at one end of the room and singing their hearts out! Though some were very shy, they let us hug them afterward!

When we returned two years later, in November 2008, this C&Y Ministry had grown to more than 50 children. Children's Supervisor Ingrid Cambridge, a regal-looking, passionate and industrious widow who owned a rental car company, sent out mini-buses into the surrounding hamlets to transport the children to come and learn about Jesus. During class Ingrid proudly showed us the boxes and packages of new craft materials recently received from our fellow Caleb (to Scotland) Helen Jane Peters. She worked through her CBS class in Orchard Lake, Michigan, to have items donated and shipped to Carriere as a love gift!

As we visited these precious children's classes, we thought of the legacy these leaders were building for eternity. While focused on encouraging them, we were the ones encouraged!

By the end of 2007, Jeff Gilbert had completed his Trinidad employment contract, and he and Donna moved home to Connecticut. Clearly, God had placed Donna in Trinidad for such a time as this. As 1 Corinthians 3:8 says, *"The man who plants and the man who waters have one purpose, and each will be rewarded according to his own labor."* Donna did both and will be doubly rewarded!

In March of 2008 while again in St. Lucia, we were joined by the new Children & Youth Ministry Area Director Darlene Winfree and her co-worker Kim Clifton, both from Orange County, California. What fun we had watching their excitement as we visited three classes, Castries Streams of Power with about 24 children and the Laborie-Banse combination with more than 40. The evening before Darlene and Kim's departure, they met at Castries Evangelical Church with all the St. Lucia Children's Supervisors and Leaders from all six programs. Wanting to help them connect with the children in their weekly mini-talks, Darlene encouraged them to use simple illustrations familiar to the kids as they taught. She demonstrated this with a calabash, a gourd-like fruit with a hard shell. She talked about how a calabash, split in half, emptied of its soft interior and dried, can be used for many purposes—as a cup, a bowl or serving utensil. She went on to say that implements made with calabash shells are often carved with beautiful designs. With the leaders nodding and agreeing, Darlene spoke of how human beings, like calabashes, must be "scraped and emptied" to be useful in God's service—and, just as there are many uses for the calabash, God uses different people for various purposes. She continued about how God carves us through the difficulties of our lives to make us unique and beautiful servants. The leaders sat in rapt attentiveness.

In 2008 when CBSI Caribbean Inc. was formed, Jacqui Bridge, the Children's Supervisor of the St. Augustine, Trinidad class, accepted a position on the Servants Team as the Caribbean Children & Youth Coordinator. She provides shepherding and training for all Caribbean C&Y Supervisors and Leaders. In July of 2009, Jacqui, along with C&Y Area Director Darlene Winfree, trained three new leadership teams—seven people from Antigua and one from Tortola. They then flew to Martinique to train seven C&Y Leaders from the French-speaking Fort de France class. Jacqui and Darlene were welcomed warmly by Pastor Doyen, who shared how they had been praying for materials to be translated into French. National Coordinator Felix Alexander willingly served as their translator. These new leaders were prepared not only with skills but with the newly translated study of the Gospel of John. This was the first French-speaking class with a children's course also translated into French. These same courses can now be used by French-speaking children and youth worldwide. *Isn't that just like the Father!*

Strong C&Y classes were formed in both Fort de France and Antigua later in 2009. The Antigua class has continued strong because of its committed, prayerful leaders and consistent meeting schedule. Ironically, though there had been strong participation by the children, the Fort de France C&Y Ministry recently went inactive because adult class participation diminished. This had been one of the larger and more vibrant classes in the Caribbean! But because of the frequent interruption of the class schedule for months on end for crusades and other church-wide activities, the perceived importance of Bible study among members was undermined. So the class withered and closed.

Children and youth are the church of the future. ***Jesus said, "Let the little children come to Me, and do not hinder them, for the kingdom of heaven belongs to such as these." (Matthew 19:14)*** Since Jesus is the Word, we obey His will by providing opportunities for children to meet with Him through Scripture study. The CBSI C&Y Ministry is one of the most effective vehicles for this. If we do not provide for the nurturing of little children in the Word, in Jesus, then the church of the future will reflect the values of the world and the bondage of its prince rather than the truth and freedom of God's love.

God used the Laborie and Banse classes to pilot this vital ministry. While some C&Y classes have closed due to lack of people willing to prioritize their time to lead children to Jesus, hundreds of others have responded to Jesus' call to make disciples of the little children. At this writing in 2011, the CBSI Children & Youth Ministry is in its sixth year with 107 classes across the Caribbean and in Australia, North, Central and South America, Eastern and Western Europe, Asia, the Pacific Rim region and Africa, with more than 2,000 children involved! Besides English and French, CBSI children's lessons are now available in Portuguese, Spanish, Dutch, Russian, Kirundi and Ukrainian. *Isn't that just like the Father!*

"Lᴏʀᴅ,...all that we have accomplished You have done for us." *(Isaiah 26:12)* To God be the glory!

Children attended Laborie class before C&Y Ministry began. Joni James (standing) taught them weekly, preparing materials herself.

After successful C&Y pilot class at Laborie, St. Lucia, Children's Supervisors were trained at 2006 Conference. Director Debbie Nilsen kneeling.

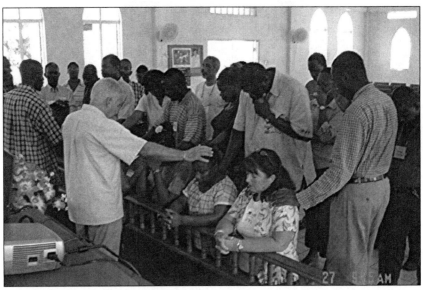

Chuck commissioning new children's leaders in prayer after training in St. Lucia.

Carriere, St. Vincent, C&Y class

Streams of Power, St. Lucia, C&Y class.

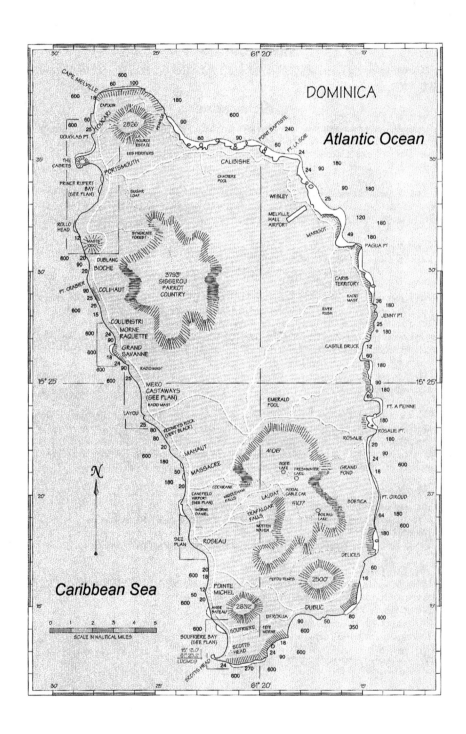

DOMINICA

Atlantic Ocean

Caribbean Sea

N

SCALE IN NAUTICAL MILES
0 1 2 3 4 5

CAPE MELVILLE
TOUCARI
CAPUCIN
2826
SOURCE ESTATE
DOUGLAS PT.
LES HERITIERS
THE CABRITS
PORTSMOUTH
PRINCE RUPERT BAY (SEE PLAN)
SUGAR LOAF
ROLLO HEAD
DUBLANC
BIOCHE
PT. CRABIER
COLIHAUT
SYNDICATE FOREST
3793' SISSEROU PARROT COUNTRY
COULIBISTRI
MORNE RAQUETTE
GRAND SAVANNE
RADIO MAST
MERO
CASTAWAYS (SEE PLAN)
RADIO MAST
LAYOU
RODNEY'S ROCK (VERY BLACK)
MAHAUT
MASSACRE
COCHRANE
CANEFIELD AIRPORT (SEE PLAN)
MIDDLEHAM FALLS
MORNE DANIEL
TRAFALGAR FALLS
WOTTEN WAVEN
SEE PLAN
ROSEAU
POINTE MICHEL
ANSE BATEAU
2832
SOUFRIERE
SOUFRIERE BAY (SEE PLAN)
SCOTTS HEAD
TETE MORNE
BEROKUA
DUBUC
FERDU TEMPS
2500'
DELICES
BOILING LAKE
BOETICA
PT. GIROUD
4107'
LAUDAT
AERIAL CABLE CAR
GRAND FOND
FRESHWATER LAKE
BOERI LAKE
4106'
ROSALIE
ROSALIE PT.
PT. A PEINNE
EMERALD POOL
CASTLE BRUCE
RIVER RUSH
CARIB TERRITORY
RADIO MAST
JENNY PT.
PAGUA PT.
MARIGOT
MELVILLE HALL AIRPORT
WESLEY
CHAUDIERE POOL
CALIBISHE
POINT BAPTISTE
PT. LA SOIE

15° 35'
15° 30'
15° 25'
20'
15'

30' 25' 61° 20' 15'

180

10

Dominica

*"And pray for us, too, that God may open a door
for our message..."*
(Colossians 4:3)

C BS International was born in Dominica on November 1, 2006,
in Paix Bouche (pronounced "pay bush") under the leadership
of Teaching Leader (pastor) Edmund George.

It has been said that if Columbus were to come back today,
Dominica is the only Caribbean island he would recognize! It is the
most unspoiled country with spectacular natural beauty. In a country
which registers 360 inches of rain annually, one can expect some
rainy days! What that means aboard *coram Deo* is to be on constant
alert to closing hatches and being quick-footed in taking down laundry drying on deck. If one happens to be working inside the boat, it
becomes a hot, humid environment—no fresh air or cool breeze. But
about the time a sailor gets ready to complain loudly, the Lord gives
a reminder of His hope for a future—another beautiful rainbow. This
is the land of magnificent rainbows!

Along with the rainbows and rain comes incredible fruitfulness.
Dominicans claim the land is so fertile that if you push a stick in the

ground, it will take root and grow a tree! We saw the trees to prove it! Flowers, fruits and vegetables—golden apples, sweet bananas, plantains, navel oranges, tangerines, limes, avocados, passion fruit, pineapple and papaya—abound. Our favorites are guava, sugar apple (with the unique look and taste of custard) and the sweetest peel-and-eat grapefruits we have ever tasted!

As cruisers we had spent two or three days at a time over the years, taking tours of the island as well as scuba diving and snorkeling in the incredibly clear waters. In November of 2005, while heading for Antigua, we followed God's leading and paused for an extended layover in St. Lucia—watching Him multiply our two leads into an island-wide CBSI introduction. When we left St. Lucia, we were in awe of what God had done but awful late getting under way to Antigua to store our boat for Christmas. To be able to catch some wind and keep our speed up in the lee of Dominica, we sailed more than five miles away from its wind-blocking mountains. As we enjoyed the beauty of its majestic scenery even from that distance, we talked about having no contacts in Dominica and wondered when God would open a door for CBSI there. Then, because of the calm seas, Chuck went below to start up our water maker while Micki kept watch on deck. A short time later she noticed a flashing blue light off the starboard stern and called Chuck on deck. It was the Dominica Coast Guard overtaking us! Over the VHF radio we were instructed to maintain course and speed, but they were going to board us. "Oh great!" we grumbled. The large inflatable with the flashing blue light pulled alongside, and two officers deftly jumped aboard *coram Deo*.

Chuck went below with one officer while Micki stayed on deck with the other officer, who reviewed our documentation and filled out some paper work. While taking our information, Micki mentioned that we were missionaries. The officer, Vincent Valerie, a bright and handsome young man, smiled warmly, saying, "Why are you passing by Dominica? We need you here!" Chuck and Officer Dominique came on deck, and we told the Dominicans about CBSI. As Christians, both were interested in Bible study! We explained our need to be in Antigua but said we could stop by in January or February on our way south if there was interest. Officer Vincent wrote out his and his wife Sylvia's email addresses and phone numbers, asking us to stay in touch while in the States. He said he would discuss CBSI with his pastor and arrange for us to meet him upon our return. So this was no random boarding. It was a divine appointment on the high seas! *Isn't that just like the Father!*

After emailing back and forth with Vincent, we saw that there was sincere interest in CBSI. So, as promised, we made a layover in Dominica in early February of 2006. We sailed into Prince Rupert Bay on the northwest coast—a huge bay more than two miles long and a mile wide. It looks idyllic but the high mountains and the warm water in the bay can combine to cause diurnal winds that will knock your hat off, sometimes coming down the mountains and across the bay at 30 knots or more. The town of Portsmouth, which overlooks the bay, was once considered for the nation's capital, but because of the swamp northwest of town, malaria or yellow fever often afflicted early settlers. Therefore, Roseau, about 25 miles south, became the capital. Prince Rupert Bay is a good cruisers' anchorage, but for us it was also the area where Vincent and his family live. Vincent and his happy, outgoing wife Sylvia, an elementary school teacher, warmly welcomed us, not just into their home but into their lives. We celebrated with them the birthdays of daughters Nery and Nissy (then ages 8 months and 3 years respectively), as well as Dominica Independence Days a couple of years, and we worshipped and went on church outings with them and their friends. Thoughtful and fun loving, they became and always will be our loving "Dominica family."

We were excited to be there for ministry and blessed to be able to enjoy this beautiful, mountainous, fertile and unspoiled island and the fellowship of its sweet people. We and other cruisers hired a local guide, Martin, to tour the cold volcano in the north and to visit Chaudiere Pool, where Chuck courageously dove off a rock cliff into the cool fresh water below a waterfall. Martin provided snacks of sweet grapefruit, oranges, bananas and coconut, giving each of us some cinnamon bark fresh off the tree! Micki learned to make two fantastic local soups—callaloo (spinach-like vegetable) and cream of pumpkin.

Vincent, as promised, contacted his pastor, Nigel Commodore, long before our arrival. Pastor Commodore arranged a meeting for us with himself, his superintendent and other pastors from their Gospel Mission denomination. Vincent, an accomplished cook, invited us to his home before the meeting to serve us a scrumptious local lunch from the bounty of Dominica! After the meal he walked us to the bus stop with instructions to get off at the Canefield Airport stop and follow his directions to the church. For quite a while we were the only passengers on the bus and began a conversation with the driver. We explained a bit about CBSI and that we were on our way to do a presentation. The driver's pastor, Bishop Michael Daniels, *just so happened* to be the President of the Dominica Association of Evangelical Churches (DAEC). Days later we made a presentation to some of the DAEC executive committee at the Bishop's church, People's Pentecostal Family Church in Roseau, the national capital. As we look back, this was a time of tilling the ground.

Cruisers who visit Dominica often use "boat boys" to assist with directions to Customs and Immigration for clearance, local information, scheduling tours, shopping etc. Some cruiser friends recommended using Martin Carriere, with his pirogue style boat named Providence, usually adding, "Martin says he's a Christian." Meeting Martin was another God-ordained appointment! Not only did we use his excellent services, but Martin invited us to his church, Lifeline Christian Fellowship, for Bible study one evening. Pastor Bernard Joseph (BJ) made some statements then about wanting his people to be equipped to teach and lead Bible study so he could sit in the pew and learn from them. Thank You, Lord, for such clear direction! We approached Pastor BJ afterward to introduce ourselves and greet him for Nath Browne from Antigua. When Nath learned we were headed to Dominica, she said to look up Pastor BJ. Nath was born and raised in Dominica, and Bernard Joseph had been her pastor! Dynamic and bright, BJ was intrigued by the fact that we lived on a boat, so we invited him aboard *coram Deo* to talk about CBSI. The next day we picked him up at a dinghy dock for a fun visit aboard.

He appreciated *coram Deo* with her beautiful and comfortable interior but was much more impressed with CBSI. He wanted it to be a vital part of his church later in the year. The congregation first needed to finish a program already started, so we exchanged information and promised to stay in touch.

Then our time in Dominica was abruptly interrupted. Micki's sister Louise had serious complications from medications after knee replacement surgery. Their mom was suffering from painful degenerated hips, and Micki was needed to help care for her during this traumatic time. Early the next morning, February 19, 2006, we raised anchor and set sail for St. Lucia, nearly a hundred miles south from which there were daily flights home. Prayers were answered regarding Louise's healing and recovery, and Micki was able to minister to her mom in a number of ways.

Two weeks later, with Micki back onboard, we sailed north to Dominica. Chuck had maintained contact with Pastor John Lambert of the Dominica Association of Evangelical Churches. From the introduction given to the DAEC executive committee in March, Pastor Lambert estimated that there would be 15 to 20 persons ready for training, making up four leadership teams. So the training seminar was set for Saturday, March 11, 2006, at People's Pentecostal Family Church in Roseau. Thinking of what God had done through the Fellowship to open up St. Lucia to CBSI, we invited Area Director Brian Burke to take part, and he flew in on March 10. When we arrived at the church, only the team from People's Church showed up. We went ahead with the training, but afterward the group was still not ready to begin CBSI. We were not discouraged. The interest was there, but the people needed time to pray and prepare. More importantly, we learned another valuable lesson. In the future, we would not set a training seminar date until the pastor of the church or prospective Teaching Leader could provide the names of persons for all leadership positions, a planned starting date and a venue for class meetings. By requiring this minimum level of planning and preparation, they would have an investment of their time and effort in CBSI. They would have skin in the game.

But this time, effort and expense were not wasted. ***"And we know that in all things God works for the good of those who love Him, who have been called according to His purpose."*** *(Romans 8:28)* While we were riding the public bus on the way to the Roseau meeting, Dominica Park Ranger Gerard Benjamin boarded. He was very friendly, and we began to chat. Soon we learned he was the pastor of the Coulibistrie Gospel Mission Church. He had been at work during the meeting with the Gospel Mission pastors and did not know about CBSI. Brian and the two of us bounced off each other in talking passionately about CBSI and its benefits. Before Pastor Gerard got off the bus 15 miles down the road in Coulibistrie, he had our business card in hand as well as CBSI brochures. This contact would bear fruit—just as a stick shoved into Dominica's fertile soil grows into a tree.

Before we boarded the bus that morning in Portsmouth, we approached a taxi driver to ask the location of the bus stop. When he looked at us, he recognized Chuck, and then we remembered him. "Victor!" He was the only taxi driver we had used in several previous layovers in Dominica, before CBSI. He had taken us on three different tours over the years. The first time we met this friendly, tender family man, we ministered to him as he shared with us the recent heartache of losing his son in an automobile accident. Then, on our last tour with Victor, he brought his lovely wife Madeline, and the four of us had a precious time of fellowship together visiting the rain forest, with the bonus of actually sighting a few Sisserou parrots, Dominica's national bird. Images of this bird appear on their flag and coat of arms. It is an endangered species, the oldest of Amazon parrots, and it is found only in Dominica. We praised God for the blessing of seeing some! Victor and Madeline talked about us attending their church Bible study that night after the tour. Some thievery was going on in the anchorage, however, and Victor nixed the plan, not wanting us to leave the boat unattended. But God had something better in store in His time!

This time, before directing us to the bus stop, Victor invited Brian and us to worship with him and his family. On Sunday morning

Victor picked us up by the dinghy dock. We had a gorgeous drive up the mountain through the lush forests and banana plantations overlooking deep valleys with rivers and small waterfalls, finally arriving at the Baptist church in the beautiful mountain village of Paix Bouche. Our praise and worship had already begun, as we were surrounded by God's spectacular creation! Arriving in time for Sunday school, we were greeted by the young and innovative Pastor Edmund George, who invited the three of us to meet with him in his office. As we shared CBSI with him, he said—excitedly and without hesitation—that CBSI would fit into his vision and plans for the church! He would introduce us during the service and wanted us to tell his congregation about CBSI. There was lots of interest, and afterward we did some planning. Brian would return the following month for a CBSI presentation to the Gospel Mission Conference as a follow-up to our earlier introduction at the pastors meeting organized by Pastor Commodore. The Lord willing, we would return in July, when we could train leadership and start CBSI classes on Dominica.

After the service Victor and Madeline invited us to their home with their family for Sunday dinner. As Micki relaxed with the ladies afterward on the porch, Madeline thanked her for sharing her personal story of childlessness when the four of us toured the rain forest. Their married daughter had not been able to conceive children and was heartbroken. Madeline had been able to encourage her daughter with Micki's story of how, although she yearned to have a family, God never blessed her and Chuck with natural children. When Micki gave that longing over to God, however, He filled her life with purpose and meaning through the teaching of His Word and in this way gave her spiritual children. In hearing Madeline tell how God had used Micki's experience to reassure the daughter, Micki was deeply touched, and now she was able to add to that story— saying that if God had opened her womb and blessed her with natural children, she said she would not be in the Caribbean with CBSI. She would want to be home with grandchildren. *"Praise be to... the God of all comfort, who comforts us in all our troubles, so that we can comfort those in any trouble with the comfort we ourselves have received from God." (2 Corinthians 1:3-4)*

It was now time to visit classes in Martinique and St. Lucia. By March of 2006, the ministry had grown to 23 classes on seven islands, and in our "spare time" we were preparing a program and syllabus for the August 2006 Eastern Caribbean CBSI Leaders Conference in Antigua. Expecting all the Caribbean leaders from those 23 classes to be there, we planned the conference to help them take CBSI to the next level across the Caribbean. But first we had a family obligation. Micki's 85-year-old mother was having her first hip replacement surgery at the end of April, and we needed to be there to help care for her during recovery. So after St. Lucia we sailed two nights and three days to Trinidad, arriving on April 23, just three days before Micki's flight to Michigan. Chuck prepared *coram Deo* for storage at Crews Inn Marina and followed shortly thereafter.

While back in Michigan, we learned that no commitments came from Brian's time at the Gospel Mission Conference in April. Chuck was in phone contact with Pastors Bill Daniel and John Lambert from the Dominica Evangelical Association, who said they wanted to embrace CBSI and asked when we could provide training. A detailed plan, with the requirements for establishing CBSI classes and a tentative schedule for leadership training, was emailed to them in June. If they were committed, we would lay over in Dominica in mid July on our sail from Trinidad to Antigua before the conference. The Training Seminar would be presented during that layover. Chuck stressed the need for the names of the persons to be trained, their proposed roles and a venue for training. When we heard nothing from the DAEC, the urgency for a seminar in mid July was lessened, but Paix Bouche Baptist Church still wanted to get started.

In the first week of October in 2006, we sailed back into Prince Rupert Bay, and Dominica was ready for CBSI. We made CBSI introductions to the leaders of Martin's church, Lifeline Christian Fellowship, the largest church in Portsmouth. Pastor BJ expressed interest in training after the first of the year. Additionally, we presented CBSI to

Coulibistrie Gospel Mission Church, led by Pastor Gerard Benjamin, the man we met on the bus. That congregation also wanted to go forward with training after the first of the year. Due to our packed ministry schedule, we turned over the training of these two classes to Area Director Brian Burke to schedule for February or March of 2007.

We then settled into Dominica for a few weeks to train the CBSI leadership team of Paix Bouche Baptist Church. Pastor Edmund George would be the Teaching Leader, and persons were identified for all other leadership roles. Training began Saturday, October 21. The four-session seminar, totaling more than 12 hours of intense training on the process and leadership roles, was not without its challenges. This was the first leadership team we trained to lead a CBSI "cell group" ministry. Thus leadership would consist of one Teaching Leader (to oversee the work and lead the Leaders Council), five Associate Teaching Leaders and five Discussion Leaders (one to teach and one to lead the discussion in each cell), and one Class Coordinator to organize for Leaders Council and provide all needed materials. The groups would meet in the village and a few surrounding hamlets. Two Associate Teaching Leaders had extenuating circumstances that could have kept them from sessions, but they did not let that happen. Clive Honore's wife underwent surgery the first day of training. After visiting with her in Roseau, one hour away, he made it not only to the first session but every session! Laurel Peterson was not feeling well during the first two seminars but trusted God's provision. She was there and attentive.

When this training was completed, we had a major encouragement! New Associate Teaching Leader Delvin Sylvester put his homiletical training into immediate use. Called on to preach the following Sunday, he used the tools he received in CBSI teaching preparation to plan his sermon. We were sorry we missed it! We heard that the message was "a powerful teaching," with a central idea and strong applications.

During that time of training, still at the height of hurricane season, we were the only cruising boat in the huge Prince Rupert Bay. We can testify that October is rainy season there! We had time to visit and grow the relationship with Vincent and Sylvia's family as well as their extended family. We anchored on the south side of the bay near Ross Medical School to pick up a WIFI hotspot. From the nearby dinghy dock we could walk to Vincent and Sylvia's home, up the mountain. One day Martin brought plantains aboard and proceeded to teach Micki the peeling, cutting and deep frying technique for making delicious plantain chips. When she served him her cream of pumpkin soup and asked for his opinion, he suggested using coconut milk. That is the secret ingredient to great cream of pumpkin soup! And talking about food, we never left our training sessions empty handed! The Dominican people love to share the bounty of their island. We would return to the boat with plantains, passion fruit, whatever was in season—and enough to feed an army!

When class night—Wednesday, November 1, 2006—arrived, a nervous but prepared and committed leadership team experienced God's faithfulness. The CBSI Paix Bouche class was the first to be born in Dominica! The 30 persons who attended that night were introduced to the CBSI process and heard Teaching Leader Edmund George's clear and compelling overview of 1 John. He is passionate about God's Word and loved the impact of homiletical teaching. This leadership was celebrating and eager to get everyone in Paix Bouche and the surrounding hamlets involved in the life transforming process of Bible study. Pastor George decided to begin as a unified class in the church for the first six-week study before beginning their cell groups in the surrounding hamlets. This would boost the confidence of the leaders. We were there for the second week of class to encourage the leadership and class before setting sail.

Six months later we returned to find the Paix Bouche class vibrant and healthy, engrossed in the study of 1 and 2 Thessalonians. They were still meeting as one class in the church, having backed off from the cell group ministry. Discussion Leader Adeline, a sharp and hospitable teacher, did an impressive job leading her group. Pastor George had made Delvin Sylvester the Teaching Leader. A retired pastor, Delvin taught with practicality from 2 Thessalonians 3, exhorting all to stand firm in the truth of God's Word.

On our arrival back in Dominica, we were just in time for the May 27, 2007 birthday celebration of one of our Dominica family, two-year-old Vinyerra (Nery) Valerie! Then on Whit Monday we joined the Valerie family and their church family for a picnic on the beautiful south shore of Scotts Head.

The two leadership teams from Lifeline Christian Fellowship and Coulibistrie Gospel Mission Church had been trained by Brian Burke in February, yet here it was June, and neither had started a class. We called Pastor BJ and learned that Lifeline's first class was scheduled for the following Wednesday, June 6. We would be there! This was exciting because this class would begin immediately, following the "cell group" approach. It would be led by co-Teaching Leaders Pastor Bernard Joseph and his wife Gloria, the church's administrative pastor. Gloria was experienced in leadership training and development from her secular job as well as within the church.

For the Leaders Council on Tuesday night, we sat in a circle with 16 cell group leaders, an Associate Teaching Leader and Discussion Leader for every group. They were planning on seven to eight cell groups meeting in homes throughout the Portsmouth area and farther away. BJ led the meeting and effectively brought out good interaction and support from the leaders. A sharp and gifted leader, he was teachable when it came to the structure of CBSI. We were impressed with his solid grasp and strong commitment to following the CBSI process. His focus with cell groups was outreach to the community with a commitment to excellence in the Lord's work. There would be weekly meetings of the Leaders Council led by the co-Teaching Leaders, who would also invest time in working with the new Associate Teaching Leaders in teaching preparation. What a great start!

The CBSI-Portsmouth cell group class began on Wednesday, June 6, 2007, at Lifeline Christian Fellowship. More than 70 persons attended, including our dear friend and boat boy, Martin Carriere, and his family. The class opened with an uplifting and worshipful time of praise singing. We helped by giving a brief history of CBSI and explaining the CBSI process of disciple making. Pastor BJ followed with an inviting, interesting and thought provoking overview of 1 John. Then there was the somewhat time-consuming process of assigning persons to cell groups. Church secretary Marissa, filling in for the Class Coordinator, finally recorded all the names of the persons assigned to each group. For the future we recommended using enrollment forms, which help people realize that they are making a commitment to the study. We so looked forward to returning to see this CBSI ministry in action!

CBSI-Coulibistrie Gospel Mission class was due to start the following week. Our schedule wouldn't allow us to stay, however, we would return.

Five months later in November of 2007 we sailed into Prince Rupert Bay. After a rough sail and *coram Deo* looking like a salt lick, she needed some TLC. When we could not locate Martin, friendly and reliable boat boy Alexis cleaned her up. While working on deck, Alexis discovered termites in our anchor locker! We later learned they were stowaways from the Antigua boatyard, which had an infestation of termites, when we made repairs while stored there. The worms destroyed a thick plywood shelf, the only exposed wood in the anchor locker. God provided Alexis and his friend Elizè to gut, fumigate, sand and paint the locker. Alexis' friend Leo built and installed a new shelf with a heavy encapsulation of FRP. This freed us for CBSI work for our short eight-day visit.

The CBSI Coulibistrie class had started back in June, and having completed their third six-week study would have their Testimony and Honors night during our stay! First we attended their Leaders Council, which was our first meeting with this leadership team. Pastor Gerard Benjamin was no longer at that church. Upon meeting the leaders, Micki said, "It's led by David and his mighty men," referring to King David and his warriors. Teaching Leader David Fritz, Class Coordinator Rennick Pousaint and Discussion Leader Malcolm St. Rose were all physically tall and muscular men with godly characters to match. Micki so named them because their might was not only seen but demonstrated in their quiet strength and commitment to and love for their people. They were passionate about helping others grow spiritually and excited when they saw it happen.

Two nights later we attended their Testimony and Honors class at the completion of their study of James. When class members were encouraged to share publicly what they had learned, the first to respond was Teaching Leader David's own seven-year-old daughter, Kasinda. She stood and confidently said, "The tongue. We have to control the tongue." They did not have a CBSI Children & Youth Ministry, but some children were doing adult lessons!

We were so disappointed to learn that the CBSI Portsmouth class was already on break until after Christmas. But Pastor BJ said he would invite the leaders to meet at the church one night to share their experiences with us. It was an impromptu meeting so not all leaders were available. We were overwhelmed as we listened for two hours to what God was doing in and through this class!

Most groups had a mixture of adults and teens. When asked if the teens were doing their lessons, there was a resounding "Yes!" Leaders spoke of good interaction, deep discussions, growing fellowship and especially how members were applying the Word of God to their lives. Discussion Leader Clare Joseph said as a shy person she has had to put away her shyness and become brave. Other leaders chimed in that it was the shy ones who became outstanding as they grew in confidence and started participating in discussions. Leaders were especially excited about visitors from the neighborhood coming to check them out. Associate Teaching Leader Jennifer Moise said that CBSI brought back her zeal to study the Word. She was getting up at 2 a.m. to prepare for her teaching!

Associate Teaching Leader Keith Thomas and his Discussion Leader, wife Yolanda, gave us an idea of their weekly format, which started at 7 p.m. and ended at 9 p.m. They had eleven in their group, adults, young adults and four children ranging in age from 12 to 16. Keith said they spent about ten to fifteen minutes in praise singing, then all participated in the three-part conversational prayer before the discussion, which lasted about an hour. He then would give a half hour interactive teaching. Both Keith and Yolanda spoke of the spiritual growth, the deep discussions and how much the children participated.

Towards the end of the time, Pastor BJ explained his agenda for coaching and shepherding the leaders. There were eight groups meeting with an Associate Teaching Leader and Discussion Leader in each. He visited each group three times. The first time he showed up unannounced to observe the group for ten to fifteen minutes. He could visit three groups in a night. What he observed that needed correction or improvement, he would deal with in a general way at Leaders Council the next week. On the second visit he would focus on the Associate Teaching Leader and Discussion Leader. He announced at Leaders Council the group he would visit that week. He would stay for the entire meeting and afterward meet with the leaders to critique and encourage. The third visit he would again attend the entire meeting and actually participate in the group. By this time the leaders were more comfortable with each other, so Pastor BJ would share what he saw during that week's visit at Leaders Council.

Then one Sunday they modeled a complete cell group meeting on the platform before the entire congregation to get everyone in the church involved. In mid November of 2007 we sailed out, praising God for His faithfulness in the cell group development that was taking place in Dominica and ready to share it with others in the Caribbean.

We remain convinced that this Portsmouth CBSI cell group experience will help many rural people in the Caribbean get into the Word. On most islands there are transportation issues due to lack of bus service in the evenings, poor roads and weather conditions. Making CBSI available to small groups in villages and hamlets would better reach the rural populations.

We were surprised after our encouraging observations in November of 2007 to learn that the CBSI Portsmouth class never started up again. Pastor BJ reverted to a mid week meeting in the church, which is an interactive discussion of Bible passages. CBSI-Paix Bouche continued, completing four studies by 2007. The class did transition into the cell group format with Pastor George and Delvin Sylvester as co-Teaching Leaders with the home cell group discussions led by Amelia Sylvester, her Aunt Madilla Sylvester and Laurel Peterson. After the completion of 1 and 2 Thessalonians, Amelia emigrated to the U.S. for further education. The other leaders could not commit to continuing, so the class went inactive until God lifts up committed leadership.

However, when we sailed into Dominica mid November of 2008, we were encouraged by the larger and still spiritually strong leadership team of CBSI-Coulibistrie. Up to that point the team had been all men, so we were delighted to see the addition of two women.

In May of 2008 when CBSI Caribbean Inc. was formed, Teaching Leader David Fritz was appointed Dominica National Coordinator and elected Treasurer of the Board of Directors to capitalize on his skills as a professional accountant. David's responsibilities as National Coordinator are to shepherd existing classes and grow the work of CBSI in his country, which he has diligently striven to accomplish.

We believe that in God's perfect time CBSI will once again grow and prosper in Dominica, fulfilling its mission of making disciples of the Lord Jesus Christ in cities, villages and hamlets island-wide. While in ourselves we can do nothing of eternal value, *"The One who calls you is faithful and He will do it."* (*1Thessalonians 5:24*) *"Therefore, my dear brothers, stand firm. Let nothing move you. Always give yourselves fully to the work of the Lord, because you know that your labor in the Lord is not in vain."* (*1Corinthians 15:58*)

"LORD,...all that we have accomplished You have done for us." (*Isaiah 26:12*) To God be the glory!

Dominica Coast Guard visiting *coram Deo* at anchor. Officer Vincent Valerie on left is who invited us to return to Dominica to introduce CBSI.

Micki training leaders at Paix Bouche, Dominica.

Coulibistrie, Dominica, leadership team with TL and National Coordinator David Fritz (back row in middle).

**Paix Bouche Leaders Council preparing for next class meeting.
TL Pastor Edmund George leading (at left in striped shirt).**

**Portsmouth Leaders introduced to the class. They led CBSI
home cell groups in their neighborhoods.**

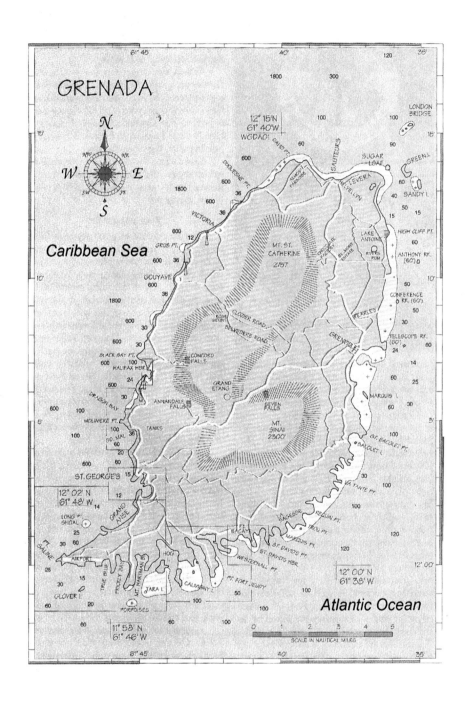

GRENADA

Caribbean Sea

Atlantic Ocean

12° 15'N
61° 40'W
WGDA01

12° 02' N
61° 48' W

11° 58' N
61° 46' W

12° 00' N
61° 38' W

SCALE IN NAUTICAL MILES

11

Grenada

"And the things you have heard me say in the
presence of many witnesses entrust to reliable men
who will also be qualified to teach others."
(2 Timothy 2:2)

CBS International was born in Grenada February 21, 2007, in Tempe under the leadership of Teaching Leader Mikey (Michael) Patterson.

Grenada is a spectacularly beautiful island with lush green mountains, crystal clear waterfalls, gorgeous yellow sand beaches and fragrant spice trees. It is well known as the "Isle of Spice." Every visit we stock up on the locally made Moses vanilla for baking and cooking for friends and ourselves! But what is by far the most important and most prominent are the twin spices of nutmeg and mace. On a spice tour we learned that nutmeg is not a nut, but actually the kernel of a fruit. The fruit looks much like an apricot. When split open the red covering on the nutmeg is actually mace. Driving anywhere north and east of St. George's, the capital, you would find yourself among nutmeg trees. Grenada had thousands of these trees and was second only to Indonesia in nutmeg exports—until Hurricane Ivan in 2004 destroyed 90 percent of the trees. Since then farmers have planted nearly 4,000 nutmeg trees in an effort to rebuild this industry.

From a yachting standpoint Grenada has good services with haul-out facilities in St. David's and Prickly Bay as well as a number of marinas from St. George's on the west to the bays on the south coast. It had been a fast growing yachting center until Hurricane Ivan ripped through in 2004, causing extensive damage. The industry took quite a hit initially when insurance companies, for hurricane season coverage, required yachts to be south of Grenada. Now with Grenada boatyard upgrades, such as storage cradles, welding of metal stands and tie-downs, insurance companies have become more willing to provide coverage to yachts stored there.

Our first hurricane season in the Caribbean in 2000 was spent moored in Mt. Hartman Bay. There we met taxi driver Percy Glaud and his evangelist friend Norma Jeremiah. They took us to the Happy Hills Berean Church where CBSI was first introduced in Grenada. But it was not God's time. He needed to put His people in place and, through a devastating hurricane, work in the hearts of the Christian community. Hurricane Ivan not only destroyed most of the nutmeg trees, but also, from our perspective, flattened many denominational walls in Grenada. After the hurricane the people and churches came together, along with churches and people from neighboring islands and the world, to help in the recovery process. When we came to Grenada in December 2006, we could still see blue tarps on many roofs and some damage to buildings, but we sensed a refreshing coming together of the Christian community.

God began putting the pieces into place for CBSI early in 2006. Area Director Brian Burke was seeking to find a Grenada contact person for a St. Vincent missions group wanting to do a youth project there in summer 2006. Through a friend in Youth for Christ, he was given the name and email address of Shane Joseph from the fishing village of Gouyave, who was active in youth ministries throughout the island. In May Brian flew to Grenada to meet Shane to lay the groundwork for the mission trip. To quote Brian, they formed an "everlasting bond." As they talked about their ministry passions, Brian mentioned CBSI and how God was using it in SVG and around the eastern Caribbean. Shane expressed interest for Grenada.

It just so happened when Brian returned that summer that he met Joachim Phillip, Associate Pastor at Market Hill Evangelistic Center. Little did Brian or Joachim realize it, but this would not be the last time they would meet in a ministry advancing the Kingdom of God. After that summer Brian remained in contact with Shane, who offered to coordinate a CBSI introduction to the heads of the denominations in Grenada. Chuck and Brian emailed Shane a detailed letter for distribution about the CBSI process and the possibility of an introduction meeting in early December of 2006. During this planning stage we were shepherding classes in St. Lucia, where both Teaching Leaders, Rev. Cleatus Henry and Rev. Wally Dantes, recommended contacting Rev. Alfred Horsford, the Grenada Moderator of the Evangelical Church in the West Indies. Chuck called Rev. Horsford, who expressed interest in learning more about CBSI and offered the church in Springs as a venue for the introduction.

On November 30, 2006, we set sail south for the Isle of Spice, anchoring in Prickly Bay on the southwestern coast. We continued to make contact with pastors on Grenada, meeting as many as we could face-to-face and encouraging them to attend the CBSI presentation. On December 5 Brian Burke arrived from SVG at Grenada's Maurice Bishop International Airport and joined us in Springs for the 10 a.m. CBSI presentation. The turnout was small—five or six pastors—but there was solid interest for leadership training early 2007. We had learned the lesson of Zechariah 4:10, *"to not despise the day of small things."* Seeds were planted. Besides, this was Micki's present from the Lord, since it was held on her birthday, December 5! Chuck made this known, and they honored her in song with their spirited version of Happy Birthday. Afterward we celebrated at lunch with Brian and special cruising friends, Gary and Sharon Simmers from sailing vessel Elusive. Excited about the interest, we sent out a *coram Deo* online requesting prayer for God to identify leaders of His choosing for training in February. Little did we know the extent of God's plans for Grenada.

With only one week before our flight home for Christmas, a decision needed to be made as to where *coram Deo* would be stored for our six-week absence. After visiting a few marinas by taxi, we decided on Clarkes Court Bay Marina. We motor-sailed into the mild east winds and seas along the beautiful southern coast, passing Mt. Hartman Bay and Hog Island before turning into the marked channel of Clarkes Court Bay, securing *coram Deo* in the marina. We loved its location in the countryside, where one awakes to the singing of birds and the bleating of sheep and goats. On our morning walks through the hilly open countryside, we would come upon pigs wallowing in mud holes, cows or horses grazing or a big ole bull lying under a shade tree chewing his cud. One morning a little colt approached Micki and allowed her to give him a pet on the head—a true Kodak moment!

While home for Christmas and in North Carolina for a CBSI Leadership Conference, Chuck stayed in contact with the pastors from the introduction meeting. Upon our return January 29, 2007, three leadership teams were committed for training. Pastor Lauriston Hosten from Praise and Deliverance Sanctuary International in Victoria on the northwest coast and Pastor Charles Douglas from the same denomination in Tempe, outside the capital, sent the names of their leadership teams. Bishop Christopher Baker, sharp and highly motivated pastor of Market Hill Evangelistic Center in St. George's, was interested in CBSI for his large and vibrant congregation. He was off island for the December meeting but wanted to learn more about CBSI. So on February 1 we met at his office and went through the PowerPoint presentation. Without hesitation he committed to identify a leadership team for the training seminar, saying it was a great program for his youthful Associate Pastor, Joachim Phillip, who has the gift of teaching. This was the same young man Brian had met the previous summer. Furthermore, Bishop Baker offered his facility for the four-session seminar. To accommodate the schedules of the trainees, three sessions would be held in the evenings and the fourth on Saturday morning. We sent out specific prayer requests for commitment of those being trained and for us to be effective communicators. Our prayer partners joined us in prayer. Thirteen delightful and attentive leaders were prepared to lead in three soon-to-be classes in Grenada. God answered. *"The prayer of a righteous man is powerful and effective." (James 5:16)*

As in St. Lucia two years prior, there would be three CBSI classes starting within one week! The day after the final training session, the Tempe class held its first Leaders Council. Up to then this church had been meeting in a home. They now rented a spacious room above the old Tempe Post Office, and the Leaders Council was the first meeting to be held in this venue. Grateful for God's provision, the leadership prayed that as people passed by the building on a daily basis, they would associate it with Bible study and the Praise and Deliverance Church. But the class was not the only birth this team anticipated. Not wanting to miss the first meeting, Discussion Leader Jason Douglas brought his pregnant wife, Doris, due any day. Later that night Doris gave birth to their first child, a son Jeshua!

In the late afternoon three days later, we attended the Victoria Leaders Council in St. George's rather than in their village more than an hour north. It was for our convenience since at 7 p.m. we needed to be at the Tempe class opening just outside of St. George's. The Victoria Teaching Leader Lauriston Hosten, a water works engineering manager, secured an office in one of the government buildings for the meeting. Only two leaders were needed for this group, so we met with Lauriston and his wife, Pansy, who would be the Discussion Leader. A gifted schoolteacher, Pansy was thrilled with the study materials, and both were eager for their class on Thursday. Since there was no lesson to discuss, we answered their questions and talked through the somewhat different format of the first class. By 6:45 p.m. we were in a taxi headed for Tempe.

The first CBSI class in Grenada was born February 21, 2007, in Tempe under the leadership of Teaching Leader Mikey Patterson. In view of the small congregation, the leaders were delighted with the attendance of 16 adults and children—even with the little family of

Jason Douglas missing! We presented CBSI, giving a brief history, especially that of the work in the Eastern Caribbean, then focused on the life transforming CBSI process and its benefits. Mikey, a banker with a Bible school diploma, gave a thorough, practical overview of 1 John with interesting personal illustrations. Clearly, he had invested time in his preparation. Word of mouth brought three intellectually sharp young men from the community the following week, eager to interact with others in Bible study.

On the following night, February 22, 2007, CBSI-Victoria was born under the leadership of Pastor Lauriston Hosten. Victoria is about 15 miles up the western coast of this 21-mile long island. It is an hour's drive or more depending on traffic to get there from Clarkes Court Bay on the south coast. The drive up the west coastline of Grenada is gorgeous, lush and green with small waterfalls cascading down rocks and small streams beside the road or in valleys below. While we ran out of daylight before nearing Victoria, the 15 men, women and teens who attended this first class were bright and friendly. The variety in ages pleasantly surprised us. They were already prepared for growth with a Class Coordinator and a Discussion Leader-in-training. We presented the CBSI history and process to the class. Teaching Leader Lauriston expressed his excitement for this new Bible study process before giving his brief but inviting overview. Afterward there was a time of fellowship with refreshments, and all happily posed for photos of this historic CBSI night.

Because of our unfamiliarity with Grenada and the fact that we were out in the countryside, we hired taxi driver, David Bartholomew, who lived nearby the marina. Dave had transported us to all the training sessions and Leaders Councils in Tempe and St. George's and told his wife, Yvonne, about us and what he knew of our work. Being a Christian, she wanted to meet us and learn more about what we were doing. So when Dave drove to the Victoria class, Yvonne joined us, and we happily answered all her questions about our ministry. When we arrived at class, Yvonne came into the church and listened to the presentation. On the drive home she was eager for us to contact her pastor, Paul Alexander, so she wrote out his cell number and encouraged us to call him. *Isn't that just like the Father!*

In the everyday routines of life—like the hiring of a taxi driver—God arranges divine appointments.

The following week Market Hill held their first Leaders Council. Teaching Leader Joachim Phillip led the most impressive first Leaders Council we had seen in our seven years! It was his grasp of the importance of Bible study in a believer's life, the consistency necessary to build that habit and his challenge for commitment that was so outstanding. He emphasized that for the next seven weeks Leaders Council would meet, and the class would meet. There would be no breaks, and all leaders would be expected to attend. In looking at a calendar, a leader noticed that one of the Leaders Council dates was on a holiday. Joachim then led a discussion of their options until they reached an agreement on an alternate day and time so class would not be interrupted. There was one comment he made that we have shared with many leadership teams because it speaks so loudly to the people of the Caribbean. He said, "Satan doesn't get excited when we Christians start a new thing." He paused, "It's when we stay with it for the long haul, week after week, month after month, year after year." This is exactly what we had experienced on many of the Eastern Caribbean islands! Many churches or people get excited and jump on the CBSI bandwagon... for a while. When the excitement and newness wear off and class becomes routine, people fall away, looking for the next exciting thing. Therein lies the vital importance of consistent, ongoing shepherding of group members by Discussion Leaders. We could not wait to see how this mature, respected, gifted 28-year-old leader would handle the class!

CBSI-Market Hill was born on February 28, 2007, under the leadership of Teaching Leader Joachim Phillip. Because this is a large, dynamic and well educated congregation, it was not surprising that more than 60 people attended the start-up. After Chuck's introduction of CBSI, Joachim did a remarkable job with a clear, compelling overview teaching. In conclusion he challenged class members to commit to the six-week study, complete their lessons and participate in discussion so the Word of God could transform their lives. The following week more than 70 attended!

Micki missed all this because the Victoria class met on the same night, and it was important for us to shepherd all classes. Here and in St. Lucia it was necessary at times for us to split up to visit two classes on the same night. So once Dave dropped off Chuck in St. Georges, he and Micki continued up the coast to Victoria's second class meeting. What an encouraging visit for Micki! Pansy Hosten was a model discussion leader, lovingly drawing answers out of the timid. For those who had not understood a question, she patiently took the time for them to open their Bibles, read the Scripture passage and the question, and help them come up with an answer. Understanding that this was a completely new way of Bible study, she took the time to train them on how to do it. Seeing this nurturing Discussion Leader in action made the long trip worth every minute. It had taken almost two hours that night for the trip because a tractor-trailer hauling a huge excavator broke down, blocking the narrow and curving mountain road.

The next morning, March 1, 2007, after spending all of February in Grenada, we set sail for St. Lucia, 150 nautical miles north to replace *coram Deo's* generator. We hoisted the mainsail and headed out the channel, only to be blasted with high winds and seas right on the nose! Beating our way through the heavy conditions, we finally got into the lee of Grenada where the wind and seas were tamer. We then enjoyed a comfortable sail, making over seven knots in 18-22 knot southeasterly winds. That was until we neared the northern tip of Grenada! High winds now north of east and matching high seas gave us a rough ride on our way to Tyrrel Bay, Carriacou.

The next morning we were off to Bequia to spend one night before the 72-nautical mile sail north to St. Lucia. Eager to get under way for Rodney Bay, we hauled anchor at 5:45 a.m., sailing out with 20-25 knot winds and six to eight foot seas, both higher than predicted, but the ESE wind direction was great. The first squall hit us within an hour, packing 30-32 knot winds. Our sail set was good, so we were prepared. *Coram Deo* loved it, reaching her all-time high speed of 9.9 knots!

We had too much sail up when the second squall surprised us at the south end of St. Lucia with angry gray-green clouds and 30-38 knot winds. To protect the sails and rigging, we had to run, so Chuck turned off course, taking the winds on the stern quarter, surfing at speeds of over 9 knots. It drove us miles away from the island! But we were dry, and all the sails and rigging were intact.

By 4:30 p.m. we were at the dock at Rodney Bay Marina, ready for the scheduled work the next day. As can be expected in the islands, the mechanic was not ready to begin our project. Once started, the four- to five-day job took ten days. In fairness, it was a difficult task. There was no easy way to get the large, heavy Westerbeke out of the engine room and on deck. First, all the accessories were removed. Then it took five "human forklifts" to manhandle the monster from the rear of the engine room over the Volvo engine, through the narrow passageway and up from below decks through the companionway. With the extra days on island we visited the seven classes and Leaders Councils spread across St. Lucia as well as helped the pilot class at Laborie Pentecostal get back on track with additional leadership training.

Finally we set sail back to Grenada, arriving on April 24, 2007, in time for the next night's Market Hill class. Eighty members in four large discussion groups were wrestling with the meaning of "worldly living" from their 1 John 2:12-17 lesson questions. What does it mean at home? In the workplace? In the church? There is no greater blessing than to provide a means for men and women not just to gain Bible knowledge but come to maturity through understanding how to apply that knowledge to their personal lives. *"Sanctify them by the truth; Your word is truth." (John 17:17)*

Having been in contact with Pastor Paul Alexander of Woodlands New Testament Church, whom we met through our taxi driver Dave's wife Yvonne, we met to discuss CBSI. In the worship service at his church the next Sunday, he called on Chuck to explain the CBSI process briefly to the congregation. Since we were due in Trinidad in a little over a week, plans were made for Area Director Brian Burke to fly into Grenada mid-June to train Pastor Paul's leadership team. First he would need to identify his leaders and plan

CBSI into his church calendar, providing Brian with the names of the leaders and a class start-up date. Our brief time in Grenada also allowed us to shepherd the CBSI Tempe Leaders Council and class, which was studying and being challenged in James. Though this class remained small, the Word was sanctifying the participants.

Setting sail from Grenada on May 3, 2007, we headed south to Trinidad to visit the four classes and Leaders Councils there. After two weeks and having visited all four classes, we sailed north, this time bypassing Grenada. We would spend the next six months shepherding the leaders and classes in SVG, Martinique, Dominica, Antigua and St. Lucia. With visits to the 16 classes on those five islands, we would log more than 900 miles before returning to Grenada in November.

On the sail south to Grenada, our single-side band radio, which we depend on for daily weather reports, stopped working. A cruising friend recommended a technician in Carriacou, just north of Grenada. Therefore, we sailed into the capital of Hillsborough, anchored and hired a taxi for the trip up the coast to the technician. On the way the driver began talking about his love for the Lord, and we smiled at each other in the back seat, happy that he was taking the opportunity to evangelize these heathen sailors! We told him that we, too, loved the Lord and were missionaries in the Caribbean helping people with Bible study, telling him a little about CBSI. After dropping off the radio, he said he wanted us to meet his pastor and drove us to the local radio station where Bishop George Guy was preparing for a broadcast. At his invitation we met him at the church office the next morning and using the PowerPoint presentation on our laptop introduced Bishop Guy to CBSI. He was interested in cell group ministry and saw how the CBSI process fit into his plans. We then learned that his church, Glad Tidings Pentecostal, is affiliated with Market Hill Evangelistic Center in Grenada. We told him about the class there and suggested he talk to Bishop Baker about CBSI. As for our radio, nothing was wrong with it. A fiber optic cable was misaligned—though it had never been touched. This was just another God ordained divine appointment for CBSI. *Isn't that just like the Father!*

Sailing from Carriacou, we arrived back at Clarkes Court Bay Marina on November 23, 2007, with only two weeks on island before flying home for Christmas. We packed our time, visiting Leaders Councils and classes in Tempe, Victoria and Market Hill, and we made a CBSI introduction.

When we visited the Market Hill class, Teaching Leader Joachim asked Micki to fill in for a Discussion Leader who was running late. Micki loved it! The women were accepting, open and talkative. We continued to grow in appreciation for Joachim. Beginning with his passion for the Bible, he loves the CBSI process and what it is doing in his life and those in his class. He shares CBSI with any who will listen and makes no apologies. He knows that CBSI can help all believers grow in their relationship with Christ and is striving to spread it across Grenada. He had shared CBSI with his friend, Pastor Royston Isaac of Grand Anse Baptist Church, who expressed sincere interest. Joachim also wanted to share CBSI with other pastors, so he had contacted us before our arrival about a CBSI presentation at Pastor Isaac's church. We agreed and November 29 presented CBSI to pastors and Christian leaders from six churches. We made the basic presentation, but it was Joachim's passionate testimony of how his life and the lives of those in the Market Hill class were being transformed through the process of CBSI that caused an overwhelming commitment. Leadership training for four CBSI teams was scheduled for February 2, 4 and 5, 2008. *Isn't that just like the Father!*

With December upon us, we stored *coram Deo* at Clarkes Court Bay Marina and returned home for Christmas and the CBS Teaching Directors Conference end of January.

Arriving back in Grenada on January 30, 2008, we hit the ground running! With much interest and leadership training scheduled to begin in three days, we expected opposition from the enemy! Sure enough, we had dead house batteries aboard *coram Deo*. That unrelenting enemy, though defeated by Jesus Christ as He rose from the grave, never gives up. Shore power gave us electricity until the new batteries we ordered would be delivered. While Chuck dealt with the power problem, Micki unpacked. That gave us one day to make our final preparations for the three-day training.

Thirty-two persons attended the six and a half hour seminar at Market Hill Evangelistic Center on Saturday. Not all were new to CBSI. Many leaders from the three existing classes came for refresher training. After leading for even a short time, the refresher training was appreciated, as it helped them become more effective leaders and shepherds.

The morning session covered a thorough explanation of the CBSI process, the responsibilities of all leadership roles and focused on the role of the Class Coordinator. After lunch the two and a half hour session concentrated on the vital role of the Discussion Leader in facilitating an effective discussion group and consistent shepherding responsibilities. The Monday and Tuesday evening sessions were for Teaching Leaders and Associate Teaching Leaders only, emphasizing their dual responsibilities to lead and teach and an interactive training on the eight-step process of teaching preparation.

Holding these training sessions immediately upon our return was possible only because of Teaching Leader Joachim Phillip and his efficient Class Coordinator, Vanessa Smith. Both are highly committed to CBSI because of its benefits in their own lives. Pastor Joachim willingly accepted the assignment of part of the first training session. Knowing his capabilities to do future trainings, we wanted Grenada leaders to see him as part of the training team. Vanessa is able, organized and energetic in making things happen! She coordinated the venue and lunch, helped in contacting all the participants, printed nametags and handled registration. As a result, three new CBSI classes began in New Hampshire, Calliste and Vincennes, areas surrounding St. George's. Joachim, with Vanessa's support, committed to help launch these new classes, shepherd them as well as the three existing classes and train additional leadership teams. These classes were birthed and continue because of their capable and committed support.

CBSI Vincennes was born on February 19, 2008, under the leadership of Teaching Leader Judith Lett. CBSI-New Hampshire came into being on February 22 under the leadership of Teaching Leader Phillip Baptiste. CBSI Calliste began on March 5 under the leadership of Teaching Leader Joel Webbe.

Once the training was behind us and we could catch our breath, Chuck turned to enlisting help to remove the dead but very heavy batteries and install the four newly arrived 4Ds at 130 pounds each. Sean Thomas, who lived nearby and did boat cleaning for us back in 2000, helped not only with the batteries but with exterior varnishing, polishing of stainless, driving us on errands and providing vegetables from his garden. In a *coram Deo* online we requested prayer that we would be effective witnesses of God's love to Sean, a hardworking, likeable young man who had suffered a tough upbringing and a failed marriage. It would not be too long before God answered. While He worked in Sean's life and the developing CBSI classes in Grenada, we sailed north to St. Lucia on February 20, 2008, for five weeks of shepherding the seven classes there.

April 9, 2008, we once more sailed into Clarkes Court Bay, Grenada, docking at the marina, which by then had become comfortable and familiar. Within two days we were involved in a whirlwind of visiting six of the eight Leaders Councils and/or classes meeting in New Hampshire, Market Hill, Vincennes, Woodlands (trained by Area Director Brian Burke) and Calliste. After a class visitation we would meet and shepherd each Teaching Leader. In our absence Joachim had trained the leadership team of Grand Anse Baptist Church, and God blessed us with the privilege of attending their first class. CBSI-Grand Anse was born on April 17, 2008, under the leadership of Teaching Leader Paul Lewis. What a beautiful and humbling gift to see the evidence of training well done by Joachim Phillip.

The creativity and caring of the leadership team in the Vincennes class was something we would share with other classes. Teaching Leader Judith Lett and her team realized their members were struggling in doing their lessons. They came up with the idea of "study groups" at the beginning of each class session. Members would meet in their discussion groups, and the Discussion Leader would lead them by reading the home study question and the appropriate Scripture passage and then encourage all to share possible answers aloud, some giving part of an answer, another completing it. Then each would write down what he felt was an answer to the question. After a prescribed time, persons from each group were chosen to sit in the large discussion group circle and participate in discussing the lesson. All others sat outside the circle to listen, watch and learn. The teaching would follow with Judith's outline projected for all to see and follow. This was their format for the first six-week study. The leaders saw growth in more members preparing their lessons ahead of time and wanting to participate in the discussion. So with the start of the second study, the regular CBSI format was followed. During this time their membership grew to more than 40 persons studying God's Word as never before.

Two and a half weeks later in the wee hours of the morning, we sailed south to Trinidad for an historic meeting. It was there, May 2-4, 2008, that CBSI Caribbean Inc. was formed. God's faithfulness came to fruition then as the Caribbean leadership took over the helm of the ministry. Over the preceding year and a half Joachim Phillip had developed into the prototype of a National Coordinator as he shepherded existing classes, trained and encouraged leaders and introduced CBSI to his friends and colleagues across Grenada. He attended the Trinidad gathering as an appointed representative for his country, but he, more than any other representative, understood what God was calling him to do with CBSI in his country. Even though he was the newest leader present at the historic meeting, we were not surprised when he was elected to the CBSI Caribbean Inc. Board of Directors as Director at Large.

When we sailed back into Grenada on June 1, 2008, it was for Joachim's continued development. The assignment could not have been easier or more rewarding! We visited classes with him, encouraging him to comment carefully on the components, but he was already an encourager. We observed how sincerely and lovingly he shepherded the leaders. Together we discussed methodologies and strategies to strengthen and expand CBSI in Grenada and elsewhere. As we worked closely, getting to know him on a more personal level, it became clear that God has anointed this committed pastor/teacher with a unique ability to lead and teach others. *"And the things you have heard me say in the presence of many witnesses entrust to reliable men who will also be qualified to teach others." (2 Timothy 2:2)*

God had one more encouragement before we stored *coram Deo* at Clarkes Court Bay Marina for part of hurricane season 2008. Sean Thomas, our boat worker, had become a special friend. We would walk to his house from the marina to visit and spend time talking and enjoying each other's company. Arrangements had been made with Joachim to visit the Grand Anse class together, and we hired Sean to drive us, picking up Joachim on the way. We invited Sean to stay for the class to see what we do as missionaries. He knew some of the men and seemed to enjoy it. Wanting to worship there on Sunday, we asked Sean if he would drive us. He agreed, and when he arrived at the marina on Sunday morning, he was dressed up. We asked if he was going somewhere after dropping us off, and he said no, he was staying for service. It was a moving service and, talking later, we both felt the message was speaking directly to Sean, but we did not want to look his way or put any pressure on him. Toward the end of the service, when Pastor Isaac invited people to step forward to accept the love of Jesus Christ, a few people did. While we were praying for him, Sean leaned over to Chuck and asked, "Should I go up?" Chuck answered, "Only if you want to. This is between you and God." As we continued praying, we did not see him slip out of the pew, but when we looked up from our personal prayer, there was Pastor Isaac with his arm around Sean's shoulder leading him in prayer. So on June 8, 2008, in Grenada it was not a CBSI class or a human baby born, but more importantly Sean Thomas was born again!

Four months earlier a prayer request was sent to our prayer partners that we would be effective witnesses of God's love to Sean.

God did it. And He blessed us with being there to see with our own eyes. *Isn't that just like the Father!*

    "LORD,…all that we have accomplished You have done for us." *(Isaiah 26:12)* To God be the glory!

Leadership training in Grenada led by Micki.

St. George's, Grenada, class at Market Hill Evangelistic Center with five groups discussing their lesson.

**Grenada annual leadership workshop led by National
Coordinator Rev. Joachim Phillip.**

**(l to r) Our boat maintenance worker, Sean Thomas, Pastor
Isaac of Grand Anse Baptist Church and TL Paul Lewis after
Sean made a commitment to follow Christ.**

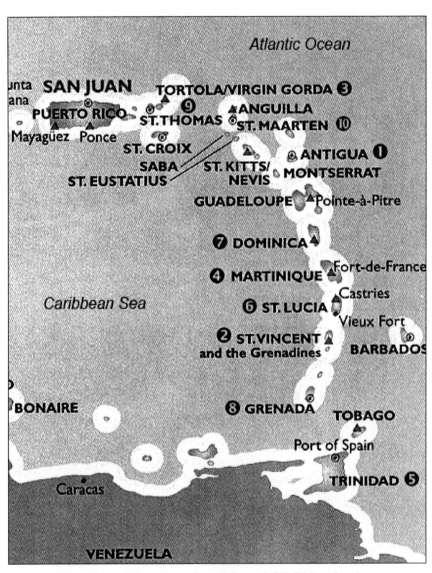

Numbers represent the order of CBSI beginning
in each country.

12

Coming Together

*"And let us consider how we may spur one another
on toward love and good deeds. Let us not give up meeting
together, as some are in the habit of doing,
but let us encourage one another—and all the more
as you see the Day approaching."
(Hebrews 10:24-25)*

As early as June of 2002, with three CBSI interdenominational classes spread 400 miles apart across the Eastern Caribbean, we began planning for the leadership teams to come together. It would be an opportunity to give them additional training, share their experiences about what was or was not working, love them, encourage them and let them know they were not alone. Coming together they would realize that their calling is not from us or their pastor or a friend, but from Jesus Christ and, thus, has eternal value! *"You did not choose me, but I chose you and appointed you to go and bear fruit—fruit that will last." (John 15:16)*

Having taught in-depth Bible study ourselves, we know the value of coming together with people involved in the same ministry who can identify or empathize with the stresses, struggles and time constraints that a CBSI commitment demands. In CBS the Teaching Directors Conferences and regional conferences serve this vital purpose. So we discussed the idea with CBSI Director Damon Martinez, who gave his wholehearted support. We emailed the idea of an Eastern Caribbean CBSI Conference to the three Teaching Leaders who responded positively and felt all their leaders would want to participate. The planning began.

CBSI Caribbean Leaders Workshop, August 21-24, 2003
Preparation for this Workshop took an entire year. Based on input from the Teaching Leaders of the three classes, we decided to hold it in August. It would be an encouragement before classes began, and, since that was hurricane season, hotel costs would be more reasonable. By December of 2002 announcements were made through emails and at Leaders Councils encouraging people to begin planning for the time and the finances. Knowing the financial situation of most of the leaders, we began soliciting scholarships for room and board through our *coram Deo* online, even before knowing the needed amount.

In March of 2003 we announced the confirmed details. The workshop would take place August 21-24 at the Jolly Beach Resort in Antigua. All inclusive double occupancy hotel accommodations and airport transfers totaled U.S. $210. In every *coram Deo* online from then until the event, we asked our partners to pray about donating funds for scholarships so that every leader could participate. On the other hand, we wanted the leaders to value this opportunity so each would be responsible for his transportation cost. Teaching Leaders made announcements to their classes, asking for extra contributions to help with airfares for their leaders. Trusting God for the finances, we began planning the agenda and preparing each session. Everything needed to be bathed in prayer, so we sent out prayer requests bi-weekly. An unexpected gift was when Bill and Judy Scott, small group leaders and dear friends from our home church, Woodside Bible, volunteered to join us in Antigua and help with the details during the workshop. Looking back at that time of planning this first-ever workshop, shepherding three new classes spread across the Caribbean and pioneering CBSI, all at the same time, we see one thing clearly—God did it! ***"The One who calls you is faithful and He will do it."*** *(1 Thessalonians 5:24)*

On August 21, a sunny humid day, 30 Caribbean leaders from six classes in Antigua, St. Vincent and Tortola as well as a pilot class from Barbados gathered at the Jolly Beach Resort. During the planning year the number of classes doubled! All leadership roles were represented—Teaching Leaders, Associate Teaching Leaders, Class Coordinators and Discussion Leaders. After dinner the first night Chuck gave an inspiring teaching on servant leadership from John 13:1-17. Then, wrapping a towel around his waist and with Micki accompanying him with a container of water, he moved around the circle of seated leaders, stooping to wash the feet of every person including Micki's. Then, to our surprise, CBSI Executive Director Damon Martinez walked over to Chuck, asking him to be seated. Damon then washed Chuck's feet. Chuck stood and repeated the words of Jesus, *"Now that you know these things, you will be blessed if you do them." (John 13:17)* The tone was dramatically set!

Our goal was for the leaders to leave encouraged and motivated with added leadership skills. More importantly, that all would return to their classes with servants' hearts to serve one another and class members humbly and lovingly. That's what shepherding is—serving. The titles for every session began with "Servants Blessed"—in Developing Leaders...by Proper Priorities...by Discussion Effectiveness...by Proper Preparation for class start-up and so on. For morning devotions each leader was given "Evaluation of a Servant of God," three pages of Scripture bringing out the attributes, requirements, goals and visible results of God's servants. Sister Esmie Potter, Tortola Associate Teaching Leader, said this was the most challenging for her.

Director Martinez shared the CBSI world vision, enlarging participants' view of the ministry. Bill and Judy Scott served humbly and perceptively with love, taking care of the needs of all in attendance. Bill was especially busy on arrival and departure days, making numerous trips in a rented van to and from the airport, even learning the shortcuts! Teaching Leaders and Associate Teaching Leaders arrived a day early for sessions on developing their teaching skills. All learned more about their specific leadership roles from breakout sessions throughout the workshop.

God faithfully provided for every need through people prompted to help in many different ways. Every leader was covered by a scholarship for accommodations through contributions of prayer partners, our Faithful Friends AFG and Woodside Bible Church. One contributor provided for the entire five-person SVG Kingstown leadership team! With the workshop venue in Antigua, the Antiguan leaders would be attending at no cost. Learning the need of some leaders, Teaching Leader Ted Martin remembered the story in 2 Samuel 24:24 of King David and the threshing floor in their recent Servants of God study. King David said, *"No, I insist on paying you for it. I will not sacrifice to the LORD my God burnt offerings that cost me nothing."* When he shared this with his leadership and class, they donated the funds, making it possible for some Vincentian leaders, who otherwise would have missed the blessing of the workshop, to attend. SVG Discussion Leader Annette Martin-Kennedy made and sold craft items to help cover her own transportation cost. The Rochester, Michigan CBS class donated binders for every leader. A friend from our home church, Jerry Prest, donated highlighters. Bruce Harris, a newly born again Antigua class member whom we met in the Jolly Harbour Boatyard, borrowed a pickup truck to help Bill Scott transport people and luggage to and from the airport. The rental car company and Jolly Harbour Marina, where *coram Deo* was docked, both got into the spirit by reducing our daily rates. *"And my God will meet all your needs according to His glorious riches in Christ Jesus."* (Philippians 4:19) Isn't that just like the Father!

Damon Martinez stayed over an extra day for debriefing, agreeing with us that the workshop was a huge success. He encouraged us to consider future workshops, not necessarily for all leadership roles but, as in CBS, for Teaching Leaders only. Exhausted, we could not think about planning another event! But we did tell him that we would consider this when we were rested. The fruit of this workshop was immediately seen in attitude and class growth as we continued shepherding classes.

Acts in August Conference, August 4-8, 2004

With two Martinique classes launched end of 2003 and a number of prayer groups meeting in Trinidad expected to result in a number of classes early 2004, we began considering Damon's suggestion. These new Teaching Leaders and Associate Teaching Leaders would benefit from additional training and coming together in sharing their experiences. Also, they would gain in skill if taught leadership and teaching preparation from a perspective other than ours. So we called our friend Dr. Bruce Fong, asking if he would be interested and available to help us out the following August. He had been well received in St. Vincent in 2001 and after checking his schedule said he would love to return to the Caribbean. Since most Eastern Caribbean classes would be studying the Acts of the Apostles, we asked Dr. Fong to point out the overall message of Acts but focus on how to approach teaching the weekly lessons. Prayer requests went out to our prayer partners for Dr. Fong and for us in the hope that in all details the conference would take these CBSI leaders to the next level in their teaching skills.

Official announcements went out by March for the "Acts in August Conference" for all CBSI Teaching Leaders and Associate Teaching Leaders to be held in Trinidad August 4-8, 2004, at Anapausis. Subesh and Debbie Ramjattan, friends and trained CBSI Teaching Leaders, own this private conference center and were excited to host the event. Again we asked for prayer for scholarships—this time U.S. $200 per leader—to cover room, board and transfers for the five-day conference.

Having flown back to the States in May to attend family celebrations, we had stored *coram Deo* at Rodney Bay Marina in St. Lucia. Early July of 2004 we returned and in less than a week began island hopping south to Trinidad to complete the details for the conference. At the end of a gorgeous day sail from St. Lucia to St. Vincent, we tied to one of Charley Tango's mooring balls in Young Island Cut and made contact with Teaching Leaders Brian Burke and Alwyn Joseph. The next morning we went on deck to sail out and found we had been robbed! While we slept directly below in the aft cabin, thieves boarded *coram Deo* and lowered our dinghy with its outboard, cranking it down from its storage davits. Since it was raining, all hatches were closed. Micki had heard a noise about 11 p.m., but when Chuck looked out, he didn't see anyone. Had he caught them in the act, it could have gone badly, so we thanked the Lord for His protection. Charley Tango took Chuck to the local police station, where we were given little hope of recovering the dinghy. We stayed long enough to file the police report for insurance purposes, leaving Brian Burke's phone number with the police.

Immediately we sent out a prayer request that we would not be unduly distracted from our upcoming conference preparation. Having spent much time in SVG and never experiencing this kind of problem, it was obviously an enemy attack to distract. With most of the day gone, we made the short seven-mile sail south across the Bequia Channel and anchored, prepositioning *coram Deo* for the longer sail the following day. As we sailed out the next morning, rounding the West Cay, a gust of wind ripped our mainsail! This confirmed that the enemy was out to discourage, but we chose to praise God. A new sail was already on order in Trinidad to be installed after the conference! Chuck shortened the sail, flying only the part above the tear, and we continued south to Union Island, where we anchored and enjoyed a quiet, star-filled night. The next morning we sailed south to Grenada before making the uneventful crossing to Trinidad, arriving ahead of schedule. God blessed us with two days in gorgeous Scotland Bay, away from the busyness of Chaguaramas, serenaded by singing birds, chirping crickets and the roar of howler monkeys. When we moved into Crews Inn Marina, *it just so happened* that we tied up on a finger dock directly across from a born again Christian family! Bob, Lona and teen-aged sons Rob and Michael had just completed a six-year circumnavigation of the world, handing out Bibles along the way. We sat on deck that night talking to them about things of God. *Isn't that just like the Father!* We were not one bit discouraged but more encouraged than ever. Take that, devil!

With the conference only two weeks away, we worked on covering the details. Our conference banner needed to be redone with the Acts in August theme. After asking around we contacted Steve, a talented local former tattoo artist with a powerful Christian testimony. He did a beautiful job on the banner and made logo labels for the nametags, all as a gift to the ministry, after learning that CBSI is about the Word. He was saved through the written Word. A customer had called asking Steve to tattoo Leviticus 19:28 on his arm. Steve's wife had started going to church, and he had recently bought her a Bible. Curious about the customer's request, he opened the Bible and read *"Do not cut your bodies for the dead or put tattoo marks on yourself. I am the Lord."* (*Leviticus 19:28*) He immediately knew he was doing wrong but didn't know what to do. The next day not one client came into his studio. He began going to church with his wife and reading the Bible. In time he closed his shop, dumping his tattoo inks down the sink at $100 per bottle! Steve became the Lord's man because of reading God's Word.

On August 4, 2004, the Acts in August Conference began with an outpouring of praise to the Lord through song and prayer. God threw open the floodgates of heaven and poured out His blessings on 28 Teaching Leaders and Associate Teaching Leaders from 15 established classes and three pilot classes on six islands! One year previously 30 leaders had gathered in Antigua representing all leadership roles. The number of classes had more than doubled!

Again through our prayer partners God provided, but this time above and beyond what we needed for scholarships because He knew our expenses would be more than anticipated. One was added airport transfers. Due to a tropical depression, typical during the summer hurricane season, flights were off schedule. A canceled flight postponed the arrival of CBSI Director Damon Martinez. The SVG airport was flooded and closed, holding back three leaders from the first day of the conference. When the airport re-opened that evening and all the stranded travelers attempted to get out of SVG, Teaching Leader Alwyn Joseph said he did not know how all three got seats on the first outgoing flight to Trinidad. But Esmie Potter, Tortola Associate Teaching Leader, told them how. She did not want to arrive in Trinidad alone at night, so she asked the Lord to give her a familiar face on the flight. As her flight made a stopover in SVG, on came not one but three familiar faces from CBSI! She laughed, saying their misfortune was her blessing. *"And my God will meet all your needs according to His glorious riches in Christ Jesus."* *(Philippians 4:19)*

Dr. Fong, empowered by the Holy Spirit, clearly explained and demonstrated the homiletical process of Bible teaching, giving many opportunities for group participation. He graciously encouraged and constructively critiqued the presentations made by participants. We didn't anticipate all the ramifications of our first bilingual conference. We had provided microphones and headsets for translators and the six non-English speaking leaders, but we didn't think of the PowerPoint presentations. God did. Trinidad Teaching Leader Kimlin Philip, recognizing the problem for the French with the presentations, came to us the first day asking to enlist her friend from Guadeloupe (then living in Trinidad). She took a CD of Dr. Fong's PowerPoint presentations which the woman translated in time for the French speakers to take with them.

The conference was not all work. One afternoon two busloads of participants went to the beautiful Asa Wright Nature Preserve for a wonderful local lunch followed by either a guided tour or relaxation on the veranda watching the variety of hummingbirds.

All participants returned to their countries to hold national or individual Pre-Class Workshops for their leadership teams. Every leader left Trinidad better equipped to make disciples for Jesus Christ through their new teaching skills acquired at the conference.

2006 CBSI Caribbean Leaders Conference, August 9-13, 2006

In late 2005, with the ministry continuing to grow and mature, we began sharing more of the shepherding responsibilities with Area Directors Ian Macintyre (Virgin Islands), Felix Alexander (French West Indies) and Brian Burke (Windward Islands). Together we agreed another leadership conference for entire teams needed to be held in 2006 for the 20 active classes on six islands. All leadership roles needed additional training and encouragement. With the potential of 100 or more persons in attendance, this was a daunting task for two people on a boat to organize while still shepherding and pioneering! We sent out a *coram Deo* online asking for prayer for wisdom.

While in Michigan for our 2005 Christmas break, three dear friends volunteered as "conference staff" to assist in planning and implementation. All three had been part of our Bible study leadership team, and we worked well together. Heidi Lynn Holz had previous experience helping with the first class in Antigua. Jon and Dionne Wemple had met on our Bible study leadership team and later married. Jon, an engineer, was an excellent administrator, preparing things before we could even ask. Dionne, also an engineer and former Discussion Leader, is organized, excellent in everything she does and familiar with PowerPoint, a skill we could use for a breakout session. God knew we would need a dependable team on which to lean heavily. Not only did we have ministry responsibilities during the time of planning but Micki would need to help with her mom's medical needs. But God knew this. *"The One who calls you is faithful and He will do it."* (*1 Thessalonians 5:24*)

We prayed and sent out prayer requests regularly, and God did it. He put together the conference details working through our team. In February of 2006 the announcement went out for the CBSI Caribbean Leaders Conference to be held August 9-13, 2006, at the Jolly Beach Resort in Antigua. Dr. Doug Schmidt, our pastor and professor at Michigan Theological Seminary, agreed to be our main speaker and teacher for the Teaching Leaders and Associate Teaching Leaders. A variety of breakout sessions were planned, not only to be led by us but by Brian Burke and our conference staff. History would be made at this conference with the Children & Youth Ministry. Director Debbie Nilsen would train Children's Supervisors for established CBSI adult classes, assisted by Donna Gilbert and Linda Baber. CBSI would be represented by Stephen Hood of the CBSI Executive Leadership Team and Dr. Glenn Collard, then Regional Director for North and Central America and the Caribbean. When we were in Michigan in June of 2006, we met with Heidi, Jon and Dionne to firm up the many details. Philippians 4:6-7 became our watchwords. *"Do not be anxious about anything, but in everything, by prayer and petition, with thanksgiving, present your requests to God. And the peace of God, which transcends all understanding, will guard your hearts and minds in Christ Jesus."*

One week before the conference we were settled nicely at the dock in Jolly Harbour Marina when we had to turn from conference preparation to further securing *coram Deo*. Tropical Storm Chris was aimed at Antigua, packing 50 knot plus winds. We and our prayer warriors prayed. God provided. Just hours away, the storm moved north, missing all the Leeward Islands. Not anxious, not worrying, we continued in peace with our preparation, and three days before the conference our staff, our main speaker and the children's trainers began arriving.

The new conference banner was proudly displayed, announcing the 2006 Leadership Conference: Totally God. Totally Given. ***"Abram believed the Lord, and He credited it to him as righteousness." (Genesis 15:6)*** All that had been and would be accomplished was totally God! "How Great Is Our God" became the theme song of this conference. While singing, Tom Gamlin, our good friend from Faithful Friends AFG back home, walked in and videotaped part of the conference. He was visiting family in St. Martin and spontaneously flew to Antigua for a few hours, surprising us and recording a little of the greatness of God for our prayer team in Michigan!

Sixty-three leaders representing 20 classes on six islands praised our great God! Teaching Leader Hortensia Alvarez-Zepeda from Costa Rica also joined us. The total attendance was 81, including our conference staff, the speaker, CBSI Directors, C&Y trainers and spouses. Even though American Airlines neglected to provide a flight crew for one of Jon and Dionne's connections, they arrived in time for the first session. Heidi Lynn worked flawlessly greeting and registering all leaders.

Antiguan Ted Martin, the first Teaching Leader in the Caribbean, gave a penetrating challenge for an uncompromising commitment to God's call as CBSI leaders. Most classes would be studying the Pentateuch, so Dr. Doug Schmidt taught from six different lessons of that study with an overarching theme of "Mission Possible." Each teaching was followed by discussion with the Teaching Leaders and Associate Teaching Leaders, helping them analyze it. The challenge for them in this study would be putting together a 30-40 minute tcaching on long passages with up to 10 or more chapters! Afterward, one Teaching Leader commented that what she learned through the sessions was that the mission is possible!

Seven Children's Supervisors were trained. Their sessions seemed to be the most fun! A highlight on the Saturday afternoon was a moving commissioning service of these newly trained Children's Supervisors.

Jon Wemple led the session entitled The Class Coordinators Handiwork, modeling and teaching from Scripture this very important servant role—that of being "the hands" that serve. During the session Jon took an incredible photo of a circle of hands that serve—the hands of all the Class Coordinators in attendance. Though that picture sends a powerful message, what spoke loudest was the modeling by Jon and Dionne serving as conference "Class Coordinators"—never complaining, always smiling and making sure we had all we needed when we needed it. The Class Coordinators were taught powerfully by word and deed.

Brian Burke led a vibrant panel discussion on shepherding entitled How to Care so Your Group will Bear. Micki led an interactive session for Discussion Leaders, encouraging them to be creative and do whatever it takes to help their members study and apply Scripture. Special interest sessions were held by Dionne on basic PowerPoint and by Heidi on praise and worship planning, showing how the message of songs could underscore the week's teaching. The many testimonies on Sunday morning were greatly encouraging to us, to the speakers and to the staff. *"And my God will meet all your needs according to His glorious riches in Christ Jesus."* *(Philippians 4:19)*

CBSI Caribbean Incorporation May 2-4, 2008

From the inception of CBSI in the Eastern Caribbean, our goal was for it to become a Caribbean ministry, not an American ministry. Every CBSI introduction included the fact that this would be a Caribbean ministry. Our calling was to help the West Indians establish CBSI and become autonomous. This goal is in sync with that of CBSI in general, which is to develop national or indigenous ministries—self-determined, self-directed and self-funded.

With that in mind in 2003, we began inviting Brian Burke to introductions and training sessions. We saw his passion and potential and his teaching abilities, so gradually we involved him in presenting portions of meetings. In 2005 he became the first Caribbean leader to provide complete training for a new leadership team at St. Augustine, Trinidad. From there he flew to The Bahamas and represented CBSI Caribbean at CONECAR.

By 2007 CBSI in the Eastern Caribbean was burgeoning with growth, vitality and experienced, committed leaders who could be brought together to begin moving toward becoming a national ministry. We were nearing the eighth year of our ten-year commitment, and continuity of leadership was essential. While we had been struggling in prayer about the future of the ministry for years, God had been maturing the leaders He would entrust with the future of CBSI. So we began to develop a strategy which, the Lord willing, would result in a concrete leadership transition.

By this time there were eight CBSI Eastern Caribbean countries with about 30 active classes. Four countries, however, had only one class. None of the countries had enough active classes to justify or support a national ministry. Numerically, Caribbean countries represented more than a tenth of the CBSI countries in the world at the time. Yet the total population of the eight island nations was a miniscule 2 ¼ million, less than a thousandth of the population of CBSI nations worldwide. Clearly God had been faithful to His calling on our lives to introduce in-depth Bible study to the Caribbean. Most of these islands had populations the size of moderately large cities in other countries. The financial burden of a national ministry in each small, relatively poor country would be too great and result in the classes closing. Obviously then, this was not an option. In Zechariah 4:10, however, we are reminded not to judge God's work by human standards. *"Who despises the day of small things?"*

Therefore, in order to maintain and grow CBSI in the Eastern Caribbean as a "national ministry," the West Indians needed to develop a creative solution using the assets that God had provided to follow the spirit if not the letter of the policy. On the positive side, the islands are predominantly Christian in religion though nominal. God had faithfully lifted up committed leaders like Area Directors

Brian Burke, Ian Macintyre and Felix Alexander who were leading vibrant classes in several countries. The obstacles were the intrinsic physical separation of the eight CBSI countries, the poverty of many of the islands and time available for effective shepherding. Unlike their counterparts in other countries, the Eastern Caribbean Area Directors could not drive to most neighboring classes. For example, Brian Burke would need to fly to St. Lucia, Grenada or Trinidad. Even though less than 70 miles separates most islands, either a boat or a plane and at least two days are required to visit one class or Leaders Council. In pioneering the ministry we had the benefit of *coram Deo* as our transportation and housing as well as full time availability. We shepherded the leaders as we traveled by boat from island to island, keeping in contact by email, Skype and cell phone when unable to physically visit. In the future, shepherding would be entirely the responsibility of Caribbean ministry leaders with full time jobs and limited travel time or funding. Thus, effective shepherding would require a different approach.

Prayerfully, a steering committee was formed from the most experienced leaders available to develop and implement a solution to provide leadership continuity that would satisfy the CBSI requirement for a national ministry. The committee included Brian Burke from SVG, Ian Macintyre from Tortola, Joe Caterson from Trinidad and Chuck with Micki's support. Each person brought his unique preparation to this committee. Brian had become Area Director for the Caribbean at the appointment of Regional Director Dr. Glenn Collard, making him a member of the Regional Servants Team (RST). In this role Brian attends biannual RST meetings at various North American venues along with other RST members from Canada, Mexico and USA-Ethnos. This was providing Brian a wider view of CBSI activities in the region. Joe Caterson spent his secular career in management of the Trinidad and Tobago phone company and currently serves as secretary of The Association of Evangelical Bible Churches of Trinidad and Tobago. Ian, as a lawyer and legislative draftsman with experience in Trinidad and Tortola, was familiar with organizing an entity under the law governing organizations. Chuck, having owned a manufacturing business and been in Christian ministry leadership for many years, had wide-ranging experience.

After many phone and Skype conversations and meetings among the committee members, with input from CBSI Regional Director Dr. Glenn Collard and Executive Director Frank Vroegop, an organizational proposal was formulated to present to the leaders of the CBSI islands. All CBSI countries in non-Spanish speaking areas of the Caribbean would band together and be represented and recognized at a national level in CBSI through a single entity to be named CBSI Caribbean Inc. (CCI) Each CBSI island would be an Ordinary Member of CCI, represented by its National Coordinator. The National Coordinators would appoint a Board of Directors consisting of a President, a Vice-President, a Director at Large, a CBSI Caribbean Director, a Treasurer and a Secretary. The President, Vice-President and Director at Large would be National Coordinators. The CBSI Caribbean Director (CCD) would be the chief executive officer of CCI or CCI's version of a National Director. The National Coordinators would also appoint a Training Coordinator, Children & Youth Coordinator and Assistant Secretary who, together with the CCD, the Treasurer and the Secretary, would comprise the Caribbean Servant's Team. The National Coordinators would also be able to appoint individuals as Honorary Members in recognition of their work for CCI.

The National Coordinators, the Caribbean Servant's Team and Honorary Members would be the Caribbean Leaders Council and would hold an Annual General Meeting to provide vision, oversight and direction for CCI activities, establish financial policy and budgets and provide the funding. The Board of Directors would support and encourage the CCD in accomplishing the vision. The CCD in turn would shepherd and work with the Caribbean Servants Team and the National Coordinators to accomplish CCI's vision, goals and objectives.

The CBSI island representatives came together at a meeting held at Anapausis Conference Center, Curepe, Trinidad on May 2-4,

2008, where the plan would be proposed. In his opening remarks Brian Burke read from the book of Joshua, challenging and encouraging those present as God did in His charge to Joshua. *"Every place that the sole of your foot will tread upon I have given you,... Be strong and of good courage; do not be afraid, nor be dismayed, for the LORD your God is with you wherever you go." (Joshua 1:3, 9 NKJV)* The successful implementation of the proposed plan would require every leader's strength, courage and commitment undergirded by this promise. The concept of the plan and the actual articles of incorporation were approved by the national representatives, who then became National Coordinators—namely Ian Macintyre of Tortola, BVI, Boris Teague of Antigua and Barbuda, David Fritz of Dominica, Robert James of St. Lucia, Chiefton Charles of St. Vincent and the Grenadines, Joachim Phillip of Grenada and Joe Caterson of Trinidad.

The National Coordinators elected the following Board of Directors: Ian Macintyre, President; Chiefton Charles, Vice President; Joachim Phillip, Director at Large; Brian Burke, CCD; David Fritz, Treasurer and Joe Caterson, Secretary.

Then, the National Coordinators appointed Marlene Thomas as Training Coordinator and Jacqui Bridge as Children & Youth Coordinator. The post of Assistant Secretary was left open. The Caribbean Servants Team (CST) is therefore comprised of CCD Brian Burke, Treasurer David Fritz, Secretary Joe Caterson, Training Coordinator Marlene Thomas and Children & Youth Coordinator Jacqui Bridge.

Representing CBSI at this historical meeting were Executive Director Frank Vroegop, Associate Director Marian Vroegop and Regional Director Dr. Glenn Collard.

With CCI established it was time to pass the baton of leadership. Since no baton was available, Caleb Chuck, in true Caribbean style, passed a maraca to the newly elected CCI President, Ian Macintyre. Thus, with confidence in God's leading, protection and calling of treasured men and women of the region, we passed responsibility of leadership to CBSI Caribbean Inc.

In theory this was a beautiful completion of God's calling on our lives for the Caribbean. However, batons have a tendency to be dropped! Relay teams practice the handoff over and over, and still races are lost because of a dropped baton. To achieve a sure-handed transition, we spent the next ten months working further with each of the eight National Coordinators.

CCI is responsible for shepherding leaders within CBSI Caribbean countries as well as introducing, training, supporting start-up and shepherding the resultant classes. As Calebs we serve CCI at their direction, primarily pioneering—that is, introducing CBSI in new island nations. The National Coordinators are responsible for keeping the classes healthy and viable in their own territories and developing new classes as God provides opportunity. Strong and vibrant classes in the eight founding CCI countries would be the launching pad for pioneering CBSI into other Caribbean islands. Therefore, before turning to pioneering, we needed to do what we could to provide continuity in effective shepherding, the key to strong and vibrant classes. Since we had been doing most of the shepherding of Teaching Leaders and had developed caring relationships, we committed to prepare the National Coordinators to replace us. In their roles as Teaching Leaders, they had been recipients of our shepherding but did not necessarily understand the process behind what they experienced. So we explained, modeled the process and provided tools for the ongoing ministry.

After the CCI meeting we first worked with Joe Caterson in Trinidad. Together, we visited the Leaders Councils and classes, introduced him as National Coordinator when needed, explained the new Caribbean leadership organization and asked for their support. We provided an observation form to help identify class strengths and weaknesses, recorded our observations, sharing and discussing them with each Teaching Leader, thus modeling this part of the shepherding process. Each National Coordinator received a CBSI "tool box" of PowerPoint presentations for introduction and training as well as forms. We did our best to repeat this process with each National Coordinator as we gradually sailed north, staying at each CBSI island as long as needed.

CCI "comes together" at an Annual General Meeting (AGM) as a requirement of the incorporation but more importantly to support and encourage one another. The first 2009 AGM was held in Trinidad, and the 2010 AGM took place in Grenada. The 2011 AGM will again be held in Grenada preceding the Tenth Anniversary CBSI Caribbean Leaders Conference at the Flamboyant Hotel & Villas in Grand Anse.

Under Brian's leadership CCI has continued "coming together" with the annual pre-class leaders workshops. Along with Marlene Thomas and Jacqui Bridge, he creates the workshop and provides a syllabus, materials and video encouragement, which are sent to each National Coordinator to organize and present. In each workshop all leadership from the island come together for a time of prayer, encouragement, refreshment and growth of leadership skills to prepare for the new course year.

At the outset the CBSI Caribbean Inc. by-laws were drafted for incorporation in Trinidad, but bureaucratic problems blocked that road. Application was then made for incorporation in SVG, and though that process was fraught with delays, the application was eventually approved. With the incorporation established in SVG, the by-laws then needed to be modified to agree with SVG laws of incorporation in order to establish a bank account. Finally, in March of 2011, nearly three years after the organizational meeting, the by-laws were in place, and in April CCI opened its first bank account at ScotiaBank, Kingstown, SVG. This bank was selected because its branches across the Caribbean provide a mechanism wherein accounts can be established in each CBSI country. Contributions then deposited locally can be electronically transferred within the bank into the main CCI account without delays or fees. Prior to this banking arrangement, while some CBSI classes gave generously, getting the funds to CCI was inconvenient and not recognized as a priority.

Another CCI obstacle has been effective shepherding. Director Brian Burke's profession as a full time school teacher has made him largely unavailable for personal visits to shepherd the National

Coordinators in the member islands. Visiting a class or Leaders Council requires two to three days because of the necessity of flying. While he is allowed a few days of release time from teaching, it requires long-range planning to get authorization from the Ministry of Education. Brian is attempting to stay in communication with the National Coordinators by phone, texting, Skype, Internet chat and email, gathering monthly prayer requests and updates on the status of classes. This provides some measure of personal interaction. However, telecommunications, for all its speed and convenience, falls way short of face-to-face communication, especially when one is trying to understand a challenging situation or get to the bottom of a problem.

So "coming together" remains essential. Conferences, national workshops and the AGM are all critical keys to maintaining strong and vibrant classes and expanding CCI. Though gathering to foster unity in the Caribbean CBSI ministry is costly in time and financial expense, by doing this we fulfill Hebrews 10:24-25: *"And let us consider how we may spur one another on toward love and good deeds. Let us not give up meeting together, as some are in the habit of doing, but let us encourage one another…"* Coming together encourages us to stand firm in the calling God has on each CBSI servant leader as together we "make disciples for our Lord Jesus Christ through in-depth Bible study available to all."

Like any newborn, CCI has had to learn to crawl before it could walk, resulting in a period of consolidation and retrenchment. Once each leader boldly and faithfully embraces his or her responsibilities in shepherding, CCI will again grow and flourish. *"The One who calls you is faithful and He will do it."* (1 Thessalonians 5:24) His ministry is indeed "God Called, God Driven."—the theme of the 2011 CBSI Caribbean Tenth Anniversary Leadership Conference. God will do it, but He expects us to take bold steps of faith in obedience to His calling. Had we remained at the dock in Tortola when God called us to this ministry in 2000, we would never have seen His awesome faithfulness as reported in this book! *"LORD,…all that we have accomplished You have done for us."* (Isaiah 26:12) To God be the glory!

2003 CBSI Caribbean leaders gathered for leadership workshop at Jolly Beach Resort in Antigua.

2004 "Acts in August" Teaching Leader and Associate Teaching Leader Workshop in Curepe, Trinidad, in preparation for Acts of the Apostles study.

Chuck passing the maraca, signifying a Caribbean gavel of leadership, to CBSI Caribbean Inc. President Ian Macintyre after establishing the corporation.

2006 CBSI Leadership Conference held at Jolly Beach Resort in Antigua.

CBSI Caribbean Inc. founders (l to r) back row: Robert James—St. Lucia, David Fritz—Dominica, Rev Joachim Phillip—Grenada, Boris Teague—Antigua, Joe Caterson—Trinidad; front row: Rev. Chiefton Charles—St. Vincent, Director Brian Burke Caribbean Director—St.Vincent, Marlene Thomas—Trinidad, President Ian Macintyre—Trinidad. Not pictured Felix Alexander—Martinique.

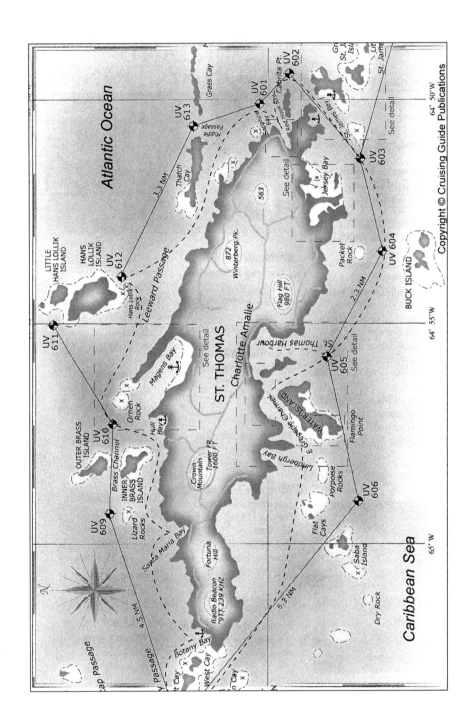

13

St. Thomas

"Let us not become weary in doing good,
for at the proper time we will reap a harvest
if we do not give up."
(Galatians 6:9)

CBS International was born in St. Thomas, U.S. Virgin Islands (USVI), on September 16, 2009 at Ebenezer Memorial Baptist Church in Contant under the leadership of Teaching Leader (pastor) Lennox Zamore.

Twenty-nine years earlier, God used a business convention on picturesque Water Island off the south coast of St. Thomas, to introduce us to His beautiful creation in the Caribbean and plant a seed. The venue was Sugar Bird Beach and Tennis Club on a hill overlooking Flamingo Bay and the sparkling waters of the sea. With a short walk across the small island we were at the ferry dock for a quick ride to the duty free shopping of Charlotte Amalie. Between meetings, we walked down to stretch out in the glorious sunshine on the beach, or swim or snorkel in the crystalline waters of Honeymoon Bay. Chuck took a SCUBA diving resort certification course and dove in the splendor of the coral reefs and abundant sea life—a dream come true! Here we were introduced to trade wind sailing as we went with others on a day charter. So our love of ocean sailing started in St. Thomas and would later draw us back to the Caribbean. Little did we know then that in just a few weeks our lives would be radically transformed by the power of the Holy Spirit and the Word of God, leading to salvation through faith in Jesus Christ. Even then, though, our eyes were being opened to the awesomeness of God in His creation.

On Sunday, we joined Chuck's brothers, their wives and two of their adult sons on the ferry to Charlotte Amalie and hired a taxi to take us to a small church. We still remember fondly the warmth and welcoming spirit of the people and the touching dedication of adorable babies. That was the first time one of the highlights of a business convention was a Sunday morning church service! *Isn't that just like the Father!*

St. Thomas and the other Virgin Islands are geographically at the high point of the curving Greater and Lesser Antilles archipelago, which swings out in an arc from Trinidad to Florida. Since their discovery by Christopher Columbus in 1493, the Virgin Islands, blessed with steady trade winds and many sheltered harbors, gradually became a center for sea routes to every point of the compass. Their location made them a welcome layover on sailing routes between Europe and the riches of South and Central America as well as a lair for the real "Pirates of the Caribbean" who plundered Spanish galleons as they sailed back to Spain loaded with gold.

While the USVI are but a stone's throw from Tortola in the British Virgin Islands (BVI) where CBSI was first introduced in the Eastern Caribbean in 2000 and the first Virgin Islands class was inaugurated in 2002, God continually opened doors in the islands to the east and south.

After the formation of CBSI Caribbean Inc. in May 2008, we gradually sailed north from Trinidad, working with the National Coordinators in each island. Our final National Coordinator training in March of 2009 was back where we started nine years earlier, Tortola, BVI. Anchoring once again in Soper's Hole at West End, we spent time with Ian Macintyre, who now held three titles—President of CBSI Caribbean Inc., National Coordinator for the Virgin Islands (U.S. and British) and Teaching Leader of the only BVI class. Ian had already assumed his responsibilities as National Coordinator by introducing CBSI to church leadership in neighboring St. John, USVI, though the presentation had not yet borne fruit.

Four days after our arrival in Tortola, Steve and Shirley Parrott from our home church, Woodside Bible, joined *coram Deo's* crew for a week in the sun, thawing out from the long, cold Michigan winter. They are leaders in our Faithful Friends AFG, strong prayer warriors and supporters of CBSI Caribbean. When they visited the class the following night, the leaders and members lovingly welcomed them, even encouraging their participation in the discussion. They saw some results of their prayers, and class members were able to put faces to two of their American prayer partners. God then blessed us with good weather for a great time together sailing, shelling, relaxing and touring around the BVI, St. John and St. Thomas. Steve proved to be a valuable deck hand, particularly when Chuck was hurt in a disastrous fall!

Anchored in St. Thomas Harbour after the Parrott's departure, we called Dr. George Phillips, the pastor of St. Thomas Assembly of God, to schedule a meeting. He was introduced to us by Grenada Pastor and CBSI Teaching Leader Joachim Phillip at CONECAR in 2007 in Trinidad. Dr. Phillips had encouraged us to come to St. Thomas and introduce CBSI, but developing work in Grenada and Dominica kept us down island. Now, two years later, on April 2, 2009 we met him for lunch at Le Petite Pump Restaurant above the seaplane and ferry terminal on the Charlotte Amalie waterfront. A friendly, focused leader with a passion for people and the Word of God, Dr. Phillips gave us contact information for Pastor Robert Nelson of Bovoni Baptist Church, then president of the St. Thomas Ministerial Alliance. When we called Pastor Nelson, he invited us to make a CBSI presentation at the Alliance's monthly meeting on April 25. With time to enjoy some of St. Thomas, we sailed to small, uninhabited St. James Island off the southern coast and anchored in beautiful Christmas Cove.

Early in the morning on April 5, we received a call from Micki's nephew, Darrin Mroz, informing us that his father, Ken, was in grave condition in a San Diego hospital. We quickly raised anchor and set sail for Puerto Rico, where we felt we could make the best airline connections. En route, we called Puerto del Rey Marina to reserve a slip. Micki's first flight was to Michigan to help her 87-year-old mother pack, and together they flew to California, arriving at noon on Good Friday. Darrin and his sweet, loving wife Myra met them at the airport, and they headed straight to the hospital. They were all at Ken's bedside as he entered eternity at 3:27 p.m. on April 10, 2009, at 65 years of age.

Chuck arrived from Puerto Rico later that evening. After comforting each other and gathering for a private memorial with the family at Ken's home, Chuck flew back to *coram Deo* early the following Wednesday. That same morning Micki's mom fell in the hotel room and cracked a rib. They were booked on a mid-day flight, and despite her mom's severe pain both made the trip back to Michigan. Micki, however, delayed her return to Puerto Rico to help her mom during recovery and time of mourning, leaning heavily on *"the Father of compassion and the God of all comfort, who comforts us in all our troubles." (2 Corinthians 1:3-4)*

Knowing that Micki would return to Puerto Rico only two days before the scheduled introduction in St. Thomas, Chuck contacted Pastor Nelson to discuss rescheduling. He was accommodating, expressing his sincere condolences, and added the CBSI presentation to the end of the agenda of a special meeting May 12. As we prepared to sail from Puerto Rico to St. Thomas, we emailed our prayer warriors to pray for "interest to be sparked in St. Thomas as a result of the May 12 introduction meeting."

The meeting was held at Church of God Holiness in the Tutu community in the east near Red Hook. We docked *coram Deo* at American Yacht Harbor Marina in Red Hook, a short walk from the ferry dock where Ian Macintyre arrived from Tortola to participate in the presentation. Since our presentation would be at the end of the meeting, Ian would miss the last ferry, so we invited him to spend the night in *coram Deo's* guest cabin. After his arrival and dinner, we drove to Tutu for the meeting. When we arrived at about 8:30 p.m., the group was in their final discussion about participation in the International Day of Prayer. Seven pastors attended, including Pastor Nelson. When he saw us, he got excited saying, "I remember you from the Layou Leadership Retreat in SVG back in July, 2001!" He had been interested in CBSI then, but we were not available for St. Thomas until now, eight years later. *Isn't that just like the Father!*

Ian, Micki and Chuck each presented part of the introduction, which did spark interest—a direct answer to prayer. In Chuck's follow-up calls two churches expressed interest in going forward with leadership training. After returning to Tortola and checking his schedule, Ian arranged to return to St. Thomas June 20, 2009, to present the first part of the four-session Leaders Training Seminar. The rest of the training, to be presented by Caribbean Training Coordinator Marlene Thomas from Trinidad with Ian's support, was scheduled for September 4 and 5. A team of six from Ebenezer Memorial Baptist Church participated in the training. Pastor Lennox Zamore trained as Teaching Leader and Associate Pastor Felix Durand as Associate Teaching Leader. Unfortunately, the team from another church misunderstood the location and missed the training.

The pilot class of CBSI in St. Thomas was born at Ebenezer Memorial Baptist Church in Contant on September 16, 2009. In late October of 2009, after CONECAR in Jamaica, CCI Director Brian Burke flew to St. Thomas. Ian Macintyre ferried over from Tortola for the Saturday meeting, and together these men introduced CBSI to the USVI Baptist Pastors Conference, an opportunity provided by Pastor Zamore. Unfortunately, neither Ian nor Brian could stay for the Ebenezer Leaders Council or class meeting to observe and give guidance.

March 29, 2010, after a serene downwind sail, we arrived and anchored in Virgin Gorda Sound, BVI in late afternoon. Exhausted from a 4 a.m. departure and a strenuous month and a half of ministry and spiritual warfare in St. Martin, we were looking forward to a good night's rest. God provided and then we set sail mid-morning for St. John, USVI to make clearance at U.S. Immigration in Cruz Bay. We moored in Caneel Bay, east of Cruz Bay, and dinghied to shore. After making clearance we wandered around the unique town, looking for some good ice cream! Settling for a Snickers ice cream bar, we headed back to *coram Deo* to relax and rest if just for one more day before sailing to Honeymoon Bay, Water Island. There we began preparing for the visit of our "spiritual kids" and former Bible study leaders from Michigan, Mark and Kristi Kirschmann, and their nine and seven year old sons Andrew and Alex. Their visit had been planned for 2009 but had to be postponed due to the passing of Micki's brother. We were looking forward to relaxation and fun in the sun with the Kirschmanns, but first there was some "heavy lifting" to do, including cleaning *coram Deo* inside and out, replacing our day fridge with a new one to be shipped to St. Thomas, provisioning, laundry, ministry communications and boat maintenance.

After the Kirschmanns' arrival April 6, the week went by in a whirl of activity—exploring Coral World as well as beaches and caves, sailing in St. Thomas, St. John and the BVIs, sunning, swimming, snorkeling and enjoying God's creation. After a fun week, the Kirschmanns flew home, and we crashed in our bunk! For two people in their second wind of life, it had been quite a change of pace!

That Sunday we worshipped at Ebenezer Memorial Baptist, the home of the CBSI class and in the evening attended their Leaders Council. Surprisingly, we were the first of any CBSI leadership to visit and shepherd this team and class since its inception seven months earlier. A new class without timely follow-up coaching is comparable to leaving a newborn baby on a doorstep to fend for itself. We praise God for the commitment of Pastor Zamore and his leadership team as they stuck with the program even though missing significant elements. Clearly there needed to be an explanation of the purpose of the Leaders Council. We pointed out the necessary agenda items, explaining that a vibrant and growing class is the result of the leaders' prayerful preparation, shepherding and planning. Hoping the purpose of the Leaders Council was now clear, we made plans to attend class Wednesday night.

The commitment and desire of this team to make disciples through CBSI was made quite clear at the Leaders Council by the presence of El John, a Haitian leader. Pastor Zamore was helping El in leading Creole-speaking Haitian nationals through the French translation of the 1 John study. El's group was having difficulty due to the differences between languages. Because this meeting was not the place for the discussion, we made arrangements to meet at a later time. Therefore, while the Leaders Council could have been more on track had they had timely coaching, we were encouraged by the leaders' commitments to strengthen and spread CBSI in St. Thomas.

At 2 a.m. Tuesday morning, Chuck awoke experiencing pressure on his chest and pain running down his left arm, characteristic symptoms of a heart attack! Since the pain was not too severe and not much could be done without putting the dinghy into the water and motoring ashore, however, he took some baby aspirins and did not disturb Micki. When she awoke about 6:30 a.m., Chuck said, "I think I had a heart attack" and explained his symptoms. Remaining calm and shooting up arrow prayers ("Help, Lord!"), we called Dr. Steve McClelland in Michigan at his home, and his wife Molly answered. Molly is as close to us as a daughter and a Ph.D. nurse. She strongly suggested we go ashore for medical assistance. Unfamiliar with the island's medical facilities, Chuck called Pastor Zamore, who advised us to go to nearby Schneider Hospital, where he *just so happened* to be a staff consultant. He called ahead so they would be expecting us. We went ashore and hailed a cab, and the driver quickly got us to Schneider. Once inside the ER, Chuck was given an EKG while Micki signed the paperwork. Pastor Zamore arrived after the EKG, prayed and anointed Chuck with oil. After a while the ER doctor reported that while he didn't know what had happened, he knew it was not a heart attack. Later in the day, it was diagnosed as a small bleb, a tiny collapse at the top of the left lung. Also from the lung scan, the radiologist detected a healed broken rib! Apparently his fall a year prior, when the Parrotts were onboard, had resulted in the broken rib and trauma that could have produced the bleb. It would heal on its own.

A medical emergency in the islands was one of our greatest fears. God knew this and through this experience spoke loud and clear: ***"So do not fear, for I am with you…I will strengthen you and help you…"*** *(Isaiah 41:10)* We were there by His calling, and He is faithful. *Isn't that just like the Father!*

The next day after a follow up appointment at the hospital, Pastor Zamore met us for lunch, the three of us praising and thanking the Lord for His protection. With Chuck feeling fine, we would visit class the next evening. Because of the number of teens attending, two separate classes had developed, with the youth going more slowly through the course than the adults. Teaching Leader Lennox Zamore led the teen class with Tyrone Reed leading his peers in the discussion. The adult class was led by Teaching Leader (pastor) Felix Durand, Discussion Leader Louisa Dickensen and Class Coordinator for both groups Janet Durand. On Friday we again met with Pastor Zamore to review the written Leaders Council and class observation form we had completed, with both encouragements and recommendations, and to listen to his ideas for ministry growth in USVI. Since National Coordinator Ian Macintyre had moved to Trinidad shortly after the training of this class, we told Pastor Zamore we would discuss with CCI the need for someone to shepherd the Virgin Island classes.

One month later, April 29, 2010, we sailed back to St. Martin to follow up the progress of new classes and from there to store *coram Deo* at the Jolly Harbour Boatyard in Antigua for hurricane season. When we returned to the boat on October 2, 2010, expecting to sail promptly, we met major delays. The sound insulating project in the engine room had hardly begun. When we finally were ready to sail, Hurricane Tomas forced us back. It was the morning of November 17 before we arrived back in Caneel Bay, St. John, U.S. Virgin Islands. We were anticipating a couple of days of relaxation with cruising friends before spending time in St. Thomas with the Ebenezer class and discussing CBSI with other interested leaders. At noon that day, however, we received a call from Micki's sister that our uncle, Vince Stanek, had just passed away! We promptly cleared into U.S. Immigration, made the short sail to St. Thomas Harbour and prepared to store *coram Deo* at Crown Bay Marina. On Saturday we flew home for the Monday funeral, returning one week later. On Sunday morning we grabbed the opportunity to worship with the vibrant and loving congregation of Ebenezer Memorial Baptist Church. Afterward Pastor Zamore invited us to join his family and friends at Walkers by the Sea for a delicious buffet and enjoyable lively fellowship.

We were looking forward to attending the CBSI class at Ebenezer on Wednesday night. Early on Wednesday, Pastor Andrew George called to set up a meeting. Chuck suggested that he and his wife Sherryl join us at class that night to see CBSI in action, and he said they would. Andrew is a church planter and professor at Blue Water Bible College & Institute in St. Thomas who was introduced to us by Pastor Zamore the previous April. He had wanted to use CBSI in the small group he was leading, but no one in CCI was available to provide training. So we invited him to attend the Leaders Training Seminar the following month in St. Martin, but he could not make it.

Meeting Pastor Andrew and Sherryl that night at the Ebenezer class, we noticed some changes since our visit six months earlier. The adult class was now being led by Karen McDowell, a passionate woman of the Word. After earning her law degree in New York, she graduated from Moody Bible Institute in Chicago. Her desire is to help class members not only learn the Word but see how each passage applies to everyday life — and then truly apply it. We were impressed and personally touched by her practical teaching! Karen is humble and unassuming, traits unexpected for one in her profession! She diligently uses homiletics to find God's truth in each passage and its application to members' lives, and she depends on the Holy Spirit to guide her preparation and teaching. At that time Teaching Leader Pastor Durand was taking courses for an advanced degree in education. He is now sharing the teaching role with Karen. Since several of the teens from the youth group had graduated and were away at college, the youth group Pastor Zamore had led was no longer meeting. Pastor Zamore, however, leads a ministry in the local prisons on Wednesday evenings, and he hopes to implement CBSI there in a way similar to the CBS InPrison Ministry in the U.S.

After class Pastor Andrew was ready to get started. We suggested that he use the If You Will Pray study as a means of introduction and identification of potential leaders since he had now experienced a class. He and Sherryl enthusiastically committed, wanting to begin immediately, so the next morning we emailed the materials and directions. After discussing follow-up with CCI Director Brian Burke, Chuck provided some coaching over the phone as Andrew implemented If You Will Pray. Once completing the eight-week study, they wanted to move into a pilot course. Again, no one was available from CCI to provide leadership training, but with CCI permission, given Andrew's strong background and with Chuck's guidance, they began their study in 1 John without receiving formal training. In late May of 2011 Brian Burke and CCI Training Coordinator Marlene Thomas provided training for Pastor George's leadership team and those preparing to bring CBSI to the local prisons, and a refresher for the Ebenezer team. Ongoing support is being organized utilizing the experience of Teaching Leader Ted Martin and National Coordinator Boris Teague from Antigua.

The CBSI-Ebenezer class is the first of several USVI classes that will eventually develop, the Lord willing, through His faithfulness to Pastor Zamore and his team. A solid foundation for CBSI in the USVI is being built, the first fruits seen at Ebenezer and in the pilot class led by Pastor George. Hopefully God will use ongoing ministry within the Haitian community, the prisons, a nearby public housing complex with many children, the Baptist Pastors Association and the St. Thomas Ministerial Alliance to open doors for CBSI. The story of CBSI in the U.S. Virgin Islands is only beginning to unfold. Much prayer and shepherding from CCI Leadership, combined with the commitment of the local leaders to disciple making through CBSI, will bring this new work to fruition. *"Do you not say, 'Four months more and then the harvest'? I tell you, open your eyes and look at the fields! They are ripe for harvest."* (John 4:35)

"Lord,...all that we have accomplished You have done for us." (Isaiah 26:12) To God be the Glory!

**Leaders Council at Ebenezer Memorial Baptist, St. Thomas.
TL Felix Durand (2nd from left), Pastor Zamore (4th from
left), Andrew George to pastor's left.**

**CBSI teen class meeting in Pastor Zamore's office at Ebenezer
Memorial Baptist in St. Thomas.**

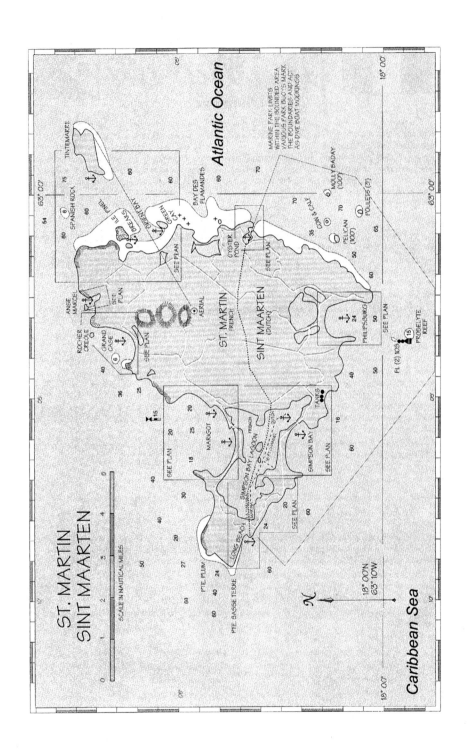

ST. MARTIN
SINT MAARTEN

SCALE IN NAUTICAL MILES

Atlantic Ocean

Caribbean Sea

250

14

St. Martin

*"Therefore, my dear brothers, stand firm.
Let nothing move you. Always give yourselves fully to the
work of the LORD, because you know that your labor
in the LORD is not in vain."*
(1 Corinthians 15:58)

CBS International was born in Dutch Sint Maarten on April 28, 2010, in Cay Bay under the leadership of Teaching Leaders (apostle) Elmead and (pastor) Aster Allen, and it was born in French St. Martin on May 12, 2010, in Marigot Bay under the leadership of Teaching Leader (pastor) Napolina Richardson.

St. Martin Island is the smallest self-contained land mass ruled by two sovereign nations in the world. The French govern 21 of its 37 square miles. The Dutch govern 16. Barely seven miles wide in each direction, it is one of the best-known vacation destinations in the region, embracing tourism wholeheartedly with casinos, condominiums, plenty of hotels and cruise ships visiting daily. The whole island is duty free—so it is the Caribbean's number one shopping mall! It is a major yachting center, especially for mega yachts, rivaling Antigua. The Caribbean's two largest chandleries are headquartered here as well as excellent facilities for most any yacht work.

Our first significant exposure to St. Martin took place after our initial shakedown cruise in 2000, which Micki called "The Crossing from Hell" in Chapter 2. While the boat was in poor shape, we were well treated by the Sunsail base manager Nick, a skilled sailor and strong, committed Christ follower. Nick put us in contact with his pastor, Tom Bartholomew, who hosted the cruisers VHF radio net every morning. But in 2000, with hurricane season upon us and the devastation from 1999's Hurricane Lenny all around us, there was no time to pursue leads for CBSI. Over the years, we made stops in St. Martin as we sailed from points south to the Virgin Islands, taking advantage of the duty free shopping or buying boat parts. Each time, though, not wanting to miss any God-given opportunity, we walked circumspectly. By mid 2003 CBSI expansion was in the central and southern part of the island chain, with God opening doors in Martinique, Trinidad, St. Lucia, Dominica and Grenada in rapid succession. Because in the north there was only the Tortola class—a long, slow sail away and under the experienced leadership of Ian Macintyre—we flew there to visit and shepherd, leaving *coram Deo* moored down island.

It was not until after the formation of CCI in May of 2008 and the training of the CCI National Coordinators well into 2009 that we could focus on new countries. After the first CCI Annual General Meeting in Trinidad in October of 2009, Chuck joined Brian Burke, Felix Alexander and Joachim Phillip on a flight to Jamaica to represent CBSI at CONECAR. On the final leg from St. Martin to Jamaica, *it just so happened* that Chuck was seated beside Rev. Wycliffe Smith, senior pastor of the New Testament Baptist Church of Philipsburg, and his associate pastor Julien John. They were not only attending CONECAR, but *just so happened* to be staying in the same guesthouse as our CBSI delegation. Chuck and the others had opportunities to talk to Pastor Smith about CBSI while learning that he was head of the St. Martin United Ministerial Foundation (SMUMF). Then, while we were home over Christmas and for the January CBS Teaching Directors Conference, Chuck stayed in contact with Pastor Smith, discussing the introduction of CBSI to the

Christian community in St. Martin. Since we would not return to *coram Deo* in Antigua until January 30, Pastor Smith invited us to make a CBSI presentation at the next possible SMUMF meeting. That was Saturday, February 27, 2010.

In mid February we sailed *coram Deo* out of Jolly Harbour, Antigua, headed to St. Martin with a layover in St. Kitts. We were sailing with new friends, Debra and Phil Stolp aboard sailing vessel Souverain. Our meeting and beginning "an everlasting bond" with Debra was another divine appointment just before entering intense spiritual warfare. She is an on-fire believer from California, a strong Scriptural prayer warrior and an encourager, our "Jesus with skin on" at the beginning of the battle for CBSI in St. Martin. *Isn't that just like the Father!*

After a horribly turbulent night in Majors Bay, where we had to hang on to stay in the bunk and Phil was kicked out of their bunk so Debra could brace herself in it, we raised anchor at 6:38 a.m. Souverain would stay to explore St. Kitts and join us in St. Martin in a few days. We set sail for the 50 mile passage north on a clear beautiful day with three to four foot seas and only eight to eleven knot southeast winds. This was nice, but with the light winds we would not have the speed to make the 5 p.m. Simpson Bay Bridge opening to enter the lagoon. The Simpson Bay anchorage is open to southern and western swells and is often unsettled, whereas the Simpson Bay Lagoon is surrounded by the island and normally calm. Therefore, we left the engine running at 1000 rpm, our spirits were high and it was great to be sailing again! About halfway into the passage, Chuck noticed the bilge pump going on. Checking it out, he found a leaking seawater cooling pump on the Volvo engine. With enough wind to make some headway, we put out all sails, and Micki kept watch on deck. Chuck set out to replace the pump with a spare, only to find that the attachment fittings were incompatible. Plan B was the removal and rebuilding of the leaking pump. Lacking a critical tool, he rebuilt the pump the best he could under the circumstances. He should have left it for the professionals for when reinstalled, it looked good but did not pump! As the winds continued to drop, we gave up the idea of making the bridge opening. At 6:15 p.m., we sailed around the reef into Simpson Bay, dropped anchor and then lowered the mainsail before starting the engine to back down and set the anchor. Whew! Thanking God for His protection and wisdom, we made dinner and relaxed. Afterward on the VHF radio we tried hailing our friends John and Ricarda Ladue on sailing vessel Drisana, who owned Permafrost Marine Services just inside the lagoon. We felt John could help source parts for the pump. They did not answer but later called us. John offered to come out mid morning in his work dinghy and tow us through the bridge into the lagoon for ease of accessing parts and doing the repair.

Up early the next day, it was relatively calm, so we were able to drop the dinghy and get the outboard off the stern rail and mounted on the dinghy. With some difficulty Chuck got the outboard started. We headed for the lagoon to visit Permafrost and call around for pump parts. We could not use our own phones since our USA SIM cards will not work in St. Martin. No sooner did we get well away from *coram Deo* when the outboard quit and would not start! Being a calm day and with the customs dock only a few hundred yards away, we began paddling. Before long a couple in a large, powerful inflatable boat from a mega yacht came near, asking if we needed help. They towed us to the Palapa Marina dinghy dock, where Permafrost is located. Chuck discussed the situation with John, who carefully instructed him on how to reroute a saltwater wash down pump temporarily to cool the engine so we could get *coram Deo* into the lagoon. John repeatedly made it clear that if this temporary pump were left running, it would flood the engine with salt water potentially ruining it. While repeating that warning, John supplied Chuck with a few potentially needed connectors for rerouting the pump. We had also determined that the problem with the outboard was probably bad fuel. Chuck replaced the fuel and it ran fine. Back onboard *coram Deo* Chuck rerouted the saltwater pump in time for us to make the 5 p.m. bridge opening, anchoring in the calm lagoon. The following day, Friday, we took the raw water cooling pump into the diesel mechanic for rebuilding. At the same time we got set up for phone and Internet communications. We then called Pastor

Smith and made a lunch date for the following Tuesday, February 23, 2010.

Over that weekend our friend John warned us about March winds, which can howl through the lagoon at 40 knots or higher. Anchored in about 10 feet, the normal scope, or length, of anchor chain is four to six times water depth, or 40 to 60 feet. John cautioned that because of the soft bottom and the probability of high winds, we needed to lay down a minimum of 100 feet to be secure. With the boats anchored around us, there was not space enough to increase our scope. So after breakfast Monday morning we started the engine, raised anchor, repositioned ourselves and dropped the anchor, carefully laying out the necessary chain. After about ten minutes, Chuck heard a pump running and asked Micki if she had turned off the saltwater pump when she killed the engine. "No!" She ran below and flipped the breaker. Too late, the engine was flooded! In hopes that it was not ruined, we headed across the lagoon in the dinghy to buy the motor oil needed to clean the saltwater out of the diesel engine. As soon as Chuck began the oil extraction, our electric oil change pump burned up because of the high viscosity of the motor oil and saltwater mixture. So it was back in the dinghy to borrow John's manual oil pump and back out to the boat. Then Chuck began the laborious task of changing oil five times over the next few days and cleaning the injectors. Micki was sick over forgetting, but oil-covered Chuck was very forgiving. Debra and Phil had arrived, anchoring behind us. We did not yet recognize these misadventures as spiritual warfare, but Debra did, knowing why we were in St. Martin. So she dinghied over to pray for and encourage us.

On Tuesday Chuck interrupted oil changing for our lunch meeting with Pastor Smith at a small restaurant across from Palapa Marina. Soft-spoken and thoughtful, this spiritual shepherd had many questions about CBSI as well as what it was like living on a boat. Chuck shared the good, bad and the ugly of our lifestyle, showing him his oil-stained hands. Discussion then turned to the details of the SMUMF meeting so we would be properly prepared.

Early on the sunny Saturday, February 27, we dinghied across the lagoon, tying to the Island Water World dock and, with both of us carrying heavy backpacks and tote bags filled with equipment and CBSI info packets, walked the short distance to Carl and Sons grocery store and restaurant. Climbing the outside stairway and entering the large, air-conditioned meeting room above the store, we were greeted warmly by Pastor Smith. Being last on a long agenda, we were encouraged when everyone stayed and listened intently as we went through the introduction. We told them how excited we were to be there because we had been waiting ten years for this opportunity. The twenty-five pastors and Christian leaders enthusiastically endorsed CBSI. Afterward Apostle Elmead Allen and his wife, Pastor Aster, said they had just created an educational approach for their church similar to the CBSI process. They wanted to implement their program but needed to write materials to support it. Recognizing the enormity of that task, they were praising God for His provision of CBSI! "We don't know about anybody else," Pastor Aster said, "but we know that God sent you to St. Martin specifically for us!"

At Pastor Smith's invitation, the following day we worshipped at his church, New Testament Baptist, one of the larger churches in the Dutch capital of Philipsburg. At one point Pastor Smith invited us onto the platform to give a brief explanation of CBSI. He then announced and encouraged all to attend our presentation the following Wednesday, March 10.

Early Monday morning we knew two things: God was going to do something great in St. Martin, and we were under spiritual attack. When Chuck went into the galley to make coffee, he found a partially eaten banana in our fruit basket. Recognizing the evidence of a rat and not wanting to upset Micki, after having coffee he broke it to her as calmly as he knew how. Because he was so calm, she thought he was kidding. Moreover, we were anchored in the middle of the Simpson Bay Lagoon at least a quarter mile in any direction from land. Nevertheless, seeing the banana, she believed! We began looking for more evidence and found a few droppings on the forward cabin floor, but nowhere else below decks. How would a rat get onboard? We could not have gotten it in Antigua. We left there two weeks ago! Going on deck, we found droppings mid ship and then more on the bow near the anchor roller. Could the rat have climbed up the anchor chain? We had heard stories of that happening in the rivers of South America but not in the Caribbean. We then recalled the last two nights, during which the lagoon was extremely calm. There was not a ripple on the water! We looked over at the airport extension being built out into the lagoon to our southwest and remembered the burning brush on the shoreline southeast of us. Also, there had been a cleanup of debris on nearby Explorer Island over the weekend which might have disturbed some rat habitat. Regardless of our visitor's origin, we had a problem. We prayed, locked up *coram Deo* and dinghied to shore to buy poison pellets. There were none on the island, according to the exterminator in Cole Bay, but maybe in a few days they would get some in. So we bought sticky traps. *It just so happened* as we were pulling away from the dinghy dock that we struck up a conversation with a couple who had just sailed in the night before. The wife mentioned being anchored in the lagoon and Micki told them about the rat. They said that two years earlier the same thing happened to them. A rat boarded their boat in the lagoon by climbing the anchor chain! Rats are good swimmers, they said. They then told us where they had found the poison pellets. *Isn't that just like the Father!*

Deciding to try the sticky traps first, we baited them and set them around below and on deck. Then we closed all hatches for the night. The next morning we thanked God there was no evidence below decks, but the bait and some of the glue was gone from a trap on deck. The rat had been able to pull itself off the trap, taking the glue with it. It must be a tough one, so we decided to go for the kill! Since the little beast was somewhere on deck, where could it be hiding? Chuck checked all lockers and vents but found no sign. Micki was growing impatient and wanted that vile thing off her boat now! We headed to shore to get a big supply of rat poison from the place recommended. Back aboard, Micki was ready to start spreading the poison on deck, but Chuck thought of one more hiding place, telling Micki to hold off until he checked under the teakwood grating on the cockpit floor. The grating has spacers leaving four inches below it to a fiberglass floor allowing plenty of space for a rat to hide. The cockpit floor is about 40" wide by 80" long and about 22" below teak seats built on both sides. The fourth side is the forward wall with a removable door to access the boat interior. When the removable door is in place, the cockpit looks like a two-foot deep box. Micki insisted on enclosing the area with the door, just in case the rat was under the grating. Chuck then tilted up the heavy 60 pound grating, disturbing the rat sleeping in one of the corners. The rat started running around the enclosure, so Chuck slammed the grating down, hoping to crush the rat with one of the supports. Missed it! OK, another plan. Adrenaline flowing, Chuck said, "Micki, you stand on the starboard seat so you can hold the grating vertical, and I'll kill it with this metal pipe handle from the deck brush." Confident from his past rat hunt here in St. Martin in 2000, Chuck lifted the grating, and Micki held it while the rat raced around and around the cockpit floor with Chuck whacking at it but missing while trying to avoid cracking the fiberglass floor! Trying to escape Chuck's murderous blows, the rat scurried under the edge of the grating. Seeing this, Micki lifted the grating and pounded it down onto the vile, squealing creature not once but twice! Both were direct hits! Chuck could not believe that his godly wife had become the ex-terminator! After a few minutes of celebration, he asked Micki to lift the grating so he could clean up the blood and scoop up the demon's remains to give him a burial at sea. She could not lift it! The ex-terminator story was an attention grabber at the opening of leadership training!

With the engine cooling pump repaired and reinstalled and the rat in its watery grave, we began the follow-up calls to the pastors at the SMUMF meeting. Four presentations were scheduled for the following two weeks. Materials needed to be photocopied, and our printer did not work. While in Antigua waiting for a good weather window for the sail to St. Martin, the active volcano on Montserrat, visible 25 miles west of Antigua, erupted, shooting heated dust and fumes more than 60,000 feet above the once blissfully beautiful and peaceful island. The winds were uncharacteristically blowing out of the west. In Antigua, the ash blocked the sun and spread a thin layer over all the boats in the marina. With all of our hatches open for air circulation, we were busily working below, missed the eruption and did not notice the dark cloud until it was too late. Our printer drew in a lethal dose of paper covered with the abrasive dust. Not a problem, we thought, since St. Martin is the shopping mall of the Caribbean. After shopping around, we found the model we thought would fit the small space above the navigation station. By the time we measured and returned, they were sold out with the next shipment two weeks away. Hearing about our predicament, Ricarda Ladue offered the use of the printer at Permafrost, but said it was low on ink. Not a problem, we can buy cartridges. What is the number? We were astounded that they had the exact printer as our dead one. We had purchased a large supply of cartridges but thought they were now scrap. We gave them all to Ricarda and John, using some for our printing needs! *Isn't that just like the Father!*

Our first CBSI presentation was on Tuesday, March 9, 2010, for the leadership of Apostle Elmead and Aster Allen's church, God's Kingdom Citizens. Twelve warm, loving and receptive young men and women listened with great interest, asking pertinent questions. Ten committed to leadership training, and they wanted it "yesterday!"

On Wednesday evening we introduced CBSI to another 30 or 40 persons at Pastor Smith's Church. Inviting pastors and leaders from SMUMF, four churches were represented. As we closed the presentation, we encouraged the pastors to identify their leadership teams as soon as possible so we could schedule leadership training within two weeks. Pastor Napolina Richardson from Repairers of Broken Walls Ministry on the French side approached us with her contact information, expressing her excitement about CBSI. She definitely wanted to be part of leadership training and would have a team ready.

The third presentation was held three days later at Pastor Lewis Constant's Christ Triumphant Church in Philipsburg. Nearly 50 attended—a lively group of young families, singles, middle-aged and elderly. After the presentation Pastor Constant gave an impassioned plea for his people to embrace CBSI and consider leadership so this could be part of their church ministry. As we greeted people afterwards, a bright eyed, young woman approached Micki asking, "Do you remember me?" Micki recognized her face but could not place from where. "From Fort de France," said Chantel Fellow, who had been a university student there and attended the class. Now graduated, she was working as a teacher back home in St. Martin. She said she loved the studies but had wanted to do them in English. Since she was now leading the youth at Christ Triumphant, we encouraged her to consider leadership and form a young adult discussion group.

With the final introduction meeting a week away at Christian Assembly Ministries in Grand Case on the French side, we followed up with the pastors and with commitments from five teams, setting the training dates. Since the training was now CCI's responsibility, we contacted Director Brian Burke and Training Coordinator Marlene Thomas for their availability. On short notice, neither was available, so we agreed to do the training. It had been two years since we last trained in Grenada. All PowerPoint training sessions needed to be updated, as did the Caribbean Training Manual. So we edited and received regional approval for changes in the manual and then had copies made and bound for all trainees.

Saturday, March 21, was an all-day seminar including sessions one and two for all leadership roles. Thirty attended at New Testament Baptist Church. After giving a brief history and explaining the CBSI process, we distributed the first lesson of 1 John. After giving the potential leaders twenty minutes to answer as many questions as possible, we formed two discussion groups, with Chuck leading the men's and Micki the women's. They got into the discussion and did not want to stop after 20 minutes, thoroughly enjoying the CBSI process. We repeated these sessions on two evenings for those not available on Saturday.

On Thursday night we trained 12 Teaching Leaders and Associate Teaching Leaders on the CBSI eight-step teaching preparation. To practice the steps taught, we used 1 John 1:5-2:6, the passage for Lesson 2 of the CBSI 1 John course, having the leaders work together through the process as they would do when teaching that lesson.

On Saturday afternoon Micki opened the final seminar with a mini-teaching from 1 John 1:5-2:6 entitled "Walking the Lighted Path" to demonstrate how well-developed Bible outlining with pointed applications can empower teaching. At the conclusion of her teaching, with tones of almost amazement, participants commented on how their teaching would be changed forever from what they had just learned. Brother Harry Jones, Associate Teaching Leader trainee from New Testament Baptist Church, said in all his years as a lay leader and with all the missionaries that had come to St. Martin, he had never received a tool that he would consider as effective as homiletical preparation. Apostle Allen wanted all the teachers in his church trained this way. Chuck then focused them on the specific responsibilities of the Teaching Leader and Associate Teaching Leader in leading the Leaders Council as well as the class and teaching in both. With training completed, one by one they reflected on what they had learned and expressed their appreciation. Apostle Allen then asked us to stand and for the group to encircle us. Anointing us with oil, all laid on hands and joined in praying for God's blessing, protection and fruition of the plans He has for us and for CBSI. Words fail to express our love for these precious people. It was a sacrifice and strenuous schedule for them as well as for us. Hugs were freely given as Pastor Janice broke out the refreshments for a time of fellowship, sharing the excitement of what God has in store for St. Martin. Two classes were scheduled to begin the following week, one on the Dutch side and one on the French. Three others planned start-ups in May.

Knowing many of the problems we had encountered since our arrival, Apostle Elmead spoke of the spiritual warfare encountered by missionaries who came to St. Martin, many of them packing up and going home. He said that was why in all of our contacts he assured us they were praying for us. The enemy has a strong hold on this island,

and Apostle Elmead knew we were in spiritual battle. Not only did we have strenuous training preparation and training schedule, but boat repairs and maintenance chores while in St. Martin never ceased. In fact they escalated with the fresh water pump, refrigeration and generator all requiring repair or replacement, just to name a few. It was exhausting. But we are promised that *"The One who calls you is faithful and He will do it."* (*1 Thessalonians 5:24*) God surely did it! He empowered our training and provided for the health and schedules of five leadership teams prepared to begin CBSI classes in St. Martin. Knowing the importance of coaching first classes on islands, but needing to meet our spiritual kids in the Virgin Islands in ten days, there was no way we could stay. We encouraged the leaders to stay in touch and promised to return for the month of May to visit, shepherd and provide any additional training.

The following day was spent stowing materials and preparing to sail before motoring through the 4:30 p.m. bridge opening out into Simpson Bay, where we anchored. Eager to be sailing again, we raised anchor at 4 a.m. on March 29, 2010, and followed the lighted path of the bright full moon. God blessed us with a serene downwind sail to the British Virgin Islands, and by 4:30 p.m. we were anchored in Virgin Gorda Sound. While in the Virgin Islands, we visited and shepherded the Tortola and St. Thomas classes. Afterward, as promised, we set sail for Simpson Bay, arriving there on April 30, primed to spend May shepherding the new classes.

As we called the Teaching Leaders for updates on classes, we learned that only the Cay Bay class had started. Pastor Napolina's class would start soon, but Pastor Janice Smith's father had passed away, and she had flown to Jamaica. Two of the teams had leaders yet to be trained. Therefore, we scheduled leadership training for May 20-22. We had discussed this training with Tortola Teaching Leader Kendolph Bobb while in BVI. He was planning on attending, as was CCI Director Brian Burke. Kendolph had recently replaced Ian Macintyre, who moved back to his homeland of Trinidad. With ministry getting under way, equipment problems again began cropping up on the boat—generator, plumbing and the dinghy outboard. Not surprised, we worked in the repairs and maintenance along with ministry, confident that God would provide for our every need.

On May 12, Chuck's birthday, we both received the gift of visiting the "firstborn" in St. Martin, CBSI Cay Bay in their third week of meeting. Cay Bay is an impoverished area of mostly uneducated immigrants on the south coast. We were anticipating seeing this loving leadership team in action and were not disappointed. Thirteen attended at God's Kingdom Citizens Ministry church. The CBSI class opened with joyful and upbeat praise singing ringing out across the area. Their building sits on a hillside above a power plant with the Caribbean Sea beyond. The building consists of a renovated shipping container with a roof built over it and an open air, latticework enclosed room beside it. This room is the sanctuary/meeting room with clear plastic roll up windows for protection against the wind and rain. The shipping container portion has been reconstructed into an office, a storeroom and rest rooms. The whole structure is painted a bright beautiful yellow.

Discussion Leaders Rene Henry and Liane Plummer patiently and cheerfully encouraged the members who were unsure of their answers, helping them understand the questions and the passages of Scripture. Given the numbers, we later recommended they meet in one discussion group rather than two for better discussion. Associate Teaching Leader Orlando Eights is a humble and friendly University of St. Martin IT instructor and systems analyst. He gave the teaching and concluded with two penetrating, challenging application questions. As we visited with class members afterwards, they were awestruck and convicted by what they were learning. This will not be an easy ministry because of the educational level. They already slowed the pace by doing half a lesson a week.

Our mission in CBSI is to make disciples for Jesus Christ, not to complete a particular number of lessons in so many weeks. CBSI helps men, women and children open their hearts and minds to the working of the Holy Spirit through the Word of God, to teach them truth and obedience. This is how believers become disciples of Jesus Christ. Over the years we have striven to adapt the CBSI process to fit the circumstances without changing the five essentials.

On the night we visited the Cay Bay class, May 12, 2010, CBSI was born in Marigot in French St. Martin. We did not know about it until the next day. Pastor Napolina Richardson emailed us that they did a test run and it went well. It is a bilingual class with three English speaking discussion groups and one French speaking. Twenty-six were in attendance for their opening class, and they were excited to get started in the 1 John study.

As we continued to follow up for the upcoming training, there was not much commitment. Two days before the first training only two previously trained St. Martin leaders committed. We were questioning whether to go forward or postpone the training and have Brian Burke and Kendolph Bobb cancel their flights. We turned to the Lord and determined to *"be still in the presence of the LORD, and wait patiently for Him to act." (Psalm 37:7 NLT)* By that evening the number grew to 16! Eighteen actually attended. *Isn't that just like the Father!*

CCI Director Brian Burke challenged the new leaders using Luke 19:30-31, where Jesus orders His disciples to go and untie the colt He would use for His triumphal entry into Jerusalem. Brian said, likewise, these new leaders needed to untie themselves from some of their activities to be used by Jesus Christ as servant-leaders for others.

The Allens once again opened their school for the training on two consecutive evenings and all day Saturday, making possible the training for five CBSI teams. As Apostle Allen was closing up the facility on Friday evening, he shared with us his excitement about how CBSI was impacting the class and his church. A young woman came to their class, he said, and told her parents about it when she arrived home that evening. In the four days following the class, the woman's parents and a friend of the mother, on separate days, called Apostle Allen asking if they could attend the class. The parents and friend are not believers. So CBSI is being used as a tool for transformation in that community.

And in the month we were away, Apostle Allen took it upon himself to contact all the other trained Teaching Leaders to find out if they had started their classes and to share what God was doing through

CBSI in his church. It was this passion to reach out to encourage and challenge his peers that prompted us, with Director Brian Burke's agreement, to partner Apostle Allen and his Associate Teaching Leader Orlando Eights to be acting co-National Coordinators for St. Martin. As with all other National Coordinators, but especially these two being so new to CBSI, Brian will need to shepherd and assist them with the work of maintaining and growing CBSI in St. Martin.

With a step of commitment in any kingdom work comes spiritual opposition. The enemy has attacked the lives of the Allens with a vengeance. In September of 2010 both of their mothers were taken ill, one living in the States, the other in England. Apostle Allen's mother was diagnosed with cancer. In mid September his radiant wife, Aster, was also diagnosed with breast cancer, and it was already spreading throughout her body. Apostle Allen sent us an email saying, "This is quite a shock to us as you can imagine... We are not sitting back and accepting this report. We are believing God for total healing of her body. We know that this is the plan of the enemy to distract, discourage and to stop the work that God has called us to." They, their church family, other churches in St. Martin and many elsewhere in CBSI Caribbean have continued to pray. Pastor Aster is a beautiful, loving, accomplished woman of God. And a fighter!

In November of 2010, we stopped in St. Martin en route to the Virgin Islands, immediately contacting the Allens. We met for a three-hour breakfast! Aster shared with us that God is not done with her yet and, changing the subject, wanted to hear about the CCI Annual General Meeting that neither of them attended due to her illness. We talked about some creative ideas bounced around at the meeting. Like other classes, the Allen's CBSI members were finding it difficult attending class on a weeknight. Their new church plant has many new believers not raised in a church environment, so we suggested integrating CBSI into their Sunday mornings, using Sunday school time for discussion groups, teaching the lessons for their "sermons" and afterwards having a time of praise and worship. Their eyes lit up! They are trying it.

Eight months after Pastor Aster's cancer diagnosis, the doctors are pleased with her progress and prayer is ongoing for a miracle of healing. Apostle Elmead continues to stay in touch with the other trained CBSI Teaching Leaders on St. Martin as well as encouraging other pastors to get involved. The only other class to start at this writing is Pastor Napolina's. But the CBSI story for St. Martin has just begun. Much prayer and shepherding from CCI leadership is needed for this new work.

"Therefore, my dear brothers, stand firm. Let nothing move you. Always give yourselves fully to the work of the Lord, because you know that your labor in the Lord is not in vain." (1 Corinthians 15:58)

"LORD,....all that we have accomplished You have done for us." (Isaiah 26:12) To God be the Glory!

Micki training leaders in St. Martin.

Teaching leader candidates concentrating on their training. Aster Allen (far right), Co-National Coordinators Elmead Allen (in pew behind) and Orlando Eights (3rd from right).

Trained leaders ready to begin CBSI classes in St. Martin.

Epilogue

Lessons Learned

*"May the favor of the L*ORD *our God rest upon us;*
establish the work of our hands for us —
yes, establish the work of our hands."
(Psalm 90:17)

*I*sn't that just like the Father to use the passions He planted within us for Bible study and sailing so that we could experience His passion for us and His people in the Eastern Caribbean? Once outside the intellectual noise of our suburban America comfort zone, we were enabled to see and learn more fully the extent of His love and faithfulness.

Our years as Bible teachers of Gen X young adults was a great learning experience in cross-cultural ministry. Our new calling in the Eastern Caribbean was one where we learned at the feet of Jesus — not so much for teaching others but for daily guidance in this multinational pioneering mission. In retrospect, we understand we were called and sent to learn. Our hope is that a few of our many "lessons learned" will be of help to you, the CBSI Caribbean leaders going forward, and to others called to be disciple makers for Jesus in their spheres of influence.

SHEPHERDING

In God's ministry in the Caribbean, we became more in tune with His ever present love and faithfulness than we had been at home in the U.S. As He poured His love into us, it flowed through us as we invested our time and lives into those He brought to us. He does the same for each of His children who take a step of faith in answer to His calling in CBSI or any Christian work. Jesus said *"A new commandment I give you: Love one another. As I have loved you, so you must love one another." (John 13:34)*

To us shepherding is being a conduit through which God's love flows to others. This is the cornerstone of the CBSI process—God's love flowing through His disciples into the lives of those He has given them to shepherd. The CCI Director shepherds those under him. The National Coordinators shepherd the Teaching Leaders in their nations. The Teaching Leaders shepherd their leadership teams. The Discussion Leaders shepherd their group members. God entrusts men and women to you, CBSI leaders, and expects you to invest sacrificially in them. You stand in the gap for the men and women God has given you to serve. You encourage. You pray. You challenge. You help each person grow in confidence in studying God's Word. You help each apply what he or she is learning to personal life.

In CBSI, making disciples is what we do. Shepherding is how we do it. We take all the gifts and talents God has poured into us and invest them in others through spending our time, our energies and our lives loving one another. *"By this all men will know that you are my disciples, if you love one another." (John 13:35)* As class members learn of God's love through the study of His Word and experience it from their leaders, lives will be transformed day by day, week by week, year by year. *"Greater love has no one than this, that he lay down his life for his friends." (John 15:13)*

COACHING

Follow-up visits within three to five weeks of a new class start-up are essential to provide the coaching needed. Anything else is like leaving a newborn baby on a doorstep! The CBSI process is markedly different from Scripture study methods leaders and class members have previously experienced. Therefore, even though thoroughly trained, new CBSI leaders will not have a firm grasp of the entire process and sometimes have difficulty explaining it to eager and well meaning new class members. At that point, a coaching visit is very helpful in getting and/or keeping the Leaders Council and class on track. Ongoing coaching at least twice a year by the National Coordinator is needed in established classes for encouragement and to keep classes on track. Encourage the Teaching Leaders to make review of the Caribbean Training Manual a regular part of their Leaders Council. Through Satan's deception there will be a temptation to change the very process that is bringing about spiritual transformation.

CONSISTENCY

Once a class is well started and following the five-featured CBSI process, the members will be bursting with enthusiasm due to all they are learning for themselves from personal time in God's Word. They will be developing the habit of daily Bible study. From personal study comes a confidence and desire to share with others what they are learning and how it applies to their lives. Interrupting the CBSI class schedule for extended periods of time for special events has two unintended consequences. First, it breaks the growing routine of daily time with the Lord in Bible study. Secondly, it undermines the perceived importance of Bible study for growing Christians.

PRAYER

The CBSI process is proven to bring about spiritual transformation in class members. The power of God's Word will be unleashed, and Satan will lose his power over the lives of some. However, he will not give up his territory without a fight. Spiritual warfare should be expected. Expect Satan's attacks on yourselves as leaders and those you lead. The enemy will attempt to deceive, discourage, distract and cause disunity. The effective weapon is prayer. Your weekly Leaders Council is a key battleground. Conversational prayer— where every leader joins in praising God for who He is, thanking God for His answers to your specific prayers and petitioning Him with the specific needs of each leader and His protection of the class and leadership—must be a priority. Also, each leader needs to pray regularly for those God has given him or her to lead. *"With this*

*in mind, be alert and always keep on praying for all the saints."
(Ephesians 6:18)*

GET COMMITMENT

Before training is held for a new class, it is important that the church or group leadership has an investment of time and personal commitment. Before CBSI training is scheduled, the leader or contact person should provide a list of the trainees including their names and potential CBSI roles, a training venue and class starting date. Class start-up should take place no more than three weeks after training because of retention. This commitment will insure a successful turnout for training and the expectation of a significant new program among those involved and usually the church as a whole.

PROCESS

Unlike spiritual conversion, which takes mere seconds in response to the anointed preaching of a pastor or evangelist, a convert becomes a disciple of Jesus Christ over a period of time if he or she grows in Christ-likeness. This growth process requires getting acquainted with who Jesus really is through the study of His Word, the Bible, as well as supplementary forms of learning. This knowledge leads to a loving relationship between the growing convert and Jesus, culminating in the convert becoming a Christ follower, a disciple. The disciple's changed life is used by Jesus to draw others to Himself, as with the apostle Andrew, who brought Peter to Jesus. This lifelong growth in Christ-likeness, known as sanctification, is a work of the Holy Spirit.

STAY ON TARGET

Always keep your mission in the forefront of your mind. Don't get distracted. CBSI exists to make disciples of the Lord Jesus Christ in our communities through caring, in-depth Bible study, available to all. When men and women come face to face with God in His written Word, lives will be transformed, and disciples will be made! As a CBSI leader you are called by God specifically for this purpose—to help men, women and children get into God's Word for themselves. Be creative. If the educational level of the class is low, try half a lesson a week, as did the Laborie, St. Lucia class. If it is an older group and the heart language is Creole, the Discussion Leader may have to read, translate and have the group do the home study questions during discussion time, as did one discussion group in Banse, St. Lucia. If necessary, start out with study groups as Grenada Teaching Leader Judith Lett did until the people learned how to do the CBSI lessons. Do what it takes to fulfill the mission in CBSI to make disciples through in-depth Bible study without compromising the five feature process.

We have learned many lessons and are confident that, just as God taught us, He will teach you as you walk in your CBSI role. We thank God for the privilege of pioneering CBSI in the Eastern Caribbean, watching Him go before us, providing for every need and transforming lives through in-depth study of His Word in ten island nations. And we thank you, the CBSI Caribbean leaders, for your acceptance, love, support and prayers over these 11 years. Through your committed lives God will continue to write the "rest of the CBSI story" in the Eastern Caribbean.

"May God Himself, the God of peace, sanctify you through and through. May your whole spirit, soul and body be kept blameless at the coming of our Lord Jesus Christ. The One who calls you is faithful and He will do it." (1 Thessalonians 5:23-24) To God be the glory!

Acknowledgments

Writing this book in eight months was a challenge. At the same time it was an immense encouragement to recount God's faithfulness in meeting and working with the Caribbean people, adjusting to the exciting and sometimes daunting lifestyle aboard *coram Deo* and receiving His provision through family and friends who supported us in a variety of ways, making it possible for us to leave our home to follow God's call.

As in the CBSI ministry, publishing a book requires a team. We thank editor Larry Haise for his advice, patience and expertise in maintaining our voices and personalities in the text while bringing the words to life for the reader. Our spiritual daughter Heidi Lynn Holz, who has been part of our CBSI ministry from the beginning, was an excellent proofreader. For her work and joyful attitude we are grateful. We thank God for providing interior formatting specialist Kathy Curtis with her gracious and professional manner, who brought insightful guidance to the page design and layout, and graphic designer Brenda Haun, with her creative talents on completion of the beautiful cover design. We also appreciate writing and design input from our friends Alison Lyons, Gray Counts, Susan M. Brown and Jim Jackson.

We give God all the glory for this ministry, but we know He works through people. During our first eight years we spent eight to nine months annually in the Eastern Caribbean. We would like to thank our families for their love and support during our CBSI ministry and in our isolation while writing. We are grateful for the patience and understanding of Micki's 90-year-old mother, Cecilia Mroz; for Micki's sister Louise and husband Chris Doherty, who carried our family responsibilities during our many absences; for Chuck's brother Bob Harding Sr. and wife Donna, who consistently prayed and encouraged us; for the love and interest of our many nieces and nephews; and for dear friends Bill and Bonnie Reeves, who saw our love for the Eastern Caribbean people while sailing with us in 1995 and thus were not surprised by God's call. We are grateful for Bill and Bonnie's unwavering support in so many ways, initially in taking care of the details of maintaining our home in Michigan. After they moved to Florida, Kristi Kirschmann and neighbors Rob and Laura Wilborn and Jerry Burge took over helping on the home front.

Reverends Clancy Thompson and David Andersen gave us invaluable cross cultural advice from their own missionary service in Latin America. We are humbled by the encouragement and financial and prayer support of our home church, Woodside Bible, and its missions board and leadership team, especially senior pastor Dr. Doug Schmidt and innovations pastor Mike Wendland. The Faithful Friends adult fellowship group, of which we are a part, took a personal interest in every aspect of our ministry, including praying us through the completion of this book.

We want to thank the many alumni of our former Bible Study Fellowship young adult class for their manifold support. Additionally, and certainly not least, we wish to thank CBSI "Caleb" forerunners Jim and Carolyn Robertson and our fellow Calebs as well as CBSI Caleb Ministry Associate Director Gordon Spaugh, Regional Director Shirley Adams and former Executive Director Damon Martinez for their advice and steadfast encouragement.

CPSIA information can be obtained at www.ICGtesting.com
Printed in the USA
BVOW041036260911

272033BV00006B/3/P